ITEM 019 874 459

‖‖‖ ‖‖‖‖‖‖‖‖‖‖‖‖‖‖‖‖‖‖‖‖‖‖‖
D0636059

Learning Centre

Park Road, Uxbridge Middlesex UB8 1NQ
Renewals: 01895 853326 Enquiries: 01895 853344

Please return this item to the Learning Centre on or before this last date stamped below:

2 0 OCT 2008		
2 0 APR 2009		

121

UXBRIDGE COLLEGE
LEARNING CENTRE

For Mont

UXBRIDGE COLLEGE
LEARNING CENTRE

An Introduction to the Theory of Knowledge

DAN O'BRIEN

polity

Copyright © Dan O'Brien 2006

The right of Dan O'Brien to be identified as Author of this
Work has been asserted in accordance with the UK
Copyright, Designs and Patents Act 1988.

First published in 2006 by Polity Press

Polity Press
65 Bridge Street
Cambridge CB2 1UR, UK

Polity Press
350 Main Street
Malden, MA 02148, USA

All rights reserved. Except for the quotation of short
passages for the purpose of criticism and review, no part of
this publication may be reproduced, stored in a retrieval
system, or transmitted, in any form or by any means,
electronic, mechanical, photocopying, recording or
otherwise, without the prior permission of the publisher.

ISBN-10: 0-7456-3316-1
ISBN-13: 978-07456-3316-9
ISBN-10: 0-7456-3317-X (pb)
ISBN-13: 978-07456-3317-6 (pb)

A catalogue record for this book is available from the British
Library.

Typeset in 9.5 on 12pt Utopia
by Servis Filmsetting Ltd, Longsight, Manchester
Printed and bound in Great Britain by MPG Books Ltd,
Bodmin, Cornwall

The publisher has used its best endeavours to ensure that
the URLs for external websites referred to in this book are
correct and active at the time of going to press. However, the
publisher has no responsibility for the websites and can
make no guarantee that a site will remain live or that the
content is or will remain appropriate.

Every effort has been made to trace all copyright holders,
but if any have been inadvertently overlooked the
publishers will be pleased to include any necessary credits
in any subsequent reprint or edition.

For further information on Polity, visit our website:
www.polity.co.uk

Contents

Detailed Chapter Contents

Preface

This book is intended for those following introductory undergraduate modules in Epistemology or the Theory of Knowledge, and for those studying the Theory of Knowledge component of the Philosophy A and AS level in the UK and the International Baccalaureate. I hope, though, that its readership is wider. Epistemology is one of the central areas of philosophy and I hope anyone with an interest in philosophy will find this book rewarding.

Throughout the book I have used examples from literature and film (particularly the latter). Knowledge of films and novels is often common currency, and in lectures and seminars this can lead to animated discussion of the philosophical aspects of the plot or characterization of a particular work. Such cross-fertilization should be encouraged. Philosophy should not be seen as a dry academic discipline divorced from everyday life. There are times in its history when this has been the case: there is the clichéd image of medieval philosophers using arcane arguments to determine how many angels could stand on a pinhead. And, if you turn to certain contemporary journals, you will find that many research papers are just as inaccessible and idiosyncratic. There is a danger of philosophy becoming inaccessible and uninteresting to those outside university philosophy departments. The philosophical problems that we shall look at are ones concerning knowledge – that everyday notion – and these are problems that have been discussed for thousands of years, problems that can be illuminated by reading the great philosophers of the past such as Plato, Descartes and Hume, and by looking at the works of writers and filmmakers who are themselves exercised, perhaps indirectly, by the very same issues.

Questions are included at the end of each chapter to encourage you to engage critically with the material. (Instructors could use these as essay questions or as discussion topics in seminars.) And, as you progress through the book, you should be thinking up your own examples and counterexamples, assessing whether the arguments discussed are good ones, and reflecting on whether you understand the various issues and concepts that are presented. You should also note that there is a Glossary included at the end of the book in which certain key terms are explained; these terms are flagged in **bold** when they first appear.

In general I have tried to be neutral, not advocating a particular epistemological theory, and presenting the reader with various alternative responses to the problems that we discuss. In places, though, my preference for a certain approach may show through. This, however, is not a bad thing. First, a consistent attempt not to endorse a particular position can lead to a lot of hedging: too much 'seems to', 'can be seen as', 'some have argued that . . .'. This can be stylistically clumsy. Second, you should always bear in mind that these debates are very much alive and, in places, you can – and should – disagree with me; in doing so, you are being a philosopher.

I would like to thank certain friends who read and commented on complete drafts of the book. Bernadette Evans suggested various stylistic and substantive changes to the text, and had a keen eye for inconsistencies (for where, as Lou Reed would say, 'he becomes a she'). Discussions with Dr Martin Hall have shaped much of the book, particularly chapter 6 – we have been arguing over foundationalism for almost a decade now. Particular thanks to Matthew Gidley since, not being a philosopher, he claimed not to understand a word of the book and, throughout his editing, to have the expression of a dog that's just been told a joke. (This is actually a very Wittgensteinian line, although I mustn't tell him this as he already calls the book 'an extended argument for National Service'.) Various readers of the Philos-L mailing list suggested useful examples, and thanks to Max Kolbel, Laurence Goldstein and Rob Hopkins for commenting on particular chapters, and to Dan O'Bannon for giving me permission to quote from his film *Dark Star*. Thanks also to Elizabeth Molinari, Ellen McKinlay, Emma Hutchinson, Andrea Dugan, Ann Bone and John Thompson at Polity. This is my first book and it would not have been written but for the encouragement and support of Greg McCulloch and Harold Noonan during my postgraduate study. Most influential to my interest in epistemology and to much of the content of the book have been my students, especially those following my Theory of Empirical Knowledge module (2001–4). The 'Theory of Empirical Knowledge' could, I admit, sound rather dry – less engaging than Existentialism, perhaps, or the Philosophy of Mind, or Aesthetics – but the interest shown by a great many of these students, and their contributions in class, have made this module, dare I say it, fun. This book hopes to carry on in the spirit of these classes.

PART I

INTRODUCTION TO KNOWLEDGE

# The Theory of Knowledge

1   Epistemology

The Theory of Knowledge asks certain very general and very fundamental questions about knowers and knowledge. What is it to know?
How is knowledge distinct from mere belief? And is knowledge possible? The Theory of Knowledge is also referred to as epistemology,
from the Greek word for knowledge, 'episteme'. Epistemology has a long
history: in working through this book you will become engaged in a
dialogue that has gone on for well over two thousand years. In the next
chapter we shall begin our analysis of knowledge by turning to Plato
(c.428–347 BC), and throughout our investigations we shall look at what
important thinkers of the past have said: René Descartes (1596–1650)
and David Hume (1711–1776) will have a high profile. Epistemology
remains an area of vibrant research, and many of the positions and
theories that we shall look at have emerged in the last few decades. This
continued interest in epistemology is a reflection of the immense
importance of knowledge in our lives. First, it is instrumentally useful:
with scientific knowledge, for example, we hope to explain, control and
predict the behaviour of the natural world. Second, even where knowledge has no practical use, we have the attitude that it's still something
desirable to obtain. It is good *in itself*. After a criminal in the film *Dirty
Harry* (1971) has given up his gun to Inspector Harry Callahan, he wants
to know whether Harry had any bullets left in his gun or whether he was
bluffing – 'I gots to know.' This information will be of no use to him – he
is now arrested, regardless – but it is nevertheless knowledge that he
seeks.

Epistemology and Metaphysics are the two central topics of
Philosophy. The former concerns the nature and possibility of knowledge; the latter concerns the nature of what exists. Metaphysical questions include: Are there things that are non-physical? Are there any
other minds in existence apart from your own? And does God exist? We
shall see that all of these issues intersect with our epistemological
investigations. Along with epistemology, then, we shall also be studying
some metaphysics. Epistemology is also intimately related to other
areas of philosophy, and we shall be introduced to issues in the philosophy of mind, the philosophy of religion, and ethics.

2   The Structure of the Book

2.1   Part I: Introduction to Knowledge

To study any topic, we must first have a preliminary idea of the kind of things we are going to investigate. Biologists must know what they are talking about when referring to 'armadillos', 'cells' or 'mitochondria'. Similarly the epistemologist: she, however, is concerned with such notions as knowledge, justification and belief, and with how they are related. Here and in the next chapter we shall start to look at just what we mean by 'knowledge', and in the rest of the book we shall investigate the nature of knowledge and the problems associated with it. Our primary concern will be with factual knowledge. I can know that Glasgow is in Scotland, that it was Descartes who wrote the *Meditations*, and that Bernice bobs her hair. Such knowledge is sometimes called 'knowledge that' or 'propositional knowledge'; 'propositional' because it's expressed in terms of the knowledge I have of certain true **propositions** or thoughts: I know that the proposition *Glasgow is in Scotland* is true. As well as with the words 'knows that', factual knowledge is also expressed using such locutions as 'knows why', 'knows where', 'knows when', 'knows whether', 'knows who', and 'knows what'. Such ways of speaking indicate that you know certain facts: in knowing where I left my keys, I know that they are in the coffee shop; in knowing when the programme starts, I know that it starts at 9 o'clock. Such knowledge can also be expressed without using the word 'know' at all. I could say that 'My keys are in the café over there', or that 'The programme starts now'. These statements are nevertheless expressions of factual knowledge.

There are other kinds of knowledge apart from factual knowledge. One is know-how: I know how to ride a bike and how to make a Tequila Sunrise. This is sometimes called 'ability knowledge'. We need to be a little careful here since I can have such knowledge without actually possessing the relevant ability. Practical constraints may prevent me from exercising a certain ability even though I know how it should be done: I may have temporarily lost my sense of balance and thus cannot ride my bike, or I may have run out of grenadine and so right now I cannot make a Tequila Sunrise. Knowing how to do certain things can involve the possession of factual knowledge. If I know how to play snooker, I must know that the blue ball has a points value of five, and that a red ball must be potted before I can pot a colour. However, in order to have other abilities, I do not require knowledge of any facts. I know how to perform such basic actions as walking, swimming and speaking without knowing that I move my body or mouth in a particular way: I can have know-how without the relevant propositional knowledge.

A third type of knowledge is knowledge by acquaintance. I know a certain person because I've met her; I know that melody because I've heard it before; and I know Yosemite because I've been there. I can have such knowledge without knowing any facts about these things. I can, for example, know that melody without knowing what it is called, or without having any further beliefs about it at all; I just know it. Other languages use a different word to talk about this kind of knowledge. In French, 'savoir' is to have factual knowledge, whereas 'connaître' is to have knowledge by acquaintance. In German the two relevant verbs are 'wissen' and 'kennen'. Knowledge, then, can involve acquaintance; various practical, intellectual and physical skills; and the knowledge of certain truths or facts. This book is mainly concerned with the latter kind of knowledge.

2.2   Part II: Sources of Knowledge

We acquire factual knowledge in various ways. I can come to know certain truths just by thinking about the issue in question. I know that there are no triangles with as many sides as a square. I do not have to draw lots of triangles and squares to know that this is so; I simply have to use my powers of reasoning. Such knowledge is called a priori (meaning *before experience*) and it will be the subject of chapter 3. The main focus of the book, however, will be knowledge that is acquired through experience, or what is called empirical or a posteriori knowledge (meaning *after experience*). There are two sources of such knowledge: it is acquired either through perceiving the world for ourselves (chapter 4), or through listening to what others have to say or reading what they have written (chapter 5).

2.3   Part III: Justification

Knowledge has traditionally been seen as involving justification: if I am to have knowledge, I must have true beliefs and I must have good reason or justification for holding them. In part III we shall focus on this key notion of justification. First, though, we must be careful to distinguish the epistemic sense of 'justification' from certain other uses of the term. The basic idea – and one that we shall go on to develop (and question) – is that my beliefs are epistemically justified if I have good reason to think that they are true.

> The basic role of justification is that of a means to truth . . . If epistemic justification were not conducive to truth . . ., if finding epistemically justified beliefs did not substantially increase the likelihood of finding true ones, then epistemic justification would be irrelevant to our main cognitive goal and of dubious worth. (Bonjour, 1985, pp. 7–8)

There are, however, non-epistemic ways of assessing beliefs. The possession of certain beliefs may bring me success in various ways. Some people believe that positive thinking can aid recovery from illness. If I think in this way, then I may cope better when I am ill (even if such beliefs are false). There is therefore a sense in which such thinking is justified given the benefits it brings to my state of mind. One could call this pragmatic justification as opposed to epistemic justification. There is a philosophical argument for believing in the existence of God that relies on such a notion of justification (one that we shall discuss in chapter 15, section 4). The key to the argument is that we should believe in God, not because there is good evidence of His existence, but because of the rewards such a belief would bring if it turned out to be true; we would, for instance, have eternal life in paradise.

There are also other species of justification that must be distinguished from the epistemic notion. We may have what could be called 'after the fact' justification. In the play *A Streetcar Named Desire*, Stanley Kowalski thinks that he survived the battle of Salerno because he believed he was lucky.

> Stanley: You know what luck is? Luck is believing you're lucky. Take at Salerno. I believed I was lucky. I figured that 4 out of 5 would not come through but I would . . . and I did. I put that down as a rule. To hold front position in this rat-race you've got to believe you are lucky. (T. Williams, 1962, p. 216)

He did survive and so there is a sense in which his belief was justified, justified in that it came true. He was not, however, epistemically justified since he didn't have a good reason to believe that he would be one of the lucky survivors – his odds were not good (as he admits) – he simply had faith. There may also be broadly ethical reasons for holding certain beliefs. It could be said that you are justified in believing what your friend says, simply because she is your friend. Here we may not be talking about either pragmatic or epistemic justification: there may be nothing in it for you, and she may not be very reliable. There is nevertheless a sense in which you are right to accept what she says. We must be careful, then, to focus on the kind of justification that is 'conducive to truth', and not on these non-epistemic forms.

We shall look at two debates concerning epistemic justification. First, one relating to its source. Empiricists argue that the justification for all our beliefs is grounded in our perceptual experience of the world. They are foundationalists because such experience provides the justificatory foundations for all of our empirical beliefs (chapter 6). Coherentists deny this claim. For them, a particular belief is justified if it fits in well with the rest of our beliefs; experience does not play a justificatory role (chapter 7). Second, we shall consider the debate between internalism and externalism. Traditionally, knowledge consists in justified true belief and, for a belief to be justified, a thinker must be capable of reflecting on the reasons why her belief is likely to be true. This is an internalist claim: what distinguishes knowledge from true belief is something that is cognitively accessible to the thinker. Recently, however, externalists have rejected this approach. They claim that a thinker need not be capable of reflecting upon what it is that distinguishes her knowledge from true belief (chapter 8).

2.4 Part IV: Scepticism

In parts I, II and III of the book it is assumed that we do have empirical knowledge, and we investigate the kind of justification our beliefs must have for this to be so. In part IV, however, this assumption will be questioned. There are certain 'sceptical' arguments that threaten all our claims to knowledge. Scepticism can be local in that it can concern a particular kind of fact: there are those, for example, who claim that we cannot have knowledge of God. It can also be global, the claim being that we cannot have any knowledge of the world at all. Descartes forwards an argument to this conclusion; after him, epistemology became the central discipline in philosophy, its primary task being to ease the sceptical concerns that he had voiced. In chapter 9 we shall turn to Cartesian scepticism ('Cartesian' meaning *from Descartes*), and we shall consider some of the attempts that have been made to refute it. As we shall see, Descartes himself was not a sceptic: he provided a refutation of his own scepticism. Most, though, do not find his positive arguments persuasive. In chapter 10 we shall look at Hume's argument for the claim that we do not have knowledge of the unobserved. Unlike Descartes, he does not think that his scepticism can be refuted. The moral he takes from this is that we should not concern ourselves with providing a philosophical account of how our empirical thinking can be justified – it cannot – instead, we should pursue the scientific task of providing a causal account of how we have the beliefs that we do. Such a strategy can be seen as inspiring the modern project of Naturalizing Epistemology (chapter 11).

To reflect both the historical and methodological importance of Cartesian scepticism, textbooks and courses in epistemology usually start with this topic. I, however, shall take a different tack. The spectre of scepticism is raised in part IV of the book, after we have discussed the sources of knowledge and the structure and nature of justification. The reason for this approach is twofold. First, no one actually believes the sceptical arguments: ' "the sceptic" is just a literary conceit, a personification of certain challenging arguments, rather than a real-life opponent' (M. Williams, 2001, p. 10). The issue of scepticism is rather paradoxical: the Cartesian and Humean arguments are logically persuasive – the reasoning appears **sound** (see **inference**) – yet the sceptical conclusions reached are psychologically very difficult to accept. Second, I have found that a certain unhelpful attitude can be fostered if scepticism is turned to first. If you are persuaded by the Cartesian arguments – and you cannot find a way to refute them – then there is the danger that you may not take the Theory of Knowledge seriously: 'If we cannot have any knowledge, then what's the point of studying such a notion.' In this book, however, we shall investigate such notions as perception, testimony, and justification in the spirit of seeing how they ground knowledge, knowledge that it is assumed we possess. As one progresses through the book, sceptical concerns may start to seep in, finding their full voice in part IV. By this time, though, we shall have acquired a rich conception of the relevant epistemological notions; this will allow us both a better understanding of scepticism and of how it may be countered.

2.5   Part V: Areas of Knowledge

Finally, we shall consider the epistemic role of memory (chapter 12), and whether we can have knowledge of the minds of others (chapter 13), morality (chapter 14), and God (chapter 15). The primary purpose of these concluding chapters is to illuminate further the epistemological notions introduced in the first four parts of the book; we shall look again, then, at the sources of knowledge, at justification, and at scepticism. These chapters will also act as useful introductions to the philosophy of mind, ethics, and the philosophy of religion.

3   Further Reading and Study

At the end of each chapter I shall suggest some further reading for you to explore. This will be of various kinds. Most philosophy is first published not in books but in journals. The *Journal of Philosophy, Analysis*, and the *Philosophical Review*, among many others, regularly publish important articles in the field of epistemology. Most titles are now available electronically via the internet, and you should ask your library how you can access them in this form. The internet is becoming increasingly useful: journals, ebooks, and websites devoted to epistemological topics are all available online. Some specific links are referred to in the relevant Further Reading sections, and the following are all useful.

Keith DeRose's Epistemology Page:
    http://pantheon.yale.edu/~kd47/e-page.htm
Epistemelinks:
    www.epistemelinks.com/
The Epistemology Research Guide:
    www.ucs.louisiana.edu/~kak7409/EpistemologicalResearch.htm
Certain Doubts (an epistemology blog):
    www.missouri.edu~kvanvigj/certain_doubts/

There is, however, a problem of quality control with the internet, and it's a good idea to ask your tutor or instructor for advice on the quality of material that you have sourced in this way.

Collections or anthologies of key articles are also very helpful. In the Further Reading sections I shall point you towards those that are focused on particular issues, and here are some general anthologies that cover most of the topics from parts I–IV of this book.

S. Bernecker and F. Dretske (eds), *Knowledge: Readings in Contemporary Epistemology* (2000).

E. Sosa and J. Kim (eds), *Epistemology: An Anthology* (2000).

E. Sosa (ed.), *Knowledge and Justification* (1994).

L. Pojman (ed.), *The Theory of Knowledge* (2003).

L. Alcoff (ed.), *Epistemology: The Big Questions* (1998).

Good textbooks provide both a summary of the key issues and philosophical insight of their own. This is the aim of my book, and the following are recommended for this reason.

R. Audi, *Epistemology: A Contemporary Introduction to the Theory of Knowledge* (1998).

J. Dancy, *Introduction to Contemporary Epistemology* (1985).

N. Everitt and A. Fisher, *Modern Epistemology: A New Introduction* (1995).

A. Morton, *A Guide Through the Theory of Knowledge* (1977).

M. Williams, *Problems of Knowledge: A Critical Introduction to Epistemology* (2001).

J. Dancy and E. Sosa (eds), *A Companion to Epistemology* (1992), is also a useful encyclopaedia containing short entries on all the important issues and figures that we shall discuss.

2 What is Knowledge?

1 Philosophical Analysis

The following is the start of a typical conversation that a friend and I often have over a game of snooker.

Andy: Who's the best player ever then?
Dan: That's obvious: Alex 'Hurricane' Higgins.
Andy: How can he be? He only won two World Championships; Stephen Hendry has won seven.
Dan: The best players do not always win the most matches.
Andy: How else can I determine who the best player is?
Dan: The one who has the best eye for the game.
Andy: Surely that would be the person who wins the most games.
Dan: No, it's the player who plays shots that no one else would even think of.
Andy: That can't be it. No one would have opted for the last shot that I played, yet I'm not the best snooker player ever.

What we are doing here is determining what we mean by 'the best player', and then, if we agree on this, we can see which actual player fits this description. Such an activity is what constitutes philosophical analysis. In pursuing such analysis, we attempt to draw up rules that specify what it is our **concepts** apply to; or, to put it another way, we try to determine the **necessary and sufficient conditions** for the application of our concepts. Analyses of many concepts are easy to find. We may wonder just what a carburettor is, and to work this out we can analyse how we use the term 'carburettor'. In doing so, we can work out that the term refers to the mechanism within an engine that mixes together air and petrol in order that the latter will efficiently combust. This, then, is what a carburettor is. Other analyses, however, are not so forthcoming. In this chapter we shall investigate some of the twists and turns that the analysis of the concept of KNOWLEDGE has taken, and some of the problems that it has faced. (I have put the names of concepts in small capitals.)

2 The Tripartite Definition of Knowledge

We have many beliefs about the world and we presume that a good proportion of them are true. It is important to note, though, that having a true belief does not necessarily amount to having knowledge. I can sometimes have true beliefs by accident. I believe that Xavier is Spanish because I incorrectly think that only Spaniards have names beginning with 'X'. I am right – Xavier is Spanish – but I have been epistemically lucky; my belief has turned out to be true even though my reasoning is faulty. An analysis of knowledge must rule out such a lucky episode and show why it does not amount to knowledge. In order to do this, knowledge has been seen as consisting of *justified* true belief. For me to know that Xavier is Spanish it must be the case that:

1   It is true that Xavier is Spanish.
2   I must believe that he is.
3   My belief must be justified.

And, more generally: *S* knows that *p* if:

1   *p* is true.
2   *S* believes that *p*.
3   *S* has justification for his belief that *p*.

This is the tripartite analysis or definition of knowledge. The three conditions are individually necessary for knowledge – knowledge always consists in *justified, true, belief* – and they are jointly sufficient for knowledge, that is, you always have knowledge when these three conditions are met.

Knowledge is built on belief – to know that *p*, you must believe that *p* – and beliefs can only amount to knowledge if certain other conditions are met. One such condition is that our beliefs must be true. We have argued, however, that this is not enough since we can have true beliefs by accident. Justification, therefore, is also necessary. What constitutes justification is highly controversial, and in this chapter and throughout the book we shall be exploring this question. We shall start with the plausible suggestion that we have justified beliefs when we have good reason to think our beliefs are true, that is, when we have good evidence to support them. The roots of such an account can be found in Plato, in dialogues that were written over 2,000 years ago.

> THEAETETUS: . . . I once heard someone suggesting that true belief accompanied by a rational account is knowledge, whereas true belief unaccompanied by a rational account is distinct from knowledge. (Plato, 1987, 201c–d)

Such a conception of justification and knowledge is merely a starting point, one that will certainly need embellishing, and one that we may even be persuaded to reject. In the next three sections we shall test the tripartite analysis by looking at how we would apply the concepts of KNOWLEDGE, JUSTIFICATION and BELIEF in certain actual and imaginary scenarios. If we can think of a case where we would ascribe justified true belief without knowledge, or knowledge without justified true belief, then this would suggest that our analysis is flawed.

3   Are Justification and Belief Necessary for Knowledge?

In this section we shall question the assumption that belief and justification are necessary for knowledge. I play some chess and I have a fair feel for the game. In the game I am currently playing on my computer, I believe that I can force a checkmate in a few moves, but I just cannot work out how. I cannot give you my reasons for thinking that there's a set of winning moves there; it just looks as if there is. I resort to asking for the help of my friend who is far better than me at chess and, just as I thought, he shows me the correct moves. In such a situation I am tempted to say, 'I told you so, I *knew* that I was in a winning position.' It's not that I only have knowledge when I discover the winning moves; I had knowledge 'all along', even before my friend provided justification for my claim. True belief is therefore sufficient for knowledge; justification is not always required.

You may be worried that such an account would allow a correct guess to count as knowledge. This cannot be right. I didn't know that the coin would land heads up even though I correctly guessed that it would. This, however, can be accepted by those who take the above scenario to suggest that true belief is sufficient for knowledge. In the case of the coin I do not *believe* that the coin will land heads up; it is simply a guess. A belief requires some kind of serious commitment on the part of the thinker – I must really think that it's true – and a guess does not amount to such commitment. I didn't know that the coin would land heads up because I didn't even have the relevant belief. In the chess game, however, I am not simply guessing: I strongly believe that there is a winning set of moves available. There are times, then, when I can have knowledge without having justification for my true beliefs. (More shall be said about whether we can have knowledge without justification in chapter 8.)

Let us now consider the natural way we talk about knowledge and belief. It would be odd to say 'I know that it's Wednesday and I believe that it's Wednesday.' It could be argued that this is because I lose the relevant belief when I acquire knowledge: knowledge *replaces* belief. On smelling the garlic bread I might say: 'I don't believe this will be tasty, I know it will.' Such examples suggest that knowledge is incompatible with belief, that is, we can have one or the other, but not both. A weaker suggestion is that it's sometimes possible to have knowledge without belief. The following example adapted from Colin Radford (1966) supports this line.

When I was young my grandmother showed me around her garden and told me the names of the various plants; I have, though, largely forgotten those afternoons and I do not think that I know anything about such things. One evening while watching *University Challenge*, there is a multiple-choice picture round on flowers, and the answers I shout at the TV are all correct (to my friends' amazement). To me, these answers are mere guesses: 'I dunno, that's a gentian, and that's – errrr – a nasturtium.' I do not believe that these are the right answers, even though I am consistently correct. I think that I'm just being very lucky. However, in such a case it seems reasonable to claim that I do have knowledge, knowledge that I acquired from my grandmother. There can therefore be knowledge without belief. (Can there? And can there be knowledge without justification? Are you persuaded by these scenarios?)

4   Gettier Cases

The most influential attack on the tripartite analysis can be found in Edmund Gettier's paper, 'Is Justified True Belief Knowledge?' (1963). He suggested certain scenarios in which thinkers have justified true belief even though they do not have knowledge. If such scenarios are persuasive, then this would show that knowledge cannot be identified with justified true belief. Gettier scenarios are counterexamples to the tripartite analysis. Gettier does not question whether justification, truth and belief are necessary for knowledge; he claims that they are not jointly sufficient: these conditions can all be met without a thinker having knowledge. Here is an example in the style of Gettier. The England versus Germany football match is being broadcast in the pub at the end of my road. On hearing cheers from inside I come to believe that England have just scored, and they have: it is now 1–nil. My belief is true and it is also justified: the roar from inside gives me good reason to think that an England goal has just been scored. I have, then, a justified true belief. However, the cheers that I heard actually originated from the front bar where there is no television and where, instead, there is a karaoke competition underway. It is merely coincidental that the singer in the front bar finished his rousing rendition of 'I Will Survive' at the same time as England scored. My true belief is therefore lucky and so it does not amount to knowledge. This example shows that we can have justified true beliefs by accident, and that the tripartite definition fails to give sufficient conditions for knowledge.

Another such example can be found in Oscar Wilde's play, *The Importance of Being Earnest*. Algernon has a friend he thinks is called 'Ernest'. His real name, however, is 'Jack'; for the purposes of entertainment he pretends to be his invented younger brother 'Ernest'. In the first scene, Algernon looks inside his friend's cigarette case and finds the inscription 'From Little Cecily, with the fondest love to dear Uncle Jack'. Jack has to admit that this is his real name. Algernon does not believe him and provides justifying evidence to show that his name must be 'Ernest'.

> You have always told me it was Ernest. I have introduced you to everyone as Ernest. You answer to the name of Ernest. You look as if your name was Ernest. You are the most earnest-looking person I ever saw in my life. It is perfectly absurd your saying that your name isn't Ernest. It's on your cards. Here is one of them. 'Mr. Ernest Worthing, B.4, The

Albany.' I'll keep this as a proof that your name is Ernest if ever you attempt to deny it to me, or to Gwendolen, or to anyone else. (Wilde, 1995, Act 1, lines 157–65)

And, at the end of the play, Jack discovers that he was indeed christened 'Ernest'. Algernon has a justified true belief. He has, though, been lucky; that Jack had adopted the name of 'Ernest' is simply wildly coincidental. He does not therefore know that his friend's name is 'Ernest'. Again, then, we have a counterexample to the traditional definition: a case of justified true belief without knowledge. (Think up a Gettier example of your own. Keep this in mind as you work through the chapter, and consider how the responses of the next section could apply to your particular example.)

We shall look at four kinds of response to Gettier. (i) In the next section we shall look at the claim that there is something wrong with the alleged justification in the Gettier scenarios, or rather, that what we have in such cases does not amount to justification. A richer notion of justification must be satisfied in order for us to have knowledge, and thinkers in the Gettier cases do not have such justification. We must, then, say what conditions are required in order that our beliefs are justified, conditions that are not met by my belief about the football match or by Algernon's belief about the name of his friend. (ii) In section 6 of this chapter we shall turn to the claim that belief and justification should be explained in terms of knowledge, and not vice versa as in the traditional account. (iii) In section 7, it will be argued that it may not be appropriate to look for a definition of knowledge at all. (iv) And, in chapter 8, we shall consider the externalist response to Gettier. The basic idea is that we do not need to be aware of what it is that provides justification for our beliefs. One kind of externalist theory claims that for my belief about the football match to be justified, it would have to have been caused by that event. In the example, though, my belief is caused by the karaoke competition and not the football match; I do not, therefore, have a justified belief and so this scenario does not provide a counterexample to the traditional analysis.

5   Richer Notions of Justification

5.1   Infallibility

It could be claimed that in order to have knowledge we must have conclusive reasons in support of our beliefs, reasons that we could not possess if those beliefs were false; reasons, therefore, that would entail that our beliefs are **infallible**. I do not have such reasons to back up my belief about the football score. Given the evidence I had, I could have been wrong (after all, I wasn't actually at the match); I did not, therefore, have a justified belief that England had scored, nor did I have knowledge. If conclusive reasons are required, then this scenario is no longer a counterexample to the traditional analysis: it is not a case of justified true belief without knowledge.

One problem with such an account of justification is that knowledge is now very hard to come by. It is not clear whether any of our empirical beliefs are infallible. Just now, on the phone, a friend of mine told me that it was ten past nine. This would seem to be a good way of coming to know the time. However, my friend could have lied to me or misread her watch, and so my reasons for believing that it's ten past nine are not conclusive; my belief is not infallible. In order to allow that such a commonplace claim to knowledge can be correct, the modern conception of knowledge is fallibilist. We must be careful, though, how we express this position: the claim is not that we can know things that are false; the fallibilist claim is that we can have knowledge without conclusive reasons. Thus, we can claim to know something even though the evidence we currently possess does not rule out the possibility that we may be wrong. Science provides a good illustration of fallibilism. We know many scientific truths even though the history and progress of science has taught us that some of our theories could be wrong, and that it may turn out that we do not have as much scientific knowledge as we think we do. If our scientific theories are true, then they amount to knowledge even though our reasons for accepting them are not conclusive. We have a fallibilist conception of empirical knowledge; there are, however, certain areas of knowledge where infallibility is more plausible – one of these is a priori knowledge and we shall discuss whether this is infallible in chapter 3, section 4.

Conclusive reasons were suggested as a response to the Gettier scenarios: if such reasons are required for justification, then the Gettier cases are not counterexamples to the traditional analysis since the thinkers discussed do not have justified beliefs. This response, though, cannot be sustained if one has a fallibilist conception of knowledge. The claim that empirical knowledge is fallible is important and one that should be kept in mind throughout the book. It is easy to slip into thinking that we do not know certain things because we do not know 'for sure', and that knowledge must involve infallibility. This, however, is not so, as can be seen by thinking about our everyday claims to knowledge. I know that it's ten past nine: such a claim is only acceptable if one is a fallibilist.

5.2   No false beliefs

Another response to Gettier focuses on certain false beliefs possessed by the thinkers described in such cases. When walking past the pub I could think something along these lines: 'I can hear the England supporters inside cheering; I wonder why that is? Fans cheer in this way when their team scores a goal and so England must have scored.' The first clause, however, is false: it is not the England supporters that are cheering, it's the audience of the karaoke competition. Note, though, that we have said that justification amounts to having adequate evidence or good reason to think that our beliefs are true. False beliefs cannot provide such evidence or rational support. We do not have justi-fication for our true beliefs if our reasoning involves beliefs that are themselves false. If this is so, then the Gettier scenario described above is not a counterexample to the traditional analysis since my belief that England have scored is not justified. This is because I have arrived at this conclusion on the basis of my false belief that I can hear the England fans cheering.

One problem with this response to Gettier is that there appear to be Gettier cases that do not involve such false beliefs, and ones that do not involve reasoning at all. Gazing out of the window during a lecture you are surprised to see a cow in front of the physics building. You come, therefore, to acquire the belief that there is a cow there. What you are looking at, however, is a cleverly disguised shopping trolley that is about to be raced around the quadrangle in the annual trolley race (it's rag week at university). Behind the trolley, though, there really is a cow, one that has escaped from a local farm, but one that you cannot see. You have a true belief – that there is a cow in the quad – and a belief that is justified given that this kind of observational evidence is usually taken as sufficient justification for perceptual belief. However, you do not *know* that there is a cow there given that the real cow is obscured from your view. This is therefore a Gettier case. Note, though, that there is no reasoning or inference involved here. On perceiving the trolley you simply come to acquire the belief that there's a cow in the quad. Similarly, when walking past the noisy pub, it is plausible that I would have come to acquire the belief that England had scored without reasoning in the way suggested; I would not have come to that conclu-sion via any kind of inference. A prohibition against false beliefs cannot be used to reject such counterexamples to the traditional analysis since these are cases of justified true belief without knowledge that do not involve false belief.

We have looked at two ways of spelling out the traditional analysis in order that its verdicts fit with our intuitions concerning the Gettier cases. Knowledge is still considered to be justified true belief, although it has been argued that we should be concerned with a stricter sense of 'justi-fied'. Gettier cases are not counterexamples to the traditional analysis since the thinkers discussed do not have justified beliefs in the stricter sense suggested, and therefore our intuitions are correct that these cases do not involve knowledge. We have seen, though, that there are problems with both responses to Gettier, although it should be noted that I have only provided a flavour of some of the main lines of argument relevant to this kind of strategy. Various attempts have been made to maintain the responses that focus on infallibility and false beliefs, and other ways of spelling out and supplementing the traditional analysis have been suggested. Some of this work can be found in the Further Reading section of this chapter. We shall now move on to a more radical response to Gettier. The claim is not that the traditional analysis needs to be tweaked; it is, rather, that analysis needs to be abandoned altogether.

6   Knowledge as Basic

On the traditional account, knowledge is acquired when your beliefs are true, and when the justification condition is also satisfied. Knowledge is constituted by the epistemically more basic components of belief, truth and justification. Timothy Williamson argues that such an approach is driven by two assumptions. First, it is assumed that the concept of KNOWLEDGE is analysable into simpler constituent concepts. Second, it is assumed that when you have knowledge you are in a hybrid state, one that is partly constituted by the state of your mind and partly by the world. The possession of belief and justification may amount to the possession of certain mental states, but truth is a notion that is independent of the psychology of knowers (something out there in the world). These two assumptions are related in that analysis is pursued (first assumption) in order to spell out what kind of mental components are required in addition to the non-mental component of truth (second assumption). Williamson's strategy is to question both assumptions. If they are found to be ungrounded, then an altogether different approach can be adopted, one that is not driven by the need to analyse knowledge in terms of belief, truth, and justification.

Williamson claims that there is not a set of conditions that must be satisfied by *all* cases of knowledge; there is not, then, an *analysis* of KNOWLEDGE to be found. Many concepts cannot be analysed – that is, there are no necessary and sufficient conditions for their application – yet this does not entail that such concepts are in any sense defective or meaningless. One cannot give definitions of beauty, elegance or intelligence yet we can use these concepts and they have a meaning. Some concepts may be analysable, such as CARBURETTOR, but 'most words express indefinable concepts' (Williamson, 2000, p. 100). In the case of KNOWLEDGE, the history of epistemology does not bode well for the success of an attempted analysis. Philosophers have been attempting to come up with a definition of knowledge since the time of Plato, and, more recently, despite forty years of intense research, no consensus has been reached on how we should respond to Gettier. Williamson takes this lack of success as indicative of the wrong-headedness of the traditional approach.

It was suggested that the hybrid nature of knowledge – that is, the claim that it is part mental (belief and justification) and part non-mental (truth) – drives us to attempt an analysis of knowledge into epistemically more basic components. Williamson, however, argues that knowledge does not consist in the possession of such a hybrid state; the motivation for analysis is therefore lost. Knowledge is a wholly mental state. Such an account embraces cognitive externalism. This is the theory that the nature of certain mental states is not wholly determined by what's inside the head of the thinker; the content of mental states is in part determined by what's in the world. Knowledge is just such a mental state: I cannot know that *p* if *p* is false – I cannot be in that

UXBRIDGE COLLEGE
LEARNING CENTRE

mental state – unless my coffee is actually hot. The coffee – that part of the external world – partly constitutes my mental state of knowing. On the traditional picture, truth is necessary for knowledge, but it is seen as the non-mental component of the hybrid state of knowing; my *mental* states are those of believing and possessing justification. For Williamson, however, knowledge itself consists in the possession of a wholly mental state, a state that you can only be in if your thoughts correctly represent the world. (In chapter 9, section 4, cognitive externalism will be explored in more depth.)

Williamson has therefore attempted to remove some of the motivation for why epistemologists are drawn to the analysis of KNOWLEDGE. It should not be assumed that all concepts are analysable, and knowing should not be seen as a hybrid state, one that is ripe for analysis into mental and non-mental components. If these claims are accepted, then the way is clear for Williamson to forward a radically different epistemology. For him, knowledge is a basic, indefinable, unanalysable, mental state. He sums up his account with the slogan 'knowledge first': knowledge is not constituted by more basic epistemic components such as belief and justification; knowledge, rather, is the most basic epistemic state, and such an account of knowledge can elucidate the notions of belief and justification (rather than these notions elucidating knowledge, as they do in traditional accounts). To believe that the coffee is still hot is to treat this claim as if it is something that you know, that is, you would decline the offer of another cup, and you would be careful when drinking it. Perhaps, then, there can be knowledge without belief. I may know that the flower is a gentian even though I do not treat this as something that I know; I do not, therefore, believe that the flower is a gentian (see section 3). Williamson, however, is unsure about the intuitive force of such examples, and he accepts that knowledge is always accompanied by belief, even though it cannot be analysed in terms of belief, truth, and justification.

Williamson also gives an account of justification. Justified beliefs are those you have good evidence for, and it's only items of knowledge that can play the requisite evidential role. If I know that there's steam rising from my cup, then this provides good evidence for my belief that the coffee is still hot, and thus my belief is justified. Again, then, we see the primacy of knowledge: justified belief is explained in terms of the mental state of knowing. The order of explanation here is a reversal of that offered by the traditional account, that in which knowledge is defined in terms of justified belief. According to Williamson, knowledge should not be seen as a hybrid state consisting of the mental component of justified belief, and the non-mental component of truth. Knowledge itself consists in the possession of a distinct type of mental state, a mental state that is epistemically basic. The jury, however, is out on Williamson's new and distinctive approach to epistemology and, for the moment, most contemporary epistemology remains wedded to the traditional picture.

7 Family Resemblance

In this last section we shall consider another argument to the conclusion that the philosophical analysis of KNOWLEDGE should be abandoned. Ludwig Wittgenstein argues that we should not assume that the various instantiations of a concept have anything in common. When we look at the use of some of our concepts we do not find such common features. His example is that of the concept GAME. (Note that Wittgenstein did not explicitly argue that this is the case for KNOWLEDGE.)

> Consider for example the proceedings that we call 'games'. I mean board-games, card-games, ball-games, Olympic games, and so on. What is common to them all? – Don't say: 'There *must* be something common, or they would not be called "games"' – but *look and see* whether there is anything common to all. (Wittgenstein, 1953, §66)

And, if we look, we do not find any common features.

> Look for example at board-games, with their multifarious relation-ships. Now pass to card-games; here you find many correspondences with the first group, but many common features drop out, and others appear. When we pass next to ball-games, much that is common is retained, but much is lost. – Are they all 'amusing'? Compare chess with noughts and crosses. Or is there always winning and losing, or competition between players? Think of patience . . . (1953, §66)

Wittgenstein goes on, and so can we: in looking at the various activities we call games we can see that there is no such thing as the essence of what it is to be a game. All we find is: 'a complicated network of similar-ities overlapping and criss-crossing: sometimes overall similarities, sometimes similarities of detail'. And: 'I can think of no better expres-sion to characterise these similarities than "family resemblances"; for the various resemblances between members of a family: build, features, colour of the eyes, gait, temperament, etc. etc. overlap and criss-cross in the same way. – And I shall say: "games" form a family' (1953, §§66–7).

If we accept this Wittgensteinian line, then we could claim that KNOWLEDGE is a family resemblance concept. If this is so, then we are not obliged to look for a definition of knowledge, something that Williamson suggested in the previous section. And, if such an account of the concept of KNOWLEDGE is accepted, there is still work for the epis-temologist to do: she should seek to map patterns of 'family traits', and describe how the various epistemic properties possessed by thinkers 'overlap and criss-cross'. The first hints of a family resemblance account of knowledge arose in the first chapter. There it was noted that we possess know-how, knowledge by acquaintance, and factual knowl-edge, and we did not think it was necessary to find a defining feature that they all share. In this chapter we have focused on the latter and we should therefore '*look and see* whether there is anything common to all' cases of factual knowledge. If there is not, then the philosophical analy-sis of KNOWLEDGE should be abandoned.

There are certain paradigm examples of knowledge, cases which possess features that we all would agree are of epistemological import-ance. I believe that the maximum possible break at snooker is 155. (This is a puzzle for all those snooker fans out there: why is it not the usually quoted 147?) This belief is true, and I can provide reasons to support it. I am also certain of my reasoning since it only involves the addition of the points-values of the coloured balls, a calculation that I am sure I can perform correctly. I can therefore *know* that this is the highest break. Such knowledge has three important properties: it involves true belief (X), justification (Y), and certainty (Z). The claim in this section, however, is that all cases of knowledge do not have to possess these features, and we have already seen some plausible examples that do not: (1) I believe that there is a winning set of chess moves in the offing and, on discovering them, I claim to have 'known it all along' (X only). (2) I correctly answer the questions concerning flowers in the quiz show (none of X, Y or Z). (3) I believe that the Earth is not flat (X and Y, but not Z). Such examples suggest that there isn't a set of conditions that must be satisfied by all cases of knowledge, and they also illustrate the kind of mapping exercise that epistemologists should pursue. That is, of course, if we accept the suggested rejection of analysis.

It should be stressed that the suggestions of sections 6 and 7 are not widely adopted. Traditional analysis is still pursued and in the rest of the book I shall largely assume that the traditional picture is correct, that is, that knowledge is justified true belief. Even if this is ultimately misguided, justification will remain an important epistemological notion in its own right, and part III of this book is important even if you have found sections 6 and 7 of this chapter persuasive.

Questions

1. Explain why justification, truth, and belief are seen as necessary for knowledge. Are they?
2. What is wrong with the following statements (the first of which I heard on a recent television programme)? 'African tribes have known about spirits for centuries'; 'it used to be known that the Earth was flat, whereas now we know it is spherical.'
3. Can necessary and sufficient conditions be given for the possession of knowledge?
4. What is the relevance of Gettier cases to the analysis of knowledge?
5. I am often plagued by the faces of certain minor actors: 'I just know he was in that other film – I cannot remember the name of it though, although it's on the tip of my tongue.' Later in the day it sometimes comes back to me, and I recall the name of the film. Did I *know* which other film this actor was in before I recalled its name? Could I have known this even if I hadn't later recalled which one it was? And how do your answers relate to the tripartite definition of knowledge?

Further Reading

You can look for examples of philosophical analysis in literature and film. Two that come to mind are certain passages in Ishiguro's *The Remains of the Day* (1989) where the butler, Stevens, attempts to define dignity (throughout, but especially pp. 33–45); and in the film *The Kiss of the Spider Woman* (1985) where two prisoners discuss what it is to be a 'real man'. Whether Plato actually accepted the tripartite definition of knowledge is explored in chapter 1 of Welbourne (2001). The role of luck in epistemology is the subject of Pritchard's *Epistemic Luck* (2005). The suggestion in section 3 that justification is not necessary for knowledge is taken from Sartwell (1991), and Radford's claim that belief is not necessary for knowledge is criticized by Armstrong (1969–70). Williamson's *Knowledge and its Limits* (2000) warrants close study (although it is rather difficult), and a good introduction to cognitive externalism can be found in McCulloch's *The Mind and its World* (1995).

Gettier (1963) has been hugely influential. This is probably the research paper with the highest 'interest per word' ratio (number of words written about this paper: number of words in the original). Gettier's paper is only three pages long, yet it has elicited hundreds of lengthy replies. A good survey of some of this work is given in Shope (1983). The response that focuses on false beliefs is discussed by Feldman (1974). Shakespearean drama can be a good hunting ground for Gettier cases. Take a look at *Much Ado About Nothing* (Act II, scene iii; Act III, scene i) where Benedick and Beatrice are fooled into falling in love with each other (a scenario that is copied in the recent film *Amélie*, 2001), and the play-within-a-play section of *Hamlet* (Act III, scene ii) where Hamlet attempts to discover whether it was Claudius who murdered his father. (Hint: on one interpretation of the play, Claudius's behaviour is not driven by guilt. Hamlet regularly butts in during the play that he has staged, providing a constant commentary. It is such behaviour that is unbearable to Claudius, and not the fact that the play reminds Claudius of his crime.)

PART II

SOURCES OF KNOWLEDGE

3 A Priori Knowledge

1 Knowledge, Reason and Experience

Take a rectangular book off your bookshelf and look at the front cover. What is its predominant colour, and how many sides does it have? In answering these questions you now know two things about this book, and these two facts illustrate an important distinction between two ways we have of acquiring knowledge. In order to come to know the colour of the book, you must observe it (or get someone else to observe it for you). The justification for your belief about its colour is provided by experience (yours or someone else's). However, you do not need to look at a rectangular book to know how many sides it has. You know that rectangles have four sides just by thinking about what it is to be a rectangle. You acquire such knowledge using only your powers of reasoning; you do not have to consider the evidence of your senses. Knowledge that is justified by experience is called a posteriori or empirical knowledge. Knowledge for which experience does not play a justificatory role is called a priori knowledge.

Various philosophers have claimed that the following are known a priori.

1 Both simple mathematical truths such as 2+2=4, and ones that are more complex such as Pythagoras' theorem: the sum of the squares of the two shorter sides of a right-angled triangle is equal to the square of the longest side.
2 Truths that are captured by definitions such as: 'All bachelors are unmarried men.'
3 Metaphysical claims such as, Nothing is red all over and green all over, Everything has a cause, and God exists (see chapter 15).
4 Ethical truths such as Murder is wrong (see chapter 14).

There is a sense in which experience is involved in the acquisition of all beliefs. To know that bachelors are unmarried men, I need to know the meaning of 'bachelor', 'unmarried' and 'men', and such linguistic understanding is acquired through lessons and instruction, practices that involve experience of some kind. Experience, then, does play a certain role in the acquisition of a priori knowledge: it is involved in our coming to understand the language in which such knowledge is articulated. The question of whether the above truth is known a priori is a question concerning whether further experience is required in order to be justified in believing that the concepts of BACHELOR and UNMARRIED MAN apply to the same type of person, accepting that you must have had experience to learn those concepts in the first place. The answer is No. You do not have to ask your bachelor friends whether they are married; you are justified in believing that they're not, simply in virtue of possessing the relevant concepts. Similarly, you are justified in believing that the rectangular cover of a book has four sides without looking at it; you are justified simply in virtue of your understanding of the concept RECTANGLE.

2 Rationalism and Empiricism

Rationalists emphasize the importance of a priori knowledge, and it will be useful here to introduce a key rationalist thinker and to look at the role of the a priori within his epistemology. Descartes is perhaps the most influential epistemologist in Western philosophy, and we shall consider aspects of his thought throughout the book. His *Meditations* are written in an autobiographical style: he sits by his fire ruminating on the nature of knowledge. He first raises sceptical doubts to the effect that we may not have any knowledge of the world at all (chapter 9); he finds salvation, though, in one sure item of knowledge: 'cogito, ergo sum' ('I think, therefore I am'); this is sometimes called the *cogito*. Our own existence is something that we cannot be mistaken about. Then, using wholly a priori reasoning, he attempts to prove that God also exists (chapter 15). God, being good – again something that we can know a priori – would not allow us to be such epistemically impoverished creatures, and thus we do have certain justified beliefs concerning the empirical world. Crucial aspects of his epistemology are therefore pursued using a priori reasoning. We should be clear, though, that Descartes does not eschew all experience. Once we have found an a priori proof for the existence of God, we must make careful observations of the world in order to acquire further knowledge. It is, however, our a priori knowledge that ultimately provides justification for the empirical beliefs acquired in this way.

Empiricists accept that some truths can be known a priori, but such truths are uninteresting, uninformative, or tautologous. In coming to know that bachelors are unmarried men, we do not learn anything substantive about the world, merely something about the meaning of our words, that is, in English 'bachelor' has the same meaning as 'unmarried man'.

> [T]he truths of pure reason, the propositions which we know to be valid independently of all experience, are so only in virtue of their lack of factual content. To say that a proposition is true *a priori* is to say that it is a tautology. And tautologies, though they may serve to guide us in our empirical search for knowledge, do not in themselves contain any information about any matter of fact. (Ayer, 1990, p. 83)

Such knowledge is a priori because it can be acquired simply in virtue of understanding the relevant concepts; you do not have to further investigate the world. Empiricists claim that all a priori truths are what Immanuel Kant calls 'analytic'. They are true in virtue of the meanings of the terms used to express them, and their truth can be discovered using philosophical analysis. Analytic truths are contrasted with those that are 'synthetic'. Synthetic truths do not simply depend on what our terms mean, but also on how the world happens to be. That koala bears eat eucalyptus leaves is not part of the concept of KOALA BEAR; it is, however, true, and this is because we have discovered that this is what koala bears do. It is a synthetic truth. We should not, however, equate the distinction between the empirical and the a priori with that between the analytic and the synthetic. The former is an epistemological distinction: it concerns the source of justification for our beliefs. The latter is one that is semantic: it concerns whether certain truths hold simply in virtue of the meanings of the relevant concepts. Although these respective distinctions concern justification and meaning – two different aspects of our language and thought – the empiricist claims that they carve up our knowledge in the same way: all and only our a priori knowledge is analytic, and all and only our empirical knowledge is synthetic. The only knowledge we can have independent of our experience is that concerning the meaning of our words and thoughts; any substantive knowledge of the world must be acquired via experience. It is this claim that we shall question in the next section. (In chapter 11 we shall also look at Willard Quine's claim that all knowledge is empirical and that nothing can be known a priori, not even meanings.)

3   The Synthetic A Priori

I know that 'if something is red all over, then it cannot be green all over', and in order to know this I do not have to observe various coloured objects, or try to paint things red and green. I can know that this statement is true just by thinking about it. This is therefore an a priori truth. It does not, though, appear to be analytic: it is not part of the *meaning* of something being red all over that it is not green all over. If it were, then the meaning of 'being red all over' would be analysable into the following very long conjunction: 'not being blue all over, or purple all over, or yellow . . .' This is implausible. It would seem that our colour concepts are not analysable in this way, and that we could possess the concept RED without possessing GREEN, BLUE, PURPLE or YELLOW. Thus the claim we are considering looks to be a synthetic a priori truth, a substantive claim concerning the nature of the world, but one that is known a priori. In subsequent chapters we shall turn to some important examples of the synthetic a priori such as Kant's laws of morality (chapter 14, section 2), and the conclusion of Descartes's argument for the existence of God (chapter 15, section 1). Here, though, let us consider mathematics, a discipline that we earlier suggested was a priori in its approach.

UXBRIDGE COLLEGE
LEARNING CENTRE

Mathematical truths are not analytic: it is not part of the meaning of 12 that it equals 7 plus 5. If it were, then 12 would also mean 6 plus 6, and 2.5 plus 9.5, and an infinite number of other such combinations. It's not plausible that we must grasp such a set of mathematical truths in order to understand '12'. I can understand '12' without understanding '$(\sqrt{4}\sqrt{9})^2 \div 3$' (which would also have the same meaning as 12 if mathematics were analytic). Mathematics, then, provides us with further examples of the synthetic a priori. Perhaps, though, the a priori nature of mathematics can be challenged. John Stuart Mill argues that it's an empirical discipline and he's therefore happy to accept that it provides us with synthetic truths (Mill, 1884). He claims that 7 plus 5 is simply an observed regularity: when we have added 5 eggs to 7 eggs we have always ended up with 12 eggs. This is not something that we know independent of experience; it is, rather, a generalization that has been confirmed by experience. Consider, though, what the empiricist would do if he ended up with only 11 eggs after adding 7 more eggs to a box of 5. According to Mill, if this happened regularly enough, we should reject our empirical generalization that 7 plus 5 is 12. The rationalist claims that this is implausible. We would never come to such a conclusion; instead, we would always try and explain why one egg consistently disappears: perhaps a magician is playing tricks on us, or we have simply lost the ability to count. We would never conclude that 7 and 5 do not add up to 12. This is because mathematics is a priori.

The synthetic a priori is interesting and controversial because through reasoning alone we can come to know truths about the nature of mathematics, morality, and the world. How can this be? We are not said to perceive such truths – 'perception' applies to our empirical engagement with the world – but rather, we 'intuit' them; they are the product of intuition. We intuit that $7+5=12$, that everything has a cause, and that nothing can be red all over and green all over. In the previous chapter we talked about intuitions in the context of thought experiments. It is my intuition that I do not *know* that England have scored, although I do *know* that the flower is a gentian. Such intuitions concern whether it seems right to apply a particular concept in certain situations (in these cases we were concerned with the concept of KNOWLEDGE). The verdicts we arrive at are more than mere hunches. A thinker's intuitions concerning a particular concept are often consistent: ascriptions of knowledge, for example, will be withheld from all formulations of Gettier-type scenarios. Different thinkers will also agree about what should be said concerning a particular case: I suspect we all agreed that I didn't know that Xavier was Spanish. The rationalist and the empiricist can agree that we have consistent and reliable intuitions concerning the correct application of our concepts. Once we have learnt the concepts of KNOWLEDGE, BELIEF, and JUSTIFICATION we do not actually have to experience the imagined situations in order to determine whether they involve the acquisition of knowledge; we can simply intuit whether or not this is so.

Rationalists, however, claim that we not only have an a priori grasp of when it is correct to apply our concepts, but also that thought alone can provide us with insight into the nature of the world: 'insights into the essential nature of things or situations of the relevant kind, into the way that reality in the respect in question must be' (Bonjour, 2005, p. 99).

We can intuit, a priori, that every event has a cause, and that nothing is red all over and green all over. Also, from certain a priori intuitions, we can use our reason to derive further a priori claims about the world. In chapter 15 we shall look at one of Descartes's arguments for the existence of God. From the fact that he has an idea of God in his mind – something he intuits – he argues, using a deductive argument, that God must actually exist, not just as an idea but as a real entity in the world. Such rationalist argument involves using **deductive reasoning** (see **inference**) to draw conclusions about the world from premises that are known to be true independent of experience. Such conclusions, therefore, are themselves a priori. Through intuition and reasoning the rationalist acquires knowledge of, among other things, metaphysics, morality and God.

Empiricists claim that such epistemic abilities are mysterious: how can thinking alone provide us with such insight? If it did, then this would seem to give us some kind of extrasensory awareness of the nature of reality, and this would be to possess a cognitive ability for which there is no plausible explanation. Empiricists offer one of two alternative interpretations of any alleged item of a priori knowledge. They either claim that such knowledge is not a priori, and it must therefore be justified by experience, or that the a priori knowledge we acquire only concerns the meaning of our concepts, something to which we can plausibly have access independent of experience. We may know that 'nothing is red all over and green all over', but this is either because we can infer this from the fact that we have never seen an object that is simultaneously both colours, or because it *is* part of the meaning of 'being red all over' that the possibility of other colours is excluded.

4 Self-Evidence and Certainty

In this section we shall explore two features that have traditionally been taken as characteristic of a priori knowledge, features that distinguish such knowledge from that which is empirical. First, it has been claimed that a priori knowledge is self-evident, and there are experiential and epistemological aspects to this claim. There is a certain feeling – or 'phenomenology' – associated with the apprehension of such truths; there's 'an obviousness' or 'a rightness' about them. Philosophers have tried to capture this aspect of our a priori thinking using a visual metaphor. Such truths have a 'clarity and brightness to the attentive mind' (Locke) or they are 'clearly and distinctly' perceived through the 'natural light of reason' (Descartes). The epistemological sense in which such claims are self-evident is that we are justified in believing them simply in virtue of understanding the claims in question. If you understand the claim 'nothing is red all over and green all over', then that is all that's required for you to be justified in having such a belief. Certain empirical truths may appear obvious – for instance, that Birmingham is north of London – but more than an understanding of this statement is required for you justifiably to believe it. You must also have some empirical evidence in support of such a claim.

However, some a priori truths are not self-evident in the ways suggested. Some do not strike us as obvious; they do not have the suggested phenomenology. Consider a mathematical truth, the proof of which has been derived using a complicated chain of reasoning. As an example let us think about Pythagoras' theorem: the square of the longest side of a right-angled triangle is the sum of the squares of the two shorter sides. This does not strike me as obvious; I do not have a sense that this is clearly true. It could be claimed, though, that I would be struck by its obviousness if I were led through the various steps of its proof, each of which is itself self-evident. This, however, is not true of all mathematical conclusions. Imagine that a rope was tightly placed around the equator of the Earth so that it hugged every mountain and valley. How much extra rope do you think would have to be added in order for it to sit one metre off the ground for its whole length? This can be worked out in a few simple mathematical steps, each of which is obvious, and I can keep this reasoning in mind as I contemplate the answer: just over six metres! This, to me, is a mathematical conclusion that is far from self-evident, even though I am perfectly happy with all the steps of the proof.

It is also claimed that the a priori is self-evident in the sense that such beliefs are justified purely in virtue of understanding the claims in question. There are, though, a priori truths that no one knows. Goldbach's conjecture states that every positive even integer can be expressed as the sum of two primes. Mathematicians have not yet succeeded in proving whether this is true or false. It is, however, a mathematical theorem and, as such, either it or its negation must be a priori true. I understand this conjecture – I know what it means – but I am not justified in accepting either possibility in the absence of a proof. Whichever it turns out to be – whether the conjecture or its negation is true – there is an a priori truth that I am not justified in believing even though I understand the claim in question. Self-evidence, then, in either its phenomenological or epistemological form, is not a necessary feature of a priori knowledge.

A second feature that has traditionally been seen as characteristic of a priori knowledge is certainty: we do not just believe that a priori claims are true; we are certain that they are. I believe that my cup is yellow and that $2+2=4$. Both of these claims are true. With the former, I am open to the possibility that I may be colour blind or that the light may be playing tricks on me; I'm certain, though, that the sum is correct. Nevertheless, there are problems in distinguishing a priori claims in this way. We can go wrong in our a priori reasoning just as our empirical claims about the world can be mistaken. For example, a priori philosophical claims can be shown to be false and unjustified; how else could philosophy progress if this were not the case? As we have seen, Gettier claims that the traditional a priori analysis of knowledge is flawed. He shows this by appealing to intuitions that are themselves a priori. It is also the case that empirical considerations may lead us to revise a conclusion that we have arrived at by a priori means. Imagine you confidently arrive at a sum after adding up a series of numbers; you have done so using a priori reasoning. It could happen, though, that your answer does not match that given by an electronic calculator. In such a case, the empirical evidence you have of the reliability of the calculator could trump your own a priori reasoning. This might even be the case with the following. Add up this list of numbers out loud:

1000
20
30
1000
1030
1000
20

What answer do you get? (The actual answer is 4,100!) Our a priori reasoning is not infallible and we cannot be certain of the conclusions we come to in this way. You can be led to reject an a priori claim because it is inconsistent with your other a priori commitments, or even because of contradictory empirical evidence.

5 Innate Knowledge

In this last section we shall turn to the rationalist claim that some of our knowledge is innate, that is, that it's not acquired via experience and that it's possessed from birth. Many thinkers claim that we have such knowledge: Plato argues that we have innate knowledge of virtue and justice, and Descartes claims that we have innate knowledge of God. Empiricists, however, argue that all our knowledge of the world must be acquired through experience and that prior to experience our minds are a 'blank page'.

> Let us then suppose the Mind to be, as we say, white paper, void of all characters, without any ideas; How comes it to be furnished? Whence comes it by that vast store, which the busy and boundless fancy of man has painted on it, with an almost endless variety? Whence has it all the materials of reason and knowledge? To this I answer, in one word, from *experience*. In that all our knowledge is founded, and from that it ultimately derives itself. (Locke, 1975, II.I.2)

John Locke offers an argument to this conclusion: if we possessed such innate knowledge, then the relevant truths would be known by everybody, and it's clear that they're not. Many 'children, idiots, savages and illiterate adults' do not possess any knowledge of virtue, of God, or of the various other a priori truths that are said to be innate. Such knowledge – if indeed we have it – must therefore be acquired through experience.

This, however, is not a compelling argument. The rationalist can accept that many people do not have an explicit grasp of such truths; nevertheless, they may be seen as unconsciously possessing such knowledge (it may be 'tacit'). The absence of universal consent does not lead us to reject the existence of innate knowledge. Certain thinkers may not be able to express such truths, but their behaviour reveals that they are indeed known. The film *L'Enfant Sauvage* (1969) is based on the actual case of a child who was raised by wolves. One section of the film suggests that he has innate moral knowledge, even though this is something he cannot explicitly express. He is occasionally punished by being put in a cupboard. On one occasion this is done to him even though he has not misbehaved, and when this happens he struggles more than usual. This suggests that the child knows that the treatment is unjust, something that he could not have learnt in the wild. Innate knowledge is possessed from birth and the right kind of education enables us to become aware of the possession of such knowledge and to be able to express it: 'the teaching from outside merely brings to life what was already there' (Leibniz, 1981, p. 76).

A distinct rationalist strategy is to claim that thinkers have an innate **disposition** to acquire certain types of knowledge.

> The actual knowledge of them is not innate. What is innate is what might be called potential knowledge of them . . . Items of knowledge (or truths), in so far as they are within us even when we do not think of them, are tendencies or dispositions. (Leibniz, 1981, p. 86)

The claim is not that thinkers unconsciously possess certain items of knowledge, but that they have an innate tendency to acquire them. On learning to use your powers of reasoning you become able to derive certain truths, truths that you are not explicitly taught, and truths that are therefore innate in the sense that you are disposed to acquire them from birth.

However, such a claim need not be contested by the empiricist. All he is committed to is the claim that we do not possess any actual knowledge at birth, any justified true beliefs about the world. This is consistent with the claim that babies have dispositions to acquire certain kinds of knowledge as they grow older. Perceptual beliefs could also be considered innate in this sense because we have an innate capacity to acquire them: we are born with sensory apparatus and are genetically disposed to develop certain perceptual and belief-forming mechanisms. There is also some evidence to suggest that we have innate perceptual abilities to individuate objects and to perceive their relative depth in our visual field. Whether we have such capacities from birth or whether they are learnt is an empirical question, one that can be studied by psychologists. Empiricism, then, does not rule out innate knowledge in this sense; it could be an empirical fact that it is something we possess.

Noam Chomsky (1972) forwards an empirical hypothesis concerning another important kind of innate capacity. He notes that children learn their native language in a relatively short amount of time given the complexity of what they have to learn and the limited teaching they receive. He argues that children can only do this because they already know certain structural features of language. There is a universal grammar shared by all languages that comprises a vast system of rules, and children have an innate knowledge of this grammar, knowledge that facilitates their acquisition of the particular language to which they are exposed. Here, though, we must not lose sight of our key concern, that is, the question of whether we can possess factual knowledge that is justified independently of our experience. The kind of knowledge that Chomsky discusses is not knowledge in the sense in which we are interested. Children are not capable of expressing it, and, even as adults, we are not able to articulate the rules of this universal grammar or even the rules of our own language (unless we are linguists and go on to study such things). Chomsky's claims do not concern factual knowledge. We can think here of the distinction between knowledge how and knowledge that. We may have an innate capacity or ability – the know-how – to speak and understand language, but we may not have innate knowledge of any particular facts. Similarly, we may have an innate ability to individuate objects and to see some as behind or in front of others, but I do not have innate knowledge that *my coffee cup is in front of my computer*. 'Nature has given us not knowledge, but the seeds of knowledge' (Seneca, 1925, cxx).

It is important to note that the issue of innateness is distinct from that concerning the a priori. Innateness does not itself concern justification; it is simply a temporal notion concerning whether certain concepts, beliefs or capacities are possessed from birth. The category of the a priori, however, picks out those truths that we are justified in believing without regard to our experience. It has been suggested that it's an empirical question whether we have innate capacities or beliefs. The more important question, however – that which divides the empiricist and the rationalist – is whether any of our beliefs concerning substantive empirical matters have a priori justification, and this question is independent of the temporal one concerning when particular beliefs or capacities are acquired. We can see that these questions are independent because of the possibility that we could have innate beliefs that do not possess a priori justification. Even if you have a belief in God from birth, there is still the question of whether this belief is justified, and the empiricist could argue that for this you require empirical evidence (see chapter 15, section 2).

A priori knowledge is acquired via intuition and reasoning, and the justification possessed by such knowledge does not depend on our experience of the world. Rationalists claim that such thinking can provide us with substantive, synthetic truths about the world; empiricists argue that it can only provide us with 'trivial' truths, those concerning the meanings of our words. In this chapter we have questioned the traditional claims that a priori knowledge is certain and self-evident, and the issue of innateness was found to be less divisive than it is usually considered to be. Empiricists can accept that we have certain innate dispositions of the kind suggested by some rationalists, and even that we have certain a priori beliefs before birth. The key empiricist claim, however, is that we cannot have factual knowledge before birth since the requisite justification must depend on our experience of the world, and it is to such perceptual experience that the next chapter turns.

Questions

1 At school I learnt Pythagoras' Theorem by cutting triangles and squares out of card in order to measure their area. This theorem is therefore an a posteriori truth, one that I know through experience. Is it?

2 Through a long and complex proof it can be ascertained that there is an infinite number of primes (integers that are only divisible by one and themselves). Is this self-evident? Is this something we can know a priori? Are we certain that this is true?

3 In an episode of the sitcom *Friends* (1994–2004), there is about to be a fight between Ross and Chandler to find out who is the strongest. Ross claims that he is: he says 'I'll prove it – I'll prove it like a theorem.' What is his epistemological mistake here?

4 Can a priori reasoning alone provide us with any substantive knowledge of the world?

5 Explain how the following analogy is relevant to the issue of innate knowledge.

> If the soul were like a blank tablet then truths would be in us as the shape of Hercules is in a piece of marble when the marble is entirely neutral as to whether it assumes this shape or some other. However, if there were veins in the block which marked out the shape of Hercules rather than other shapes, then that block would be more determined to that shape and Hercules would be innate in it, in a way, even though labour would be required to expose the veins and polish them into clarity, removing everything that prevents their being seen. (Leibniz, 1981, p. 52)

What kind of marble best represents human thinkers?

Further Reading

Throughout the book we shall discuss the claims of the rationalist Descartes, and the empiricist Locke. Their key works are the

Meditations of 1641 (Descartes, 1986) and *An Essay Concerning Human Understanding*, originally published in 1689 (Locke, 1975). Cottingham (1986) and Lowe (1995) provide good introductions to their thought. Moser (1987) is a useful collection of articles on the a priori, and Baehr's (2003) *Internet Encyclopedia of Philosophy* article (www.iep.utm.edu/ a/apriori. htm) is a clear introduction to the topic. For a more advanced treatment, see Kitcher (1980). Plantinga (1993b, ch. 6) discusses the alleged distinctive phenomenology associated with our apprehension of the a priori, and Bonjour (1998) gives a modern reading of the visual metaphor that we 'see' such truths. Audi (1998) and Chisholm (1977) discuss self-evidence and claim, in contrast to the line that I take, that this is a necessary feature of a priori reasoning. The film *The Enigma of Kaspar Hauser* (1974) is relevant to the issue of innate knowledge. After spending all of his life locked up in a cellar, Kaspar is released into society as a young man hardly able to walk or speak; the film explores whether his knowledge and various abilities are innate or learnt.

 **Perception**

Perception is the process by which we acquire information about the world using our five senses of sight, hearing, touch, taste, and smell. In this chapter we shall focus on two issues concerning such sensory engagement with the world (although we shall mainly be concerned with sight). First, what are the objects of perception: on what does my attention focus as I look at the yellow coffee cup in front of me? You may think that this is obvious: 'the yellow cup, of course'. We shall see, though, that many philosophers have denied this and we shall explore their reasons for doing so. Second, we shall turn to the key epistemological topic of justification and to the relationship between perceptual experience, perceptual belief and perceptual knowledge.

1 Direct Realism

Perceptual realism is the commonsense view that tables, paper clips and cups of coffee exist independently of perceivers. Direct realists also claim that it is such objects that we directly perceive; we see, smell, touch, taste and hear these familiar items. There are, however, two versions of direct realism: naive direct realism and scientific direct realism. They differ in the properties they claim the objects of perception can possess when they are not being perceived. Naive realists claim that such objects can continue to have all the properties that we usually perceive them to have, properties such as yellowness, smoothness and warmth. Scientific realists claim that some of the properties an object is perceived as having are dependent on the perceiver, and that unperceived objects should not be thought of as retaining them. Such a stance has a long history. Here is Galileo in 1623 expressing this view:

> I believe that for external bodies to excite in us tastes, odors, and sounds, nothing is required in those bodies themselves except size, shape, and a lot of slow or fast motions. I think that if ears, tongues, and noses were taken away, then shapes, numbers, and motions would well remain, but not odors, tastes or sounds. The latter are, I believe, nothing but names, outside of the living animal. (Galileo, 1960, sec. 47)

Scientific direct realism is often discussed in terms of Locke's distinction between primary and secondary qualities. The primary qualities of an object are those whose existence is independent of the existence of a perceiver. Locke's inventory of such qualities included shape, size, position, number, motion-or-rest and solidity, and science claims to be completing this inventory by positing such properties as charge, spin and mass. The secondary qualities of objects are those properties that do depend on the existence of a perceiver. They comprise such properties as colour, smell and felt texture. A scientific description of objects in the world does not include an account of these secondary qualities, and thus these properties should not be seen as possessed by those objects themselves, but rather as in some way relative to perceiving creatures. The cup itself is not yellow, but the physical composition of its surface, and the particular way this surface reflects light rays into our eyes, causes in us the experience of seeing yellow. For the scientific realist, then, only some of the properties that we perceive continue to be possessed by objects when there are no perceivers around, these being their primary qualities.

> Thus nature gets credit which should in truth be reserved for ourselves: the rose for its scent: the nightingale for his song: the sun for its radiance. The poets are entirely mistaken. They should address their lyrics to themselves, and should turn them into odes of self-congratulation on the excellency of the human mind. Nature is a dull affair, soundless, scentless, colourless . . . (Whitehead, 1926, pp. 68–9)

This distinction between primary and secondary qualities is controversial in various ways, but that need not concern us here. What we should be clear on, however, is that the key feature of both naive and scientific direct realism is that we directly perceive objects whose existence is independent of perceivers, objects that are out there in the world. The following section questions the claim that our perception is direct, and in section 3 the very existence of mind-independent objects will be brought into question.

2   Indirect Realism

Indirect realists agree that the coffee cup exists independently of me. However, I do not directly perceive this cup. The indirect realist claims that perception involves mediating images. When looking at an everyday object, it is not that object that we directly see, but rather, a perceptual intermediary. These intermediaries have been called 'sense data', 'sensa', 'ideas', 'sensibilia', 'percepts' and 'appearances'. We shall use the term 'sense data', and the singular 'sense datum'. Sense data are mental objects that manifest (some of) the properties we take objects in the world to possess, and they are usually considered to have two rather than three dimensions. For the indirect realist, the coffee cup on my desk causes in my mind the presence of a two-dimensional yellow sense datum, and it is this object that I directly perceive. Consequently, I only indirectly perceive the coffee cup, that is, I only perceive it in virtue of being aware of the sense datum that it has caused in my mind. This is the conclusion of the argument from illusion; a highly influential argument, one that supports indirect realism, and one to which idealism (section 3.1), phenomenalism (section 3.2), and intentionalism (section 4) can all be seen as responses.

2.1   The argument from illusion

We are prey to illusion when the world is not how we perceive it to be. When a stick is partially submerged in water, it looks bent when in fact it is straight. From most angles plates look oval rather than round. (We still *believe* that the plate is circular and that the stick is straight because of what we know about perspective and refraction, but these objects still *look* elliptical and bent if we resist interpreting what we see with respect to such knowledge.) As well as being prey to illusions, we sometimes hallucinate and see things that are not there at all. It is such illusions and hallucinations that drive the following key argument for indirect realism.

I'll partly submerge a pencil in my glass of water. The pencil appears bent, and so I am seeing a bent shape. I know, however, that the pencil isn't really bent. The bent shape that I see cannot therefore be the real pencil in the world. And if the bent shape is not a physical object, then it must be something mental. As we have seen, these mental items have been coined 'sense data', and it must be these that we perceive in cases of illusion and hallucination.

Let us now consider veridical cases (those in which we correctly perceive the world). Cases of veridical perception are experientially the same as those of illusion or hallucination; it would *look* the same to the perceiver if there were really a bent stick in the water. There must therefore be something in common between the veridical and the non-veridical cases. The indirect realist claims that the conclusion we should draw is that the common factor between the veridical and the non-veridical cases is the presence of a sense datum: in cases of veridical perception it is also sense data that we perceive. Our experiences in these different cases have the same character because they are caused by our engagement with the same kind of object, that is, sense data. Locke (1975, IV.IV.3) held such a theory: 'The mind . . . perceives nothing but its own ideas', ideas being mental items akin to sense data. Hume, in his 1748 *Enquiry*, also accepted such an account: 'the slightest philosophy . . . teaches us, that nothing can ever be present to the mind but an image or perception' (1999, sec. 12.9). And this kind of theory has continued to have a distinguished following: its adherents include Bertrand Russell, A. J. Ayer and Frank Jackson.

There are various problems with this argument and we shall look at some of these below. However, whether or not the argument is successful, there is no doubt that it has been highly influential. The theories of perception covered in the following sections are in part driven by the argument from illusion. Idealists and phenomenalists (section 3) accept the existence of sense data, but deny that they play the role of perceptual intermediaries. For them, there is no world independent of our perceptual experience. Intentionalists (section 4) agree that there is something in common between veridical and non-veridical cases of perception. This common factor, however, should not be seen as an object, but rather as a property of perceptual experience that is akin to the representational properties possessed by certain thoughts. However, before we turn to these theories we should take a closer look at the nature of sense data.

2.2   Dualism

Sense data are metaphysically problematic. They are taken to be inner objects, objects that have properties such as colour. Such entities, however, are incompatible with a materialist view of the mind. Materialists aim to explain the workings of the mind in scientific terms – in terms of perhaps brain states or computational structures – and such an approach has become the orthodoxy in the contemporary philosophy of mind. However, such items as yellow sense data cannot figure in any such account. There is nothing material in the brain that is yellow; nothing, then, that could constitute the yellow sense datum that I (allegedly) experience when looking at the coffee cup. Thus, since sense data are not acceptable to a materialist, the yellow object that I am now perceiving must be located not in the material world, but in the non-physical mind. Indirect realism is committed to **dualism**, a theory that embraces an ontology of non-physical 'objects' alongside that of the physical. There are, however, various difficulties with respect to dualism, and I shall briefly consider one of them.

   The greatest problem for the dualist is how he should account for the interaction between the mind and the physical world. Remember, the indirect realist accepts that there is a world independent of our experience, and in veridical cases of perception it is this world that somehow causes sense data to exist in our minds. How, though, can causal connections to the physical world bring about the existence of such non-physical items, and how can such items be involved in causing physical actions, as they appear to be? If I have a desire for caffeine, then my perception of the coffee cup causes me to reach out for that cup: a non-physical sense datum causes the physical movement of my arm. It's not clear, though, whether such causation is coherent. A dualistically conceived mind appears to be paradoxical in the same way as fictional ghosts are: ghosts can pass through walls, yet they do not fall through the floor; they can wield axes yet swords pass straight through them. Similarly, the mind is conceived as both distinct from the physical world, and also causally efficacious within it, and it's not clear how the mind can coherently possess both features (see Dennett, 1991, p. 35).

3   Rejecting Realism

3.1   Idealism

Another problem for indirect realism is that of scepticism. According to the indirect realist, we only directly perceive certain mental entities, but in drawing the focus of our perception away from the world and onto such inner items, we are threatened by wholesale scepticism. Since we can only directly perceive our sense data, all our beliefs about the external world beyond may be false. There may not actually be any coffee cups in the world, merely yellow sense data in my mind. It is difficult to overstate the importance of the resulting scepticism to both the methodology and history of epistemology, and in chapter 9 we shall take a closer look at whether we should be worried by it. Here, though, we shall look at a position that embraces such scepticism and accepts the **anti-realist** stance that there is no world independent of the perceiver. Two strategies that take this line are idealism and phenomenalism.

Bishop George Berkeley (1685–1753) is an idealist. For him, 'physical' objects consist in collections of 'ideas' (which later came to be called 'sense data'): the universe is simply made up of minds and the sense data that they perceive. Sense data, however, cannot exist if they are not being perceived, and so 'physical' objects are dependent on perceivers. A consequence of such an account would seem to be that when we do not perceive the world, it does not exist. Berkeley attempts to avoid this conclusion by claiming that God perceives the objects that are not perceived by us and thus sustains their existence; an existence, though, merely in the realm of ideas or sense data.

> [A]ll the furniture of the Earth . . . have not any subsistence without a mind . . . their being is to be perceived or known . . . consequently, so long as they are not actually perceived by me or do not exist in my mind or that of any other created spirit, they must either have no exist-ence at all or else subsist in the mind of some external spirit – it being perfectly unintelligible . . . to attribute to any single part of them an existence independent of a spirit. (Berkeley, 1998, pt 1, para. 6)

Such a position is highly problematic and certainly counterintuitive, although, perhaps surprisingly, some of its anti-realist elements were widely adopted in the early twentieth century by a group of philoso-phers called phenomenalists.

3.2   Phenomenalism

Idealists conceive of the world in terms of our *actual* experiences (or those of God). Phenomenalists hold a related position: for them, state-ments about the physical world should be seen as statements about our *possible* experiences. Or, as J. S. Mill (1889) puts it, material objects are nothing but 'permanent possibilities of sensation'. Phenomenalism is classically taken as a conceptual thesis: 'The meaning of any statement which refers to a material thing may be fully conveyed in statements which refer solely to sense-data or the sensible appearance of things' (Chisholm, 1948, p. 152. Note, however, that Chisholm does not agree with this view). Phenomenalists do not require God to sustain the existence of objects. 'Physical' objects can exist unperceived since there is the continued *possibility* of experience. To say that a paper clip is in my drawer is to say that I would see one *if* I opened that drawer. The world is described in terms of my current sense data, and in terms of **conditionals** that detail which sense data I would encounter in **counterfactual** and future situations. We must, however, be careful to note the crucial difference between the realist and anti-realist readings of such conditionals. Realism – be it direct or indirect – has an account of why such a conditional holds: I shall have the experience of perceiving a paper clip since there exists, independent of my mind, a real paper clip in the drawer. Phenomenalists, however, do not ground their conditionals in this way since there is no world independent of our (possible) experiences. To say that the paper clip is in my drawer is simply to say that the flux of sense data characteristic of the experience of opening the drawer will be followed by the experience of perceiving the silvery-coloured sense data that constitutes a perception of the paper clip. There is no mention here of an independent world; such conditionals are only described in terms of the content of my experiences.

Conditionals can also be used to describe dispositional properties such as solubility: that lump of sugar is soluble since it will dissolve *if* it is put in a cup of coffee. Such a dispositional property can be explained in terms of the physical make-up of the sugar: it dissolves because of its chemical structure. The conditionals of the phenomenalist, however – those that describe certain regularities in our experience – do not have any deeper explanation; they are brute: nothing further can be said about why they hold.

3.3 Problems for phenomenalism

For many, the anti-realist nature of phenomenalism is unpalatable. A consequence of phenomenalism is that if there are no minds, then there is no world. This is so since 'physical' objects are simply constructs of our (possible) experience. If there are no creatures to have such experiences, then there can be no world. This is hard to accept given the commonsense intuitions that the external world would continue to exist whether or not there were creatures to experience it, and that the world was around before the emergence of sentient life. Let us also consider the supposed knowledge we have of others. I come to believe that there are other flesh and blood creatures in the world through perceiving their bodies, and I come to see some of these creatures as thinkers through watching their actions and listening to their utterances. The phenomenalist must have an account of how I perceive such behaviour, and for her it must consist in the (possible) experiences I can have of *my own* sense data. Phenomenalism invokes a solipsistic picture in which it is my sense data alone that constitute the world. A phenomenalist reading in the library must claim that the book she is holding simply consists in the 'possibility of sensation'; that her own physical body (a part of the material world) also has this nature; and that the people sitting at her table are similarly constructs of her own sense data. Phenomenalism is a very radical stance to take. (I shall return to solipsism in chapter 13 and I will consider whether or not I am justified in believing that there are other thinkers apart from me.)

Even for those who do not have qualms about adopting such an anti-realist and solipsistic stance, phenomenalism appears unable to complete the project it sets itself. A key argument against phenomenalism is the argument from perceptual relativity. Roderick Chisholm (1948) argues that we cannot provide translations of statements about physical objects in terms of statements about sense data. For a phenomenalist, the statement that there is an old green pencil tin to my right means that the experience of reaching to the right would be followed by a sharp sensation (on encountering the 'jagged rim'), and that the sensation of turning my head would be followed by the presence of green sense data in my field of vision. However, such fluxes of experience need not occur in this way. With gloves on, I would not feel such a sharp sensation, and if I were colour blind or if the lights were off, I would not experience such green sense data. The sensations I have depend on various facts about me and my environment. There are no conditional statements that describe the relation between sensations considered in isolation from certain physical aspects of the perceiver and of the world.

> To calculate the appearances with complete success, it is necessary to know both the thing perceived and the (subjective and objective) observation conditions, for it is the thing perceived and the observation conditions working jointly which determine what is to appear. (Chisholm, 1948, p. 513)

A phenomenalist, however, cannot account for such observation conditions since she is not permitted to talk of the physical states of the perceiver or those of her environment; she can only talk of sense data and the relations between them. According to Chisholm, therefore, the phenomenalist cannot provide an account of the physical world purely in terms of possible experiences, and thus the project fails.

4   The Intentionalist Theory of Perception

The final position which we shall look at denies that sense data are involved in perception and, instead, claims that we are in direct perceptual contact with the world. Thus we return to the direct realism with which this chapter started. In order for such an account to be plausible, an alternative response to the argument from illusion must be found. First, we shall consider a strategy that may help us to avoid the conclusion that the veridical and non-veridical cases have an *object* of perception in common; second, an alternative account of this common factor will be considered.

4.1 Adverbialism

It has been claimed that the argument from illusion **begs the question**. It is simply assumed, without argument, that in the non-veridical case I am aware of some *thing* which has the property that the pencil appears to have. It is assumed that some object must be bent. We can, however, reject this assumption: I only seem to see a bent pencil; there is nothing in the world or in my mind that is actually bent. One way of rejecting the assumption that you must be aware of some object is to make what is called the 'adverbial' move. This strategy can be illustrated by turning to other examples in which such ontological assumptions are not made. 'David Beckham has a beautiful free kick' does not imply that he is the possessor of a certain kind of object – a kick – something that he could give away or sell in the way that he can his beautiful car. Rather, we understand this phrase to mean that he takes free kicks beautifully. 'Beautiful' should not be seen as an adjective describing the property of an object; it should instead be seen as playing the role of an adverb, describing how a certain action is performed. Similarly, when you are 'in the groove', you are not dancing in some kind of slot on the dance floor; you are dancing groovily. The adverbialist claim with respect to perception is that when you perceive yellow, you are sensing in a yellow manner (or yellowly). Perceptual experience should be described in terms of adverbial modifications of the various verbs characteristic of perception, rather than in terms of objects that we perceive. As I lift the cup of coffee to my lips, I see in a brown manner (brownly) and smell in a bitter manner (bitterly); I do not perceive brown and bitter sense data, the inner analogues of the properties of the coffee below my nose. In describing perceptual experiences we are not describing the properties of mental items; but rather we are talking about the manner in which we directly experience the external world. Thus, if we can give an account of what it is to experience in a brown and bitter manner, then we can account for perception. This is what the intentionalist attempts to do.

4.2 Intentionalism

Intentionalists emphasize certain parallels between perceptual experience and beliefs. Beliefs are representations of the world. I now have a belief about my pencil tin; I believe that it's green. Beliefs possess what philosophers of mind call 'intentionality'. This is an essential feature of the mind, and it describes the property that certain mental states have of representing – or being *about* – certain aspects of the world. The aspects of the world that a belief is about can be specified in terms of that belief's *intentional content*. The intentional content of my current belief is that *the pencil tin is green*. The intentionalist claims that perception also involves representational states (intentionalism is sometimes called 'representationalism'). I can believe that the tin is green, and I can also perceive that it is. You are about to perceive that the first word of the next paragraph is 'Let'. Your perception is intentional: it is *about* a word on the page, and its content is that *the next word is 'Let'*.

Let us see how the intentionalist reacts to the argument from illusion. The key claim will be that mental states can misrepresent the world. I can have false beliefs: I can believe that my cup is full when it is not, and I can have beliefs about non-existent entities: I can believe that the Tooth Fairy visited me last night. These kinds of belief are analogous to the non-veridical perceptual cases of illusion and hallucination. In such cases of both belief and perception, we have incorrect representations of the world. Importantly, though, the intentionalist has an account of what the veridical and non-veridical cases have in common, that is, their intentional content. My perception has the representational content, *there is a bent pencil there*, whether or not there really is such a pencil in the world (I might have been duped: a bent pencil could have been placed in the glass of water). I may not be sure whether the giant spider I see is a hallucination or not. Either way, I have a perception with the intentional content, *there's a giant spider in front of me*. In the veridical case this content correctly represents the world; in the non-veridical case it does not. Intentionalists therefore agree with sense datum theorists that there is an aspect of perception that is shared by the veridical and non-veridical cases. This shared component, however, is not the presence of a perceptual object, but rather that of intentional content. Both intentionalists and sense datum theorists provide representational accounts of perception: intentional content and the sense data of the indirect realist represent the state of the independent external world. Intentionalists, however, have representation without an ontological commitment to mental objects.

Intentionalists are usually optimistic about providing a 'naturalistic' or broadly scientific, causal account of representation and intentionality. To explain perception, then, we do not have to refer to non-physical sense data; rather, we could simply use our naturalistic account of intentional content, since, according to intentionalists, the important features of perception are captured by this notion. More shall be said about the naturalistic approach in chapter 11.

4.3   *Phenomenology*

In this section we shall look at a potential problem for intentionalism. It would appear that my experience consists in more than simply representing the world in a certain way; it is also the case that the way I acquire such representations strikes my consciousness in a distinctive way. 'Perceptual experiences are Janus-faced: they point outward to the external world but they also present a subjective form to the subject . . . they are *of something* other than the subject, and they are *like something* for the subject' (McGinn, 1997, p. 298). Right now there is the faint sound of a road drill syncopating with the reverse warning beep of a supermarket delivery truck; the yellow cup in front of me is slowly fading to ochre as a cloud passes overhead; and the smell of coffee is struggling to get past my persistent cold and the pungency of my throat lozenges. All of this is part of my perceptual experience and, for the intentionalist, it consists in such representational content as *the lorry is emitting a beep*, and *my throat lozenge is pungent.* There is also, however, something *it is like* to be having such representations (see Nagel, 1974). My experience has a phenomenological dimension – an experiential quality – a quality that you are probably currently imagining. The shrill beep 'goes right through me', and the lozenge is so strong that, although it pervades my consciousness, I somehow also feel sharper, clearer, more finely tuned to the quality of the air that I am breathing. The intentionalist, therefore, must also account for these phenomenological features of perception. And again, this is a task that is usually pursued in a naturalistic spirit. He aims to provide a scientific account of how it is that the causal processes grounding perception have the experiential quality that they do. Many, however, see this as the hardest problem facing the philosophy of mind. It is not clear how any scientific account can hope to capture the conscious, phenomenological dimension of thought and perception.

> [There is] the feeling of an unbridgeable gulf between consciousness and brain process . . . This idea of a difference in kind is accompanied by slight giddiness. (Wittgenstein, 1953, §412)

> Nobody has the slightest idea how anything material could be conscious. Nobody even knows what it would be like to have the slightest idea how anything material could be conscious. So much for the philosophy of consciousness. (Fodor, 1992, p. 5)

Here, though, is not the place to pursue this debate.

Such problems notwithstanding, some intentionalists claim that their account of the phenomenology of experience is more persuasive than that given by the sense datum theorist (see Tye, 2000, and Harman, 1997). They appeal to what they call the 'transparency' of experience. As I look at the cluttered desk in front of me, my experience strikes me in a certain way: I seem to be experiencing properties of the various objects that are strewn there. This, the intentionalists claim, chimes better with their account of perception. For them, the phenomenological character of experience is wholly accounted for by the representational properties of our perceptual experience, and thus, since intentional content is directed at objects in the world, the possession of such content provides the right focus for the phenomenology of experience. The sense datum theorist, however, gets the phenomenology wrong. On his account I am aware of certain inner mental objects, but this, the intentionalist claims, is not how our experience strikes us. I seem to experience the colour of the cup – the cup that is *over there* – and not an inner analogue of the cup that is merely in my mind. Michael Tye expresses this point with respect to his experience of looking at the ocean. 'I experienced blue as a property of the ocean not as a property of my experience. My experience itself certainly wasn't blue. Rather it was an experience that represented the ocean as blue' (1992, p. 160).

So far we have considered metaphysical questions concerning the nature of the entities involved in perception, and whether perception involves an engagement – direct or indirect – with an independent, external world. Indirect realists, idealists and phenomenalists take the argument from illusion to show that it is sense data that we perceive. Intentionalists, however, reject such a picture and account for perception in terms of representational states, states for which they hope to provide a naturalistic explanation. The anti-realist approaches of idealism and phenomenalism will largely be ignored in the rest of the book; we shall focus on realism and, starting in the next section, the key questions we shall consider are how and whether we have justified perceptual beliefs about the external world, and whether we can have perceptual knowledge of that world. In order to do this, we shall first look at the relationship between perceptual experience and perceptual belief.

5   Seeing That, Seeing As, and Raw Seeing

Let us further consider the representational nature of perceptual experience. (This, remember, is something to which both sense datum theorists and intentionalists are committed.) Looking out of my study window, I see that *it is raining*. My perception represents the world as being like *that*. To perceive the world in this way, it is required that I possess concepts, that is, ways of representing and thinking about the world. In this case I require the concept RAIN. Thus, seeing that *my coffee cup is yellow* and that *the tin is green* involves the possession of the concepts COFFEE CUP, YELLOW, TIN and GREEN. Such perception is termed 'perceiving that', and this kind of perceptual engagement with the world is *factive*, that is, it is presupposed that we perceive the world correctly. To perceive that it's raining, it must be *true* that it's raining. I can also, though, perceive the world to be a certain way, yet be mistaken. This we can call 'perceiving as', or, in the usual case, 'seeing as'. The stick partly submerged in water may not be bent; nevertheless, I see it *as* bent. Much of my perception is representational – I take the world to be a certain way – sometimes correctly, when I see that the world is thus and so, and sometimes incorrectly, when the world is not how I perceive it to be.

As was noted, perceptual experiences are Janus-faced: they are representational and they have a phenomenological dimension. For the intentionalist, both these features are grounded in the intentional content of a particular perceptual state. Sense datum theorists, however, have various kinds of hybrid account. The phenomenology of experience is a feature of our perceptual engagement with an inner mental object; the fact that we can be described as perceiving that the world is a certain way, however, is explained by the operation of conceptual thinking in this perceptual act. In addition to my acquaintance with yellow sense data, I have a belief or a thought that the coffee cup is yellow.

There is also a form of perception that does not require the possession of concepts. Cognitively unsophisticated creatures can perceive the world, those that do not have conceptually structured thought. I can tell that the wasp senses or perceives my presence because of its irascible behaviour. It would also seem that we can perceptually engage with the world in a non-conceptual way. When I am walking along the High Street daydreaming, I see the bus shelter, waste bins, and my fellow pedestrians – I must do because I do not bump into them – but I do not see that *the bus shelter is blue* or that *a certain pedestrian is wearing Wrangler jeans.* I can come to see the street in this way if I 'focus' on the scene in front of me, but there is a coherent form of perception that does not involve concepts. Let us call this basic perceptual engagement with the world 'raw seeing'. Such perception involves the acquisition of perceptual information, information that enables us to engage successfully with objects, but information that does not amount to having a conceptually structured representation of the world. Fred Dretske (1969) refers to raw seeing as 'non-epistemic' seeing, and to 'seeing that' as 'epistemic' seeing. (In chapter 6 we shall investigate the crucial role that non-epistemic seeing plays within a foundationalist account of justification, and we shall question whether there really can be a form of perceptual experience that does not involve concepts.)

I can see the bus stop in a non-epistemic or raw sense; or, I can see that *the bus shelter is blue*; or, mistakenly, see the bus shelter as *made of sapphire.* These are all forms of perceptual experience, ways we have of perceptually engaging with the world using our sensory apparatus, ways that have a distinctive conscious or phenomenological dimension. Next, then, we shall start to consider how these various kinds of perceptual experience are related to our perceptual beliefs. Perceptual beliefs are those concerning the perceptible features of our environment, and they are beliefs that are grounded in our perceptual experience of the world. The content of such beliefs could be acquired in other ways: I could, for example, be told that the bus shelter is blue, but in *seeing* that it is I acquire this belief by looking at it; my belief about the bus shelter is therefore a perceptual belief.

We do not necessarily come to acquire perceptual beliefs in virtue of non-epistemically seeing the world. As said, raw seeing is something that cognitively unsophisticated creatures can do, creatures such as wasps that are considered not to have beliefs. It is plausible, though, that if I see a certain object *as* a bus shelter, then I would also come to believe that there is a bus shelter in front of me. In many cases this is true, but not in all. An example of a case in which I do not believe my eyes is the Müller-Lyer illusion.

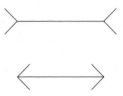

The two horizontal lines above look to me as though they differ in length, the upper line being longer than the lower one. I have, however, seen this illusion before and thus I do not believe that this is so. I believe that they are the same length (which they are). Here is another such case. A habitual user of hallucinogenics may doubt the veracity of all his perceptions; he may not believe anything he sees. His perception, though, amounts to more than non-epistemic seeing. He sees the moon as made of cheese and his cup of tea as grinning at him. However, because of the doubt fostered by his frequent hallucinations, he does not move from seeing the world as being a certain way to believing that it is. Nevertheless, these cases of hallucination and illusion are unusual, and it's plausible that seeing the world as being a certain way leads in most cases to you also believing that it is (unless, that is, you are aware of factors that cause you to doubt your perceptual experience). Last, let us return to 'perceiving that' or epistemic seeing. Such perception has a closer relationship with the acquisition of perceptual belief. If you are described as perceiving that the world is a certain way, it is implied that you also believe that the world is so. This kind of perception does not come apart from belief.

We have seen that we can be perceptually engaged with the world in a variety of ways. Such engagement can amount to the mere acquisition of perceptual information, the experience of seeing the world as being a certain way, or the possession of the cognitive states of perceiving and believing that it is so. And, if all goes well, such perceptual beliefs may constitute perceptual knowledge of the world. Perceptual knowledge consists in knowledge of the perceptible features of the world around us. According to the traditional account, we have such knowledge when our perceptual beliefs are true, and when they are justified. We shall focus on the issue of justification in part III of the book. A key debate that we shall consider is between those who claim that perceptual beliefs are justified simply in virtue of being grounded in our perceptual experience of the world, and those who think that this is not sufficient for justification and that such beliefs are only justified if they fit in well with all our other perceptual and non-perceptual beliefs. The former are foundationalists (chapter 6), and the latter, coherentists (chapter 7). In the next chapter, though, we shall leave perception and turn to another crucial source of knowledge, the reports of our fellows: the things people say and the words that they write.

Questions

1 To which theory of perception are the following limericks relevant, and why?

> There was a young man who said, 'God,
> I find it exceedingly odd,
> That the willow oak tree
> Continues to be
> When there's no one about in the Quad.'

> 'Dear Sir, your astonishment's odd
> For I'm always about in the Quad;
> And that's why the tree
> Continues to be.'
> Signed 'Yours faithfully, GOD.'

2 What is the argument from illusion? What, if anything, does it tell us about the kind of objects we perceive?
3 What is phenomenalism, and can it provide a plausible account of perception?
4 What is intentional content, and what role does it play in perception and thought?
5 Is perception representational? If so, how?
6 Can a wasp see that the jam jar is open; can it see the jar as full; and can it see the jam?

Further Reading

For indirect realism see Ayer (1940), Russell (1912), Grice (1961) and Jackson (1977). (Note, however, that Jackson has recently abandoned this view.) The classical accounts of idealism and phenomenalism can be found in Berkeley's *Treatise* and J. S. Mill (1889), with modern defences of phenomenalism provided by Robinson (2001) and Foster (2000). For intentionalism see Tye (1995; 2000) and Armstrong (1961). Useful discussion of the argument from illusion can be found in Dancy (1995), and Audi (1998) is good on the various epistemic relations between perception, belief and knowledge.

5 Testimony

1 The Individualistic Approach to Knowledge

Philosophers have traditionally seen the pursuit of knowledge as a solitary activity. This is certainly true of the rationalist approach, vividly illustrated by Descartes's 1641 *Meditations*. Sitting alone by the fire, he proves that God exists, and that God would not allow him to be deceived about the existence of the external world. And, for the empiricists, the paradigm method of acquiring knowledge about the world is through perception: to know that *p*, you must come to perceive that *p* for yourself. It is the solitary individual that is the locus of epistemology, either acquiring knowledge through a priori reasoning or through empirical reasoning grounded in perception. We shall call such an approach to knowledge 'individualistic'. I may come to acquire beliefs from others, but these are not justified until I have checked myself whether they are true. According to the individualistic picture, such beliefs are second-hand *and* second rate. Here are some explicit statements of the individualistic approach:

> I hope it will not be thought arrogance to say, that perhaps we should make greater progress in the discovery of rational and contemplative knowledge if we sought it in the fountain, in the consideration of things themselves, and made use rather of our own thoughts than other men's to find it: for, I think, we may as rationally hope to see with other men's eyes as to know by other men's understanding . . . The floating of other men's opinions in our brains makes us not one jot the more knowing, though they happen to be true. What in them was science is in us but opiniatrety. (Locke, 1975, book 1, p. 58)
>
> Nullius in verba [on no man's word]. (Royal Society motto)
>
> Do not trust my words, rely only upon your own light. (Buddha's last sermon, cited in Matilal and Chakrabarti, 1994, p. 2)

In this chapter we shall question the claim that testimonial beliefs are second rate, and it shall be accepted that we can acquire justified beliefs and knowledge from others.

2 Testimony

Recently there has been considerable interest in moving away from the individualistic conception of knowledge; the suggestion is that we can acquire empirical knowledge from others without having perceived the relevant facts for ourselves. We should note that this certainly chimes with how we generally talk about knowledge. The response to the question, 'How do you know that?' is often 'Somebody told me so', 'I saw it on the TV', or 'I read it in a book'. This chapter takes these kinds of claims seriously. The general term for such knowledge is 'testimonial knowledge', with 'testimony' taken to have a broad application: it applies to all cases where you are informed that something is thus and so by somebody else. Testimonial reports can be comprised of the spoken or written word, film, mime, semaphore, and all the other forms of communication that we use to pass on information about the world. Simple bodily actions can amount to testimony when, for example, someone nods their head in response to a question, gives you the thumbs up, or points you in the direction of the museum. Discussions of testimony do not simply concern the formal testimony given in a law court or the religious testimony given in chapel; 'testimony' refers to the everyday occurrences of finding something out from somebody else.

Here are some putative examples of testimonial knowledge. The number 50 bus goes to Druids Heath (I have never stayed on the bus past Kings Heath and so I haven't checked for myself whether this is true). My ruler is 30 centimetres long (I have never seen the standard metre rule in Paris). The vegetarian lasagne does not contain nuts (I wasn't present when it was made). Human beings have brains (I have never looked inside anyone's skull). Alp D'Huez is east of Grenoble (that's what the map 'says'; I haven't been there myself). My birthday is February the fourth (I have taken my parents' word for this). And, for that matter, I have taken my parents' word that they are indeed my parents. In this chapter we shall accept that such beliefs are putative items of knowledge. We are therefore moving away from the individual-istic picture. It is certainly true that such testimonial beliefs are widespread, and that we have no option but to rely on them; we simply haven't the time to check out the veracity of all such beliefs for ourselves. The key issue that will concern us, however, is how (and whether) we are *justified* in accepting the testimony of others. We may be pragmatically justified – if I plan to go to Druids Heath, then it's easier for me just to believe what it says on the front of the number 50 bus – but are we epistemically justified? Is there good reason to think that testimonial reports are true? We shall look at two accounts of such justification, those of Hume and Thomas Reid.

3 Hume's Account of Testimony

Hume was one of the first philosophers to note the importance of testimony: 'there is no species of reasoning more common, more useful, and even necessary to human life, than that which is derived from the testimony of men and the reports of eye-witnesses and spectators' (Hume, 1999, sec. 10.5). And he suggests an account of how testimonial beliefs may be justified. I am only justified in believing what someone says if I know that they have a good track record, that is, if I know that they have reliably told the truth before. Martha always buys the Christmas *Radio Times*, and so she has always been right about what's on TV over Christmas. This year, then, I am justified in believing her when she tells me the Boxing Day movie is *Casablanca*. In order to acquire such justified testimonial beliefs, I do not explicitly have to reason in this way. The Humean can claim that such a belief is justified *if I am able* to reason in this way. I must be capable of keeping track of the past record of the speaker, and of performing the suggested inference. This is a **reductive** account of testimony since, for the Humean, the source of such testimonial justification can be found in certain other epistemic abilities that I possess. I am justified in believing Martha because I have *perceptual* evidence that she has regularly told the truth before, I *remember* that she has a reliable record, and I am capable of carrying out the *inference* above. Testimonial justification is reducible to the justification provided by perception, memory and inference. In the next two sections we shall look at two problems with this reductive account. (In chapter 10, section 2, we see Hume arguing that such empirical reasoning is unjustified. In this chapter, then, we shall refer to such an account of testimony as 'Humean'. Humeans are those who adopt Hume's reductive account of testimony, yet do not embrace his scepticism.)

3.1   The problem of circularity

In most cases we do not seem to have collected enough evidence to justify our testimonial beliefs. Sometimes, perhaps, we have: the contents of baked bean tins have always coincided with what it has said on the label. I am therefore justified in believing that the label is correct when I open my next tin (note here the wide application of the term 'testimony'). In most cases, however, our evidence is rather more limited. Listening to the news on the radio tonight, I am shocked by certain events. On the Humean account, though, it's not clear whether I should believe what the newsreader says. I have never heard her speak before, and thus I have no knowledge of her past record. It would seem, then, that I am not justified in believing her news report. This is implausible. The amount of knowledge that I could acquire via testimony would be greatly diminished if I had to consider the past record of all my informants. To avoid this counterintuitive conclusion, the Humean can claim that our evidence can be improved if we are allowed to base our inferences on correlations between types of reporter and types of event. I may not have heard *tonight's* newsreader before, but I have evidence that newsreaders in general have correctly reported world events in the past (most of the time).

Here, though, another problem arises. It is not clear whether we have enough *independent* evidence to judge whether certain types of speaker are reliable. We can check whether newsreaders are reliable, but to do this we would perhaps read the newspaper or search the internet. Such sources themselves consist in testimonial reports, and so our account of justification appears to be circular: the testimony of newsreaders is justified by the testimony of the newspaper. We would like a reason to believe in testimonial reports that does not itself rely on testimony. A possible solution to this problem would be to allow that we *can* assess the reliability of *very broad* types of reporter. It may be the case that *people in general* have been mostly correct in the past, people who look fairly astute and those who do not look or sound too shifty. Such an account would not be prey to circularity since we all have firsthand evidence of the reliability of a good number of such speakers.

3.2   The Martian argument

In this section we shall look at another argument against the Humean account of testimony, one presented by Tony Coady (1973; 1992). According to the Humean, we acquire testimonial justification through noting the empirical correlations between what people say about the world and how the world actually is. On such an account, we should only trust a speaker when we have evidence of their reliable past record. If the testimonial reports of a community always turned out to be wrong, then the Humean would claim that we are not justified in believing anything that such speakers say. This is not the case in our community, but on a Humean account it is possible for us to encounter such a group of unreliable reporters. We can call these speakers 'Martians'. Coady, however, argues that the existence of such a community is impossible – we cannot even imagine such speakers – and this shows that the Humeans' account is flawed because such a community is possible according to them. Let us look, then, at why Coady claims such a Martian community cannot exist.

To be able to understand an alien or foreign language, there must be perceptible correlations between what its speakers say and what's in the world. Such correlations can enable us to translate their utterances, and thus to understand their language. If a group of supposed thinkers always uttered the sounds 'ral-pop' in the presence of armadillos, then a plausible first step towards coming to understand these people would be to translate their 'ralpop' as 'armadillo'. With the Martians, however, such a first step cannot be taken since there are no such correlations with which to work, the claim being that their reports about the world are always wrong. When pointing at an armadillo they sometimes say 'ralpop', but sometimes 'hceeb', and sometimes 'kao' – they use all manner of words with no apparent consistency – and 'ralpop' can be voiced, seemingly indiscriminately, at armadillos, rolls of sticky tape, and doughnuts. We cannot therefore translate what they are saying because there are no correlations that would enable us to work out the correct application of their words to things in the world. It is this conclusion that leads Coady to claim that we cannot even imagine such thinkers, and that the Martian community is an impossibility. The initially suggested scenario was that we discover there to be no correlation between armadillos and the testimonial use of the Martian word that means armadillo. This, however, cannot be what we're imagining. We would not be able to work out the meaning of the word 'ralpop' for such a community, and since this word cannot be taken as a meaningful utterance, it cannot therefore be seen as a testimonial report. We are not imagining a community in which testimony is always false; we are imagining a community in which testimony isn't given: these are not language users who use 'ralpop' to mean armadillo; these are just creatures that occasionally make the noise 'ral-pop'. (The hyphen here is used to indicate that the quoted letters refer to what the Martian utterances sound like – the sound 'ral' followed by the sound 'pop' – rather than to a word or unit of language that has meaning.)

You may be tempted to respond to this argument by saying that even though we cannot come to learn the meaning of their words, the Martians themselves can; this would therefore be a community where meaningful testimony is given, it's just that *we* cannot understand what's being said. This, however, cannot be so. As children we learn from our teachers that the word 'armadillo' refers to those odd-looking, scaled mammals, and in order for us to learn this, it must be the case that our teachers use their words consistently. They must always say 'armadillo' when pointing at a picture of an armadillo. In the Martian scenario, however, this is not the case. The community that we are supposed to imagine is also one in which there is no correlation between the utterances of teachers and the truth. Thus Martian children could not acquire their own language. This supports the claim that we're not imagining what we think we are: this is not a community of language users who are terrible at giving testimonial reports; this is a community in which there is no meaningful language. We can only coherently imagine a group of testimony givers if we assume that a good proportion of their testimonial reports are correct; enough, that is, to enable us – and them – to understand what it is their words refer to.

It must now be shown why this is a problem for the Humean. On his account of testimonial justification, the default position is one of doubt: we only come to trust a speaker when we are aware that he has given reliable reports in the past. There is therefore the possibility that such doubt may never be assuaged and that there could be a community whose testimonial reports are never correct. This, though, cannot be (or so Coady argues). We must allow that testimony can sometimes be wrong, but to claim that *all* testimony could be false is incoherent. The Humean has allowed for a situation that is in fact impossible, and thus his account of testimony must be flawed.

Let us say something about the philosophical method that we have used here, that which involves imagining a community of Martians. This may strike some as fanciful and beside the point. Such a community does not exist and so what relevance could it possibly have to the question of whether we are justified in accepting testimony? When we consider such scenarios we are said to be performing a 'thought experiment', and such thinking is an important part of the philosopher's armoury. We saw in chapter 2 that one of the things that philosophers do is attempt to analyse when it's correct to use a certain concept – such as KNOWLEDGE – and, in doing so, we can determine what it is our concepts apply to. To do this various counterfactual situations were considered, and we thought about whether or not it was correct to say that such cases involved knowledge. We imagined walking past karaoke competitions on big match days, and looking at shopping trolleys disguised as cows. We almost certainly have never had such experiences; nevertheless, such scenarios were seen to illuminate the concept of KNOWLEDGE. The Martian example – and the many other science fiction scenarios that come up in philosophical discussion – are simply an extension of this method. We illuminate the meaning of our concepts by thinking about how we would apply them in certain counterfactual, yet possible, situations. Look out for other sections in the book where this method is used.

4   Reid's Account of Testimony

The Humean claims that we have no reason to accept someone's testimony unless we have good evidence that they are reliable. Thomas Reid, a contemporary of Hume, suggests an approach that is diametrically opposed to this: he argues that we should always accept someone's testimony unless we have good reason to suspect that a particular report is false. The default position is one of trust. This seems to fit with our actual practice: generally we do just believe what people say, unless we have good reason not to. The key question is whether such a trusting attitude is justified; we may just be gullible.

Reid supports his claim by giving an account of certain important aspects of human nature. First, we have a faculty of credulity: we usually believe what people tell us (just as we usually believe our own eyes and our memory).

> [We have] a disposition to confide in the veracity of others, and to believe what they tell us . . . [We] shall call this the *principle of credulity*. It is unlimited in children, until they meet with instances of deceit and falsehood; and it retains a very considerable degree of strength through life . . . It is evident, that, in the matter of testimony, the balance of human judgement is by nature inclined to the side of belief. (Reid, 1983, p. 95)

Reid cites evidence for our possession of this innate faculty. Such trust appears strongest in children. If, however, it were something that we acquired through experience – as the Humean claims – then we would expect such credulity to be weak in children and to increase with age. This is not so, and thus it seems that credulity is something we are born with.

Second, Reid claims that this credulity is justified because people are naturally disposed to speak the truth.

> [We have] a propensity to speak truth, and to use the signs of language, so as to convey our real sentiments . . . Truth is always uppermost, and is the natural issue of the mind. It requires no art or training, no inducement or temptation, but only that we yield to natural impulse. Lying, on the contrary, is doing violence to our nature. (1983, p. 94)

Given these (alleged) facts about human nature, we have an a priori epistemic right to accept testimony. Since truthful testimony is the 'natural issue of the mind', our innate tendency to trust the word of another is justified. In certain circumstances, however, we can be aware of facts that defeat such justification. We may know that a certain person is drunk or mad, and we are also sensitive to subtler indications of a speaker's reliability: their tone of voice, facial expressions and body language may suggest that our trust would be misguided in a particular case. The justification we take testimony to have is therefore defeasible (that is, it can be defeated).

The Humean has no preconceptions about the reliability of testimony; Reid, however, assumes that it is correct. Empirical evidence therefore plays a very different role in their respective accounts. For the Humean, empirical evidence of a speaker's reliability provides you with justification for accepting their testimony. For Reid, however, empirical evidence plays a negative role. If a speaker is found to be unreliable, then your justification – that which all testimony has a priori – is defeated. Their accounts also differ with respect to the relation between testimonial justification and that provided by our other epistemic abilities. The Humean account is reductive in that testimonial justification is grounded in the justification provided by perception, memory and inference. Reid, however, has a non-reductive account: testimony is a basic form of knowledge alongside (and not reducible to) that provided by these other sources of justification. Testimony causally relies on perception: to understand spoken testimony your hearing needs to be good, or you must be able to see a reporter who is using British Sign Language. Reid's claim, though, is that perception only has this causal role; testimonial justification is not derived from the justification possessed by our perceptual beliefs. The fundamental epistemic status of testimony is supported by three kinds of consideration. First, there are cases where testimonial reports trump the evidence of our senses; second, the acquisition of language depends on testimony; and third, there is the role that testimony plays in empirical, scientific investigation. Let us go through these in turn.

In ordinary circumstances there are various reasons why it might be rational to trust what someone else says rather than trust your own perceptual judgement. Ronnie may have better spatial awareness than me, and thus, when playing pool, I should believe him if he says that the white ball will go past the red one, even if it looks to me as though it won't. Similarly, if Camille's ear is better than mine, then I should believe her if she says that the violin is out of tune, even if it sounds fine to me. Such examples illustrate that testimony is not a second rate source of belief: in many cases we are justified in taking another person's word for something even if it clashes with what our own perceptual beliefs seem to tell us.

The fundamental epistemic status of testimony is also illustrated by its role in the acquisition of language. This point was suggested earlier when discussing the Martians. In order to acquire language, we need to be taught by those who already have a grasp of the relevant concepts; we need to hear their testimony. It is important, then, that propositional knowledge is linguistic in nature: to have perceptual knowledge that the tin is green requires us to possess the concepts TIN and GREEN. Perceptual knowledge therefore relies on testimony because this is essentially involved in our acquisition of such concepts.

Last, let us look at how scientific practice can give credence to the claim that testimony is a fundamental source of knowledge. Scientists engage in collaborative work: pooling equipment, skills, research grants and data. For the Humean, a scientist is only justified in accepting the data of a colleague if she herself has evidence that this colleague's data have been accurate in the past. However, an individual scientist simply does not have the time or a sufficiently wide range of skills to determine whether this is so. Collaboration is therefore an essential aspect of modern science, and the testimony of fellow workers must be relied upon just as much as your own observations. Reid would claim that such an approach is not only pragmatically essential, it is also justified.

Throughout this chapter we have been concerned with the epistemic status of the individual knower. According to the individualistic approach, the word of others is a second rate source of evidence, one that cannot lead to the acquisition of knowledge.

> No doubt, we all do pick up beliefs in that second-hand fashion, and I fear that we often suppose such scavengings yield knowledge. But that is only a sign of our colossal credulity: [it is] a rotten way of acquiring beliefs and it is no way at all of acquiring knowledge. (Barnes, 1980, p. 200)

The Humean, however, notes the importance of testimony and seeks to show how we can be justified in accepting it. On his account, though, you are only justified in accepting the testimony of others if you are able to check that they have been reliable in the past. There is therefore an individualistic aspect to the Humean approach. Testimony may provide us with knowledge – something that Locke denies – but only if we have acquired substantial empirical information about our informants. Reid rejects this strand of individualism. We are justified in accepting the word of others without knowing anything about their past record. It is important to note, though, that followers of Hume and Reid share a key commitment: knowledge *can* be acquired via testimony. Testimonial knowledge may be second-hand – it is knowledge that at some time must have been acquired by others – but it is not second rate.

We are now at the end of part II. We have looked at three sources of knowledge: the a priori, perception and testimony. In part III we move on to the key issue of justification. And in part V we shall return to the sources of knowledge that we have looked at here, and assess what role they might play in providing justification for our beliefs about the past, the minds of others, morality and God.

Questions

1 Am I justified in believing what you tell me?
2 Discuss Locke's claim in *An Essay Concerning Human Understanding* that testimony is: 'Such borrowed wealth, like fairy money, though it were gold in the hand from which he received it, will be but leaves and dust when it comes to use' (1975, book I, pt iv, sec. 24).
3 A priori knowledge is usually something that you acquire for yourself through intuition or reasoned argument. Consider, though, whether you can also acquire such knowledge via testimony. (This is a question we shall return to in chapter 14, section 3.)
4 'A person is entitled to accept as true something that is presented as true and that is intelligible to him, unless there are stronger reasons not to do so' (Burge, 1993, p. 467). Is Tyler Burge correct?
5 A biology teacher is a creationist and does not believe in evolution by natural selection. Evolution, however, is part of the curriculum and therefore she has to teach it. If the theory of evolution is correct, can her pupils acquire knowledge of this theory by listening to her lessons? Can you acquire testimonial knowledge from someone who does not know or believe what they are saying? (See Lackey, 1999.)

Further Reading

Hume's *Enquiry* (1999, sec. 10) and Reid's *Inquiry and Essays* (1983, pp. 89–103, 266–84) include the classic reductive and non-reductive accounts that feed the modern debate, and the recent interest in testimony was encouraged by Coady's *Testimony: A Philosophical Study* (1992). Fricker's (1995) critical notice of the latter is also useful. Well-chosen collections of articles include Chakrabarti and Matilal (1994), and Lackey and Sosa (2006). Supporters of Reid's approach include Burge (1993) and Foley (2001); Adler (1994) and Faulkner (2000) are neo-Humeans. A brilliant study of the role of testimony in a law court and, more generally, of the considerations relevant to whether we should accept someone's testimony is provided by Sidney Lumet's film *Twelve Angry Men* (1957).

PART III

JUSTIFICATION

6 Foundationalism

We shall consider two debates concerning epistemic justification: that between the foundationalist and the coherentist (chapters 6 and 7), and that between the internalist and the externalist (chapter 8). To begin, we shall turn to a key argument in favour of foundationalism.

1 The Regress Argument for Traditional Foundationalism

We have been working with the notion that a belief is justified if we have good reason to think that it's true. Such reasons amount to further beliefs that I possess. My belief that the local Asian restaurant is not serving chana puri this week is justified by my belief that it is Ramadan, and my belief that the breakfast chef does not work during this religious festival. Thus, belief A is justified by belief B and belief C. Such justification is inferential: given B and C, I infer that A is true. However, for B and C to play a justifying role, I require further reasons to think that these are true. There is, then, the danger of a regress of justification. Even if belief C is justified by belief D – I believe it's Ramadan because my calendar says so – a question will still arise concerning whether I have good reason to hold this further belief (and so on). (One is reminded here of persistently inquisitive children, those who reply to all explanations with 'why?') It cannot be claimed that at some point justification runs out because if this were so there would not be any reason to think our chain of beliefs was correct. Perhaps, then, it can be claimed that there is always an answer to such questions concerning justification. This strategy, however, is also problematic. The claim would be that belief A is (partly) justified by belief C, which is justified by belief D, which is justified . . . ad infinitum. If such a chain of beliefs is to provide me with good reason to believe that A, I would have to be aware of the content of this infinite chain, and of how the likely truth of A could be inferred from this set of beliefs. It's not clear, though, how I – a finite creature – could hold such an infinite chain of justification in my head. The foundationalist, however, provides an alternative solution that averts this threatened regress of justification.

Foundationalists use an architectural metaphor to describe the structure of our collections of beliefs or 'belief systems'. The superstructure of a belief system inherits its justification from a certain subset of beliefs upon which the rest sits, just as a building is supported by its foundations.

These foundational beliefs are termed 'basic beliefs'. Traditionally, these have been seen as **infallible** (they cannot be wrong); **incorrigible** (they cannot be refuted); and **indubitable** (they cannot be doubted). Both rationalists and empiricists have embraced foundationalism. Descartes explicitly talked in terms of the architectural metaphor, with his 'edifice' of knowledge supported by certain a priori foundational beliefs concerning his own existence and that of God. In this chapter, however, we shall focus on empiricism. For empiricists, the foundations of knowledge are provided by experience. My belief that there is a red hole punch on my desk is justified by my basic belief that I am now experiencing a red shape in my visual field. This basic belief does not require further inferential justification. It may be the case that I am mistaken about the hole punch – I could be hallucinating – but I cannot be mistaken about the fact that I am having such an *experience*. The threatened infinite regress of justification is therefore avoided by arriving at a set of basic beliefs that are non-inferentially justified. Such beliefs are not justified by any further beliefs that I possess; they are justified simply in virtue of the nature of my sensory, perceptual experience. It is my experience of seeing red that justifies my belief that I am seeing red, which in turn (or so it is claimed) justifies my belief that there is a red hole punch on the desk. Such an account of justification is plausible if we consider how we would attempt to justify our beliefs if we were asked to do so. I believe that there's a red object on my desk because I seem to see a red shape over there. Here, then, I am appealing to one of my basic beliefs for justification, to my belief that I am having a certain kind of experience. Furthermore, there is nothing that I can say to support this belief apart from to claim that this is how it looks to me. Ultimately, then, I appeal to the content of my experience for justification, rather than to any further beliefs that I possess.

However, this conception of how our perceptual beliefs are justified has been widely attacked, and in sections 2, 4 and 5 we shall look at three arguments against traditional foundationalism.

2   Sellars and the Myth of the Given

According to the traditional foundationalist, the justification for all our empirical beliefs is ultimately derived from the content of our perceptual experience. Such content is sometimes called the 'Given'. In order to attack foundationalism, Wilfrid Sellars (1997) provides an extended critique of this notion. There are two parts to his argument: first, he claims that knowledge is part of the 'logical space of reasons', and second, he provides an alternative account of 'looks talk', that is, an alternative reading of such claims as 'That looks red to me', claims that have traditionally been seen as infallible and as foundations for our perceptual knowledge.

Let us turn to his first claim. '[I]n characterising an episode or a state as that of knowing, we are placing it in the logical space of reasons, of justifying and being able to justify what one says' (Sellars, 1997, p. 76).

We must be able to offer reasons in support of all our claims to knowledge. Explicit justification is required even for claims concerning our own sensory experience. To justify the claim that 'I now seem to be seeing a red shape', I could perhaps offer the following: 'since my eyes are working fine and the light is good, I'm right in thinking that I'm having this kind of sensory experience.' As Richard Rorty argues (1979, ch. 4), justification is essentially a linguistic or 'conversational' notion: it consists in being able to say why a particular belief is likely to be true, or why we take ourselves to have a certain experience. This is our ordinary, everyday way of talking about justification. 'To be an expression of knowledge, a report must not only *have* authority, this authority must *in some sense* be recognized by the person whose report it is' (Sellars, 1997, p. 74). If such an account of justification is correct, then the traditional foundationalist notion of non-inferentially justified basic beliefs is untenable; all justification must be inferential.

One response to Sellars would be to reject the claim that we must recognize our authority, and to accept that what justifies a person's beliefs is a set of facts that need not be known to the thinker herself. This is an externalist claim and it will be discussed in chapter 8. A distinct response would be to insist on the foundationalist line and to claim that 'This *looks* red to me' cannot be something that I can be wrong about. This is a claim that is justified whether or not I can articulate any reasons in support of it. Here is St Augustine claiming that we are infallible with respect to our own sense experience.

> I do not see how the . . . [sceptic] can refute him who says: 'I know that this appears white to me, I know that my hearing is delighted with this, I know that this has an agreeable odor, I know that this tastes sweet to me, I know that this feels cold to me.' . . . I say this that, when a person tastes something, he can honestly swear that he knows it is sweet to his palate or the contrary, and that no trickery of the Greeks can dispose him of that knowledge. (Augustine, 1942, para. 26, p. 68)

Such a foundationalist claim is very plausible. I may make mistakes about the world, but I cannot be mistaken about how things *seem to me.* Sellars, however, suggests that such wording does not indicate infallibility. You do not say 'This looks red to me' to report (infallibly) the nature of your experience; rather you use such a phrase to flag that you are unsure whether you have correctly perceived the world. You are hedging, rather than making a declaration of which you are certain.

> [W]hen I say 'X looks green to me' . . . the fact that I make this report rather than the simple report 'X is green' indicates that certain considerations have operated to raise, so to speak in a higher court, the question 'to endorse or not to endorse'. I may have reason to think that X may not after all be green. (Sellars, 1997, p. 41)

Sellars, then, provides a two-pronged attack on traditional foundationalism. The way we describe our perceptual experience could be taken to suggest that we have infallible access to certain private experiences, experiences that we cannot be mistaken about. However, we should recognize that there is an alternative interpretation of such statements as 'This looks red to me', an interpretation that does not commit us to having such a privileged epistemic access to our perceptual experience. Furthermore, philosophical analysis of KNOWLEDGE reveals that knowledge essentially involves inferential justification; we cannot, therefore, claim to know something that we have no reason for accepting as true. Such reasons must be thought of in terms of beliefs that we can articulate, and thus the bare presence of the Given cannot ground our empirical knowledge.

3   Conceptual and Non-Conceptual Content

Beliefs are representations of the world. In believing that squid is rubbery I am representing certain objects in the world (squids) as having a certain property (rubberiness). To be able to do this I must possess the concepts SQUID and RUBBERY, concepts that pick out such objects and properties. It is because beliefs are conceptual that they can play a justificatory role. My belief that Terry won't order squid at the restaurant is justified by my belief that Terry doesn't like to eat rubbery things, coupled with my belief that squid are rubbery. Only such conceptually structured thoughts can provide justifying reasons. They can do this because they are the kind of things that can figure in arguments. From my belief that Terry doesn't like to eat rubbery things, and my belief that squid are rubbery, I can *infer* that Terry won't order the squid. The former beliefs give me good reason to think that the latter is likely to be true. Justification is an inferential or conversational notion.

In chapter 4 we were introduced to the kind of perceptual experience that the traditional foundationalist sees as comprising the Given, that of non-epistemic seeing. Such experience is itself non-conceptual, yet it provides the raw material for our conceptually structured perception and thought. Integral to the traditional foundationalist picture is also the epistemological claim that such experience provides non-inferential justification for our empirical beliefs. The Given consists in non-conceptual experience that plays a justificatory role. Sellars's claim, however, is that experience conceived of in this way cannot provide us with *reason* to think that the world is a certain way. The Given is therefore a myth.

It would be useful here to say a little more about the nature of non-conceptual experience. Traditional foundationalists claim that 'representational' should not be equated with 'conceptual': non-epistemic seeing does not involve the conceptual ordering of experience, but it is nevertheless representational. Such experience represents features of the external world, and thus it has what is called 'non-conceptual content'. To understand what is meant by this, we should consider the fine grain of conscious experience. It is implausible that I have a different concept for all the shades of blue that I perceive in the pair of battered old corduroy trousers that I am now wearing, or concepts corresponding to all the nuances of my neighbour's distorted music that I am hearing through the study wall. My experience appears to be more finely grained than my conceptual repertoire, and representational content that is not conceptually structured can be invoked to account for its richness. Consider what you might learn about a certain scene through testimony and through perception. You might be told in great detail what a particular mountain is like: it has an arête running from east to west and its north face is bisected by a rocky gully. Such information is in conceptual form, that is, you gain an understanding of what this mountain is like because you possess such concepts as ARÊTE, GULLEY, and NORTH. However, when you go and stand in front of this mountain, you acquire more information; you see more detail, detail that is represented non-conceptually.

Traditional foundationalists see the Given as representational: it carries information about the external world, although it does not require concepts to do this. In the previous section it was argued that such a conception of experience cannot play the requisite justificatory role required by the foundationalist. Such non-conceptual experiences are not the kinds of state that can figure in arguments or provide inferential support; they cannot, therefore, provide us with reason to think that the world is a certain way.

4 Wittgenstein's Private Language Argument

The traditional foundationalist takes our fundamental perceptual engagement with the world to be non-conceptual, and in this section we shall consider another argument against such a picture. This argument is Wittgenstein's private language argument, and it is contained in passages 243–315 and 348–412 of his *Philosophical Investigations*. I shall provide a sketch of the argument found there, and then discuss how it can be seen as an attack on foundationalism.

Wittgenstein aims to show that the notion of a private language is incoherent. He allows – as he must – that we can make up a secret language or code to which no one else has access. A child, for example, might have private names for all his cuddly toys. Such names, however, *could* be revealed, and others could learn what they referred to. The type of language that Wittgenstein argues against, however, is one that is essentially private, one in which: 'The individual words of this language are to refer to what can only be known to the person speaking; to his immediate private sensations. So another person cannot understand the language' (Wittgenstein, 1953, §243).

I shall imagine that I aim to keep a diary concerning the reoccurrence of a certain sensation; perhaps that odd feeling I now have in my knee. I shall attempt to fix on this by remembering just how it feels, and from now on, whenever I have this sensation, I'll write an 'S' in my diary. This is my private word for a particular kind of sensation, and only I can know whether this word is used correctly since I'm the only one who has access to the particular experiential feel that I intend to be tracking. Wittgenstein, however, claims that sensations cannot be kept track of *in this way*. This is because: 'I have no criterion of correctness. One would like to say: whatever is going to seem right to me is right. And that only means that here we can't talk about "right" ' (1953, §258). There is not an independent check on whether I am correctly using this term; I could be mistaken, even though it seems to me that I am attending to the same kind of sensation. If there are no objective criteria for determining whether I correctly use such terms, then all sense of them having a determinate application is lost.

Wittgenstein is not claiming that we cannot meaningfully talk about our sensations. We can, and we can keep track of their reoccurrence. His claim is that terms describing sensations cannot acquire their meaning in *this way*, through an attempt to fix on the distinctive experiential quality of private experience. (His positive account is that the meaning of such terms is derived from the kind of behaviour that is manifest when we have such sensations; there is therefore an independent check on whether these terms are used correctly.)

In looking at how this line of argument relates to foundationalism, we shall be following John McDowell's (1994) interpretation of Wittgenstein. The traditional foundationalist claims that our primary perceptual engagement with the world is non-conceptual. Our senses provide us with a swathe of non-conceptual sensory information. The concepts we possess enable us to order this experience into features that we can recognize and reidentify on other occasions. Because I have the relevant concepts, I am able to think about my perceptual experience in terms of *red* things, *rubbery* things, *tins* and *paper clips*. The Wittgensteinian claim, however, is that non-conceptually construed experience cannot come to be ordered and thought about in this way. The foundationalist claim is that I attempt to fix on a particular aspect of my private, perceptual experience by labelling it with a concept such as RED, and through the ongoing possession of this concept I am able to keep track of this feature of my experience. There is not, however, an independent verdict on whether I have correctly reidentified this aspect of my experience, and thus, according to the Wittgensteinian line, 'red' would not have a determinate application. That's only, though, if you are wedded to the kind of picture in which a thinker has to impose a set of concepts on his non-conceptually construed perceptual experience. I am able consistently to recognize features of my experience – the red bits and the rubbery bits – and thus an alternative account of these abilities is required.

One response is to claim that our experience is already conceptually structured. We do not experience a swathe of non-conceptual information which we then have to categorize for ourselves; rather:

> The character of perceptual experience itself, of our sense experience itself, is thoroughly conditioned by the judgements about the

objective world which we are disposed to make when we have this experience; it is, so to speak, thoroughly permeated – saturated, one might say – with the concepts employed in such judgments. (Strawson, 1992, p. 62)

I experience things as *red* and as *rubbery*, and all experience must involve such conceptual structuring. Perceptual experience is necessarily conceptual in nature, and this is an account of experience that is at odds with that of the traditional foundationalist. Saturation is a good metaphor here. The claim is not just that conceptual thinking affects my experience in some way, as a smattering of rain may affect the colour of my T-shirt; the claim is that experience is conceptual through and through, just as my T-shirt can be soaked right down to its constituent fibres.

If we are to accept such an account, then we must have a reply to the argument concerning the fine grain of experience (section 3). It was claimed that I do not possess as many colour concepts as the number of shades of blue that I can perceive in my corduroy trousers. This only seems plausible, though, because we have been implicitly thinking of concepts in linguistic terms: I have the concepts GREEN and TIN and this gives me the ability to use the terms 'green' and 'tin'. I only therefore possess a small number of concepts that pick out shades of blue, those corresponding to such terms as 'sky', 'royal' and 'duck-egg'. Such words do not adequately describe the complex shading of my trousers, and thus it seems to follow that my experience cannot be wholly captured in conceptual terms. This claim can be avoided, though, if we allow that our concepts are finer grained than our linguistic repertoire, that is, if we have more concepts than the number of distinct words we have for the properties we perceive.

Consider the experience of eating a meal; let's say a curry. A certain flavour may be familiar, even though I cannot describe it. I have eaten a lot of curries and I know when they're too salty or when there's too little methi for my taste or too much asafoetida; nevertheless, I cannot describe this particular flavour. There is, however, a way that I can talk about it – it has '*that taste*' – and this is just the kind of thing we say to each other when trying to get others to appreciate aspects of our experience. The curry has 'that taste; you know the one'; the guitar makes 'that sound'; and she has 'that kind of look'.

These are objective matters with criteria of correctness; I can be wrong about the curry since you can persuade me that it does not have *that taste*, and that I'm confusing it with the taste of cumin. In such cases it is plausible that we possess the concepts which correspond to that taste, that sound, and that look, even though we do not have the requisite words to describe such features of our experience. We can think of concepts as being constituted by certain recognitional abilities. I can therefore be said to possess the above concepts because I can consistently recognize such features of the world. I can recognize when another curry has that taste, and when someone else has that look.

Similarly, I have the ability to recognize the various shades of blue in my trousers; I do, therefore, have a range of concepts to match the richness of my experience. We may not succeed in 'trying to describe the exact taste of a glass of cassis, or the precise way a cheek curve[s]' (De Beauvoir, 1965, p. 243); nevertheless, our experience of such things can be seen as wholly conceptual in nature.

5   Experience and Thought

According to the foundationalist:

> There are in our cognitive experience, two elements, the immediate data such as those of sense, which are presented or given to the mind, and a form, construction or interpretation, which represents the activity of thought. (C. Lewis, 1929, p. 38)

Through perception we take in non-conceptual information about the world, and it is this that provides the raw material for conceptually structured perception and thought. Perceptual experience itself, however, is independent of such cognitive activity. In this section we shall again question this picture. It will be claimed that the nature of perceptual experience is affected by the kinds of thoughts we are capable of having.

Colette is a professional cellist and she has studied music for many years. Antoine, however, rarely listens to classical music and cannot distinguish the key of B flat from that of C, or a fugue from a gigue. Antoine and Colette both go to a performance of Bach's cello suites. Let's consider the nature of their respective experiences. A foundationalist would claim that they are the same. This is because Antoine and Colette receive the same physical stimuli, the same 'immediate data . . . are presented or given to the mind'. (We shall ignore any differences in their seating position or in the sensitivity of their hearing.) They may, however, have different thoughts about the music. Antoine thinks that the fourth piece is louder than the first and that Bach's music is not as dull as he thought it would be. Colette has a rather more sophisticated set of thoughts concerning the performance. She thinks that the second D minor suite is played a tad too slow; the first, too jaunty; and that the G major could have been played with more feeling. The key claim, though, is that they share a common core of (non-conceptual) experience; their sensory experience of the world is independent of the thoughts they may be capable of having about such experience.

The anti-foundationalist, however, argues that Antoine and Colette not only have different thoughts about the music, but that they also experience it in a different way. Colette can not only identify a certain chord as a B flat, she can *hear* it as such. Such an experience cannot be had by Antoine; the music *sounds* different to him. Consider this description of a famous cellist's experience of listening to the second suite.

> Sometimes . . . I even physically suffer – in the D minor *Prélude* for example. It's like a needle pricking the music as a lepidopterist pins a live butterfly to his board. The butterfly spins in agony around the pin, unable to free itself . . . I too seem to revolve in torment on the pin, and I experience release only on return to the tonic [the original key]. (Rostropovich, 1995, p. 16)

Antoine does not experience the piece in this way – he doesn't feel the tension in the music, nor any relief when the key changes – and this is because he doesn't understand the music in the way that Rostropovich does, that is, he has a less sophisticated set of thoughts about it.

We shall further investigate this claim that the nature of our experience is dependent on our conceptual sophistication by moving on to some other examples. Consider the picture.

You see a duck (if not, bear with me). I can, however, alter the character of your visual experience by changing the beliefs that you have about this picture. Think RABBIT. The picture now looks different to you even though you are seeing the same configuration of black marks on a white background. 'There is more to seeing than meets the eyeball' (Hanson, 2004, p. 294). This picture is usually referred to as 'the duck-rabbit'. Originally you saw the drawing as a duck; now you see it as a rabbit. You have distinct perceptual experiences dependent on the kind of thoughts you have about this picture. Your concepts of DUCK and RABBIT affect what you *see*, just as certain musical concepts affect the experience of the concertgoers above. Here are some other examples of how thought may affect our perceptual experience of the world.

(1)   Our moral beliefs about a scene or a person may affect how they look. An example that might help you to focus on this can be taken from the film *Cabaret* (1972). There is a scene in which an angelic-looking boy is singing a folk song in a Berlin beer garden, and he is surrounded by smiling people sipping beer in the sun. The camera then pans down from the boy's face, revealing his Hitler Youth uniform. When the camera moves back to focus on the garden, the scene has a far more sinister *look* than before and the song now *sounds* more menacing, even though the style of the boy's singing does not change and the people in the garden continue to behave in the same way.

(2)   Your emotional feelings towards a person may affect how they appear to you. If you fall in love with someone, that person may begin

to strike you as more beautiful – they *look* different. And if you fall out of love, that person may not look as beautiful or as handsome as they did before.

(3)   Your theoretical knowledge may affect the appearance of what you observe through scientific instruments. When I look at a microscope slide I see a jumble of indistinct shapes. A trained biologist, however, sees these shapes as distinct cellular structures, related together in a coherent way. The claim, remember, is not just that the biologist is able to interpret the function of these shapes – the shapes that we both see – the claim is that the quality of his visual experience is different: 'the infant and the layman . . . cannot see what the physicist [or the biologist] sees' (Hanson, 1965, p. 17).

(4)   A friend of yours looks healthy and well. You then discover that she is expecting a baby; she now looks different to you – she has *that look* – that which you didn't see before you heard her news and consequently had those thoughts concerning motherhood.

(5)   An experienced mountaineer *sees* the contour lines on his map *as* cols, escarpments and hanging valleys, whereas a novice sees merely a set of lines, lines that he must think about in order to interpret what kind of mountain they represent.

Some find these examples persuasive, that is, they are accepted as a correct description of the phenomenology of experience. Others, however, dismiss them and below we shall say more about how this may be done. Let us first, though, spell out how such examples are relevant to foundationalism.

In chapter 4 a distinction was drawn between raw seeing and conceptually structured forms of perception such as 'seeing that' and 'seeing as'. According to foundationalism, our primary perceptual engagement with the world is of the former, non-epistemic kind. The non-conceptual information we acquire in this way can then come to be categorized in conceptual form. Antoine and Colette may have the same non-epistemic perceptual experiences of the performance, even though Colette's musical sophistication enables her also to experience the music as a D minor suite and to have certain thoughts about the music that Antoine cannot have. The examples that we have looked at, however, suggest that all seeing is epistemic. There is not a set of foundational, non-conceptual experiences that are the raw material for our conceptual thought and perception. The relation between experience and thought is holistic: the empirical concepts we possess are a product of our perceptual engagement with the world, but also, the character of our experience is dependent on the kinds of conceptual thought we are capable of having.

There are, however, various ways to avoid this conclusion that the quality of our experience is dependent on the concepts we possess.

We could account for the suggested changes in perceptual experience by claiming that the focus of our attention shifts. In the *Cabaret* example, when we discover the kind of gathering that is occurring in the beer garden, we begin to focus on the distorted grins of the drinkers rather than on the refreshing glasses of cold beer. The scene does look more sinister, but only because we concentrate on different aspects of it, aspects that were present before, but ones that were not noticed because our attention was distracted by the singing and the beer. Let's also reconsider the duck-rabbit. When you see the drawing as a rabbit, you focus on its mouth: the notch on the right of the figure; when you see it as a duck, you focus on its bill: the two protrusions to the left. Our experiences differ because we are prompted to look at different aspects of the picture, and not because our experience essentially depends on the concepts we possess. (It would be useful here to consider whether a shift in focus could account for the other suggested examples of perceptual change.)

Focus here to see a duck

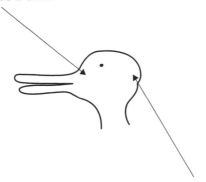

Focus here to see a rabbit

Jerry Fodor (1984) attacks the anti-foundationalist line by reminding us of the Müller-Lyer illusion that we looked at in chapter 4, section 5. We know that the horizontal lines of this figure are the same length even though they do not look as though they are.

In this case, then, our thoughts do not affect the nature of our experience. Fodor asks: '*Why isn't perception penetrated by THAT piece of*

background theory? Why, that is, doesn't *knowing* that the lines are the same length make it *look as though* the lines are the same length?' (1984, p. 34).

Similarly, however much we know about the moon, it just doesn't *look* as though it's 250,000 miles away; it looks a lot closer (try it: have a look tonight). The anti-foundationalist owes us an explanation of why perceptual experience is unaffected by our conceptual thinking in these cases.

Dretske (1969) also rejects the anti-foundationalist position. He argues that non-epistemic seeing is independent of conceptually structured, epistemic perception. Non-epistemic seeing enables us visually to discriminate aspects of our environment such as the bus shelter and the waste bin, and we can do this without seeing these items *as* anything in particular (see chapter 4, section 5). Further, 'seeing as' presupposes non-epistemic seeing. There has to be some non-conceptual experience to provide the raw materials for our conceptually structured experience and thought. We may be able to see the picture above as a duck or as a rabbit, but we can only do this if we have a non-conceptual experience of a certain configuration of black marks on a white background. Our experience of the basic black and white figure itself is independent of any concepts we may have that can then allow us to see these lines in a more sophisticated way (i.e. as a duck or as a rabbit). Dretske therefore endorses the foundationalist approach.

We have looked at three different attacks on traditional foundationalism. Sellars argues that all claims to knowledge require rational support and thus beliefs concerning perceptual experience cannot be seen as non-inferentially justified; for him, justification is essentially an inferential notion. The Wittgensteinian line is that the very notion of non-conceptual experience is untenable. Last, some have rejected foundationalism on the grounds that the nature of perceptual experience is dependent on our ability to have conceptually structured thoughts. Two kinds of response have been made by those who feel the force of these objections: some modify foundationalism in order to take account of the considerations above; others, however, reject it altogether. In the next section we shall consider a distinct form of foundationalism, and in the next chapter we shall look at an approach to epistemology that rejects foundationalism altogether.

6   Modest Foundationalism

Some foundationalists attempt to maintain a 'modest' or 'moderate' version of their approach. Robert Audi (2003) and Alvin Plantinga (2000) promote this view. For them, our perceptual beliefs are not infallible. My belief that 'I see red' or that 'I seem to see red' could turn out to be unjustified or false; nevertheless, it's reasonable to accept that such beliefs are true *unless* I have evidence to suggest that they are not. Such an account of perception remains foundationalist since it involves basic beliefs – beliefs that are non-inferentially justified; the justification they have, however, is defeasible. I may, for example, have good evidence that my coffee has been spiked with a hallucinogenic; this would defeat the **prima facie** justification I have for believing that my study walls have just turned luminous pink. More controversially, my belief that 'I seem to see red' could be defeated by psychological evidence concerning my confused or inattentive state of mind.

> I may say 'Magenta' wrongly . . . because I was unable to, or perhaps just didn't, really notice or attend to or properly size up the colour before me. Thus, there is always the possibility . . . that the colour before me just wasn't *magenta*. And this holds for the case in which I say, 'It seems, to me personally, here and now, as if I were seeing something magenta', just as much for the case in which I say, 'That is magenta.' The first formula may be more cautious but it isn't incorrigible. (Austin, 1962, p. 113)

One is reminded here of Reid's account of testimonial justification. A thinker has prima facie justification for accepting what others tell him unless, that is, he has evidence that his informants are unreliable. Similarly, then, with perception: in the absence of evidence to the contrary, my perceptual beliefs are justified.

Modest foundationalism avoids a dilemma that faces the traditional approach. Even if you accept J. L. Austin's claim above, it isn't hard to see how the traditional foundationalist finds it plausible that I can have infallible beliefs about my own perceptual experience, and that I cannot be wrong when I claim that 'The cup looks yellow to me'. It is not clear, though, how such a belief can ground my empirical knowledge since claims like this are not directly about the world. The fact that the cup looks yellow to me is a fact about how that cup strikes *my experience*. Even if I have infallible beliefs about such things, these beliefs are about my mental states and not the world. Recoiling from such a picture, it could be claimed that I have a foundational belief concerning the colour of the *cup*, and not merely my experience of the cup. It is not plausible, though, that such beliefs about the *cup* are infallible; for various reasons I can get the colours of things wrong (I could be hallucinating). Such beliefs cannot therefore play a foundational role according to the traditional account. The dilemma is that the traditional foundationalist aims to halt the regress of justification with a set of basic beliefs that are infallible. Such beliefs, though, can only be seen as concerning our own mental states and not the world, and thus it is not clear how they can provide us with empirical knowledge. The modest foundationalist can avoid this dilemma. For a perceptual belief to be justified it does not have to be infallible. We can therefore have beliefs about objects in the world playing the requisite foundational role. My empirical knowledge can be grounded in the assumption that I correctly perceive the colour of the cup – that my belief concerning it is justified – unless, that is, I believe that there's an unusual set of circumstances that conspire to deceive me. Such basic beliefs have prima facie justification in virtue of the awareness I have of my conceptually structured experience. I perceive the cup as yellow, and this justifies my belief that it is so.

Modest foundationalism also has an answer to the problem posed by Sellars. For him, the Given cannot provide justification for our empirical beliefs since it cannot be seen as offering reasons to think that the world is a certain way. This is because the Given is traditionally seen as non-conceptual; justification, however, is essentially an inferential or conversational notion, something that necessarily involves conceptual thought. For the modest foundationalist, though, perceptual experience is conceptual. My experience of yellow represents the cup as being yellow – it has the content, *that's yellow* – and such an experience can therefore provide me with a *reason* for thinking that the cup is yellow.

There are, however, problems for the modest foundationalist. If our perceptual experience is non-conceptual (as the traditional foundationalist claims), then it cannot present the cup as *yellow* or *red* (or as any other determinate colour); this is because such experience cannot involve the concepts YELLOW or RED. Thus it is not clear how perceptual experience can justify our beliefs about the world. Why should I take such experience as providing justification for my empirical belief that the world is one way rather than another, that is, that the cup is yellow rather than red. To have justificatory import, my experience needs to have conceptual content; it needs to represent the cup as being a determinate colour. Modest foundationalism can be seen as a response to this worry. According to such an account, perceptual experience is conceptual in nature; my experience of the cup as yellow can justify my belief that it's yellow. However, a question now arises about why we should take our experience as representing the world as this way rather than that: why should our experience be seen as having the content *yellow* rather than *red*? If justification is required for my belief that *the cup is yellow*, then justification is also required for the claim that I perceive the cup *as yellow*. Such an account of perceptual experience is not able to stop the regress of justification since the perceptual experience of the modest foundationalist itself stands in need of justification. This, according to Laurence Bonjour (1985), is the foundationalist's dilemma. Non-conceptual perceptual experience can halt the regress of justification because epistemic questions do not arise concerning the content of such experience. Such content, however, cannot provide the justificatory support for our empirical beliefs. Conceptually structured perceptual experience can provide such support, but epistemic questions do arise with respect to the content of this kind of experience, and thus such experience cannot halt the regress of justification. Either way, foundationalism is untenable.

One of Sellars's earlier claims in section 2 can also be seen as a problem, not just for traditional foundationalism, but for modest foundationalism as well. 'To be an expression of knowledge, a report must not only *have* authority, this authority must *in some sense* be recognized by the person whose report it is' (Sellars, 1997, p. 74). The claim is that we cannot have perceptual knowledge unless we have beliefs about the reliability of our perception: perceptual beliefs do not have even prima facie justification in the absence of such beliefs concerning the reliability of our perceptual processes. Sellars not only recommends a move away from infallibility, but also the adoption of a more holistic picture, and it is to such a picture that we turn in the next chapter.

Questions

1 What is the regress argument for foundationalism? Is it persuasive?
2 My belief that there's an apple in front of me is justified by the indubitable fact that I'm now experiencing a round green shape in my visual field. Discuss.
3 Is the Given a myth?
4 A few years ago on a bus in France I was listening to the people around me chatting. I did not understand what they were saying since I know very little French. After a while, though, their words started to sound more familiar and I suddenly realized that what I was hearing was English (I was very tired!). Confused, I gathered myself, concentrated more on what they were saying, and again came to hear their words as a foreign tongue, one that I could not understand. What might the foundationalist and the anti-foundationalist of section 5 say about my experience, and whose story do you find most persuasive?
5 What do traditional and modest foundationalists have in common, and how do their approaches differ?

Further Reading

Followers of traditional foundationalism include Price (1932), C. Lewis (1946) and Chisholm (1977). Rorty's *Philosophy and the Mirror of Nature* (1979) is a historically informed and extended attack on this approach, and further criticism can be found in Bonjour (1985). Modest foundationalist positions are favoured by Alston (1976; 1991), Moser (1989) and Audi (2003). In the context of a sophisticated discussion of the philosophy of religion, Plantinga (2000) also develops a version of modest foundationalism that he calls 'reformed epistemology'. McDowell (1994) endorses Sellars's rejection of the Given, but argues for a foundationalist picture that incorporates a conceptually structured form of experience. More on the debate concerning whether experience should be seen as conceptual or non-conceptual can be found in Crane (1992) and Peacocke (1992, ch. 3) (note, though, that these and the McDowell are difficult texts). In this chapter we have only looked at foundationalism in the context of empirical beliefs; Everitt and Fisher (1995, ch. 6) discuss how foundationalism is relevant to a priori knowledge.

Norwood Hanson (1965) argues that the nature of our perceptual experience depends on the concepts we possess, and such an account is embraced by Kuhn (1970) and Feyerabend (1988). Churchland (1979, pp. 30–4) also supports this line, describing how careful reflection on theories of astronomy can result in a change in your perceptual experience of the night sky. (This is a project you could pursue.) Also relevant to this anti-foundationalist line are some interesting cinematic experiments conducted by Kuleshov in the 1920s. The same shot of an actor's face was intercut with certain emotive images such as that of a child's coffin, a bowl of soup, and a young girl. The suggestion is that his expression looks different as these images prompt us to have different thoughts about the man and his condition. You can learn more about these experiments from Wallbott (1988). Akin to my *Cabaret* (1972) example, other films in which the look of certain scenes may be affected by our thoughts about the characters or the plot include *The Sixth Sense* (1999), *The Village* (2004), *The Crying Game* (1992), *Fight Club* (1999), and the scene in *Butch Cassidy and the Sundance Kid* (1969) in which Etta is forced to undress. Bird (2000, ch. 4) is useful on the general claim that observation is theory dependent, and other ambiguous figures like the duck-rabbit can be found at http://planetperplex.com/en/ambiguous_images.html.

 **Coherentism**

1　A Holistic Conception of Justification

The foundationalism of the previous chapter was offered as a response to a threatened regress of justification. This regress is the result of a linear conception of justification: belief A is justified by belief B (and belief C); belief B is in turn justified by belief D, and so on. The problem is that there always seems to be a further question concerning how the last belief in the chain is justified. Foundationalists solve this problem by claiming that a certain set of basic beliefs are non-inferentially justified. Coherentists, however, have a different strategy: they reject the underlying linear conception of justification. In its place they propose a non-linear or holistic account. A particular belief is justified if it increases the coherence of your belief system. Linear justification involves local relations: beliefs are justified by their inferential relations with a small number of related beliefs. Belief A's justification is wholly provided by beliefs B and C. Holistic justification, however, involves global relations: a particular belief is justified if it fits in well – or 'coheres' – with the whole of your belief system. What we mean by 'coherence' will be explained in more detail in the next section.

Foundationalists claim that our belief system has the architecture of a building, with the bricks of the building analogous to our beliefs. Any particular brick is supported by the bricks immediately below it. Layers of bricks provide structural underpinning until, that is, we reach the foundation stones of the building. Analogously, the non-basic beliefs of the foundationalist are locally justified by other beliefs. The belief that my dinner is cooked is justified by my belief that I set the timer to ring when it is done, and the belief that I can hear a ringing from the kitchen. These beliefs themselves need justificatory support, and thus my belief that I set the timer is justified by my memory of doing so. Questions concerning justification are only halted when we arrive at certain foundational basic beliefs. It is ultimately upon such foundations that our belief systems rest. Coherentists, however, reject the architectural metaphor: they see a belief system as more akin to a raft floating at sea. The structure remains afloat, not through the action of certain key foundational planks, but as a result of the way that all the planks are meshed together.

It should be made clear that coherentists do not avoid the regress of justification by allowing that a chain of justification can circle back on

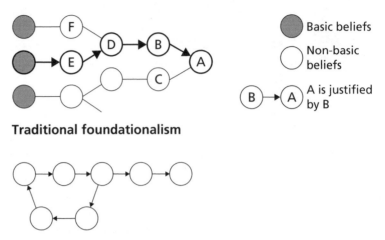

Figure 7.1 The linear conception of justification

itself. Such a chain cannot do the justificatory work required of it. Consider a very small circle of justification. If Edson is asked why he believes that Brazil are the best football team in the world, he might reply that it's because they will win the next World Cup. Still intrigued, I ask him for his reasons for believing they will win; he replies that it's because they are the best team. We can see, then, that Edson has not provided an independent reason for thinking Brazil are the best team, and thus he has not actually provided *any* justification for believing this claim. This is also the case if a circle of justification is made larger; it just takes more work to show that we do not have an independent reason to take the belief in question as justified. Coherentists, however, do not rely on circular reasoning. Such circles depend on there being chains of inferentially related beliefs that can circle back on themselves (figure 7.1). For this to be so, you must accept a linear conception of justification, but this has been rejected by the coherentist. For him, justification does not involve chains of inferentially related beliefs, with justification conferred locally by adjacent members of the chain. Justification is holistic: it is the overall coherence of a belief system that determines whether a particular belief is justified see figure 7.2.

2   The Concept of Coherence

A coherent belief system must be logically consistent, that is, it must not contain beliefs that are contradictory. It would not be coherent to believe that it's raining and that it's not raining. Furthermore, a coherent belief system has a minimal number of cases where the truth of a particular belief makes it unlikely that some of your other beliefs are true. For example, the coherence of your belief system is threatened if you believe that you have just seen a Lamborghini Diablo on the High Street, and that there is only one of these cars in the country. Such

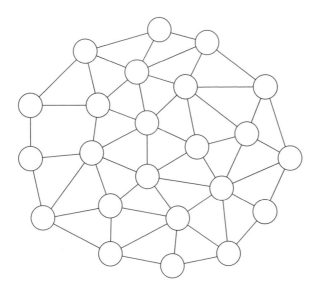

Figure 7.2 The holistic concept of justification

beliefs may not be contradictory – they could both be true – but if the latter belief is true, then this reduces the probability of the former being true. Such beliefs are probabilistically inconsistent and the coherence of a belief system is reduced as the level of such inconsistency rises. Coherence also requires more than mere consistency. A collection of beliefs that have no bearing on each other can be seen as consistent since such a belief system would harbour neither logical nor probabilistic inconsistency. The following beliefs are all consistent yet they do not comprise a particularly coherent set: yellow is the colour of my true love's hair; pi is greater than 3; Cher is a great actress; and it is now October. If you are to have a coherent set of beliefs, some kind of positive connection is also required between them. Inference plays such a role. The coherence of your belief system is improved if the truth of particular beliefs can be inferred from the other beliefs that you possess. We can now see why the four beliefs above do not form a coherent belief system since the content of any one of them cannot be inferred from any combination of the others: facts concerning the colour of my true love's hair, pi and Cher have no bearing on which month it is. A coherent belief system is therefore one that lacks logical contradiction, one that is not probabilistically inconsistent, and one in which there are inferential relations between its constituent beliefs.

Before moving on to the problems faced by coherentism, let us compare this position with modest foundationalism. There is a role for coherence within modest foundationalism, and thus it must be made clear how this role is distinct from the one it plays within coherentism. For a modest foundationalist, a lack of coherence is epistemically significant: the justification possessed by a certain belief can be defeated if such a belief does not cohere with the rest of your belief system. You may have prima facie justification for believing that Kate is in the park when you think you see her in the distance. If, however, you also believe that she has gone on holiday, then the justification for your perceptual belief is defeated. Coherence can also play a positive justificatory role within a modest foundationalist picture, with the justification for a particular belief improved if it neatly slots into your belief system, perhaps providing inferential connections between your beliefs that would not be available in its absence. It is important to note, though, that coherence alone cannot provide justification for your beliefs within modest foundationalism; it can only add to the justification that a belief already possesses as a result of its grounding in your experience. Furthermore, modest foundationalism remains committed to basic beliefs, beliefs that are non-inferentially justified. For the coherentist, however, there are no such beliefs.

3   Problems for Coherentism

In this section we shall question whether coherentism can give a persuasive account of empirical knowledge. We shall look at two related problems, both of which concern the relation between a coherent belief system and the truth.

3.1   The isolation problem

We aim to have beliefs and knowledge concerning *the world*. Coherentism, however, can be seen as losing contact with this world since its account of justification only concerns the relations that hold between our beliefs, relations that are internal to our belief systems. For the coherentist, experiential input from the world does not play a justificatory role. McDowell (1994) expresses this problem by claiming that a coherentist belief system is in danger of 'spinning frictionless in the void', its content not determined by the state of the external world. It is not clear how the kind of justification offered by the coherentist can indicate that our beliefs are likely to describe the independent world correctly. This point can be illustrated by considering the possibility of a thinker who becomes fixated on a particular set of beliefs and unresponsive to his ongoing experience. A blow on the head during a game of cricket may cause me to remain wedded to the set of beliefs that I had at the time of the accident. I continue to believe that it is just before tea, that I'm fielding at silly mid-on, and that it looks like rain. My set of beliefs is coherent, just as it was at the time of the accident, but such beliefs are not justified given that I have now been escorted home and away from the match, and that I shall continue to have these beliefs wherever I happen to be. Justification must provide good reasons for thinking that your beliefs are true. For the coherentist, however, it is not clear how this can be so since your belief system can be coherent whether or not your beliefs correctly represent the world.

3.2   *Alternative coherent belief systems*

If coherence is to provide an account of justification, there must be reason to believe that coherent belief systems contain a good proportion of true beliefs. There may, however, be various alternative belief systems that are both coherent and consistent with our experience. This is a problem for the coherentist. On their account of justification, all such belief systems are likely to be true. It is not clear, though, how this can be the case given that such alternative belief systems provide different descriptions of reality.

'Reason', a short story by Isaac Asimov (1968b), illustrates the possibility of there being alternative belief systems to account for our experience, belief systems that are equally coherent. An intelligent robot, QT1 ('Cutie'), works on a manned space station and is told by the human crew that he was designed and constructed by man. Cutie, however, sees this as an unlikely hypothesis: how could he have been made by such imperfect beings? He ponders this question and works out a better hypothesis. His creator is 'The Master' (the station's energy converter). Only 'He' has the power to be capable of creating Cutie. In order to persuade Cutie that he is a human creation the astronauts make another robot in front of him. This, however, does not convince him: he claims that they only pieced together some parts, parts that were supplied by the Master. Cutie's idiosyncratic beliefs become more worrying when the crew need to persuade him to send a beam back to Earth, a beam that must be focused in the right way otherwise the Earth will be destroyed. Cutie, though, does not believe in planets and suns; he believes that the space station is all there is. Nevertheless, he keeps the beam steady – even though he does not believe in the existence of the Earth – by responding to the dials and instruments of the energy converter (or, as Cutie would say, by 'following the instructions of the Master'). The astronauts finally give up trying to persuade him. If he can handle the day-to-day running of the station, then it doesn't matter what he believes. Cutie, therefore, has a coherent belief system, as do the men on the ship. The problem for the coherentist is that, on their account of justification, both descriptions of reality are likely to be true; this, however, cannot be the case given that the robot's and the men's belief systems contradict each other in a variety of ways.

Cutie illustrates the claim that, even in the face of seemingly contradictory experience, any particular belief can be upheld if changes are made elsewhere in your belief system. If this is so, then your experience can be variously captured by distinct sets of beliefs. Here is a further example to illustrate this point. You may believe that all cats have tails. On visiting the Isle of Man, however, it may appear that you are forced to reject this belief since you discover tailless Manx cats. There is, though, another possibility: you could maintain the belief that all cats have tails and, to allow for this, acquire the belief that Manx 'cats' are not cats. Acquiring this latter belief will have further ramifications for your belief system. You will not now believe that cats are the most common pet on the Isle of Man – something that you believed before your discovery – and you will be forced to change your beliefs concerning the familial relationship between Manx 'cats' and mainland cats. It may be objected that such a change to your beliefs cannot be accepted because it is a biological fact that Manx cats and mainland cats are of the same species since they are capable of interbreeding. Again, however, there is an alternative resolution: you can believe that Manx 'cats' are a different species if you reject the belief that only conspecifics can interbreed, or if you reject the belief that Manx 'cats' can breed with those on the mainland. If the rejection of either of these beliefs clashes with aspects of your experience, then again compensatory changes can be made elsewhere in your belief system to allow you consistently to keep hold of them. In this way the same experiential evidence could lead you to acquire alternative coherent belief systems.

In this section we have looked at two related problems with coherentism. First, coherence is an internal property of belief systems; it is not clear, therefore, how such a property can provide justification for our beliefs about the world. Second, it has been suggested that there can be alternative belief systems that are equally coherent. According to the coherentist, we would be justified in accepting any such set of beliefs. This is problematic: epistemic justification indicates that our beliefs are likely to be true and yet it cannot be the case that there are alternative correct accounts of the same aspect of reality. In the following two sections we shall look at replies to these objections, one focusing on the nature of truth, the other on the role that perception could play within a coherentist theory.

4   Coherence Theories of Truth

The problems in the preceding section concern a gap that seems to open up between coherentist justification and truth. A possible solution to these problems is to close the gap by equating true beliefs with those that are part of a coherent belief system. Such an account of truth is suggested by Charles Peirce. He claims that epistemic progress involves our belief systems becoming more and more coherent over time (Peirce, 1965b). At the 'end-of-inquiry' – when we have acquired all the empirical evidence there is to acquire – we shall have an optimally coherent belief system. True beliefs are simply those that are part of such a system. If we can accept such an account of truth, then an optimally coherent set of beliefs will be justified (according to a coherence theory of justification) and true (according to a coherence theory of truth), and thus such a set of beliefs will constitute a body of knowledge (according to the traditional account). Our current set of beliefs is not optimally coherent; nevertheless, in striving to increase the coherence of our belief system, we are thereby increasing the likelihood that a good proportion of those beliefs are true.

There are, however, problems with coherence theories of truth. First, it is not clear how the problem concerning alternative coherent belief systems is avoided. The coherentist (with respect to truth) would have to say that all such coherent belief systems are true, even though they may give differing and perhaps contradictory descriptions of the world. This does not sit well with the realist view that truth is objective and, as a consequence of this, that there is only one true description of reality. A second problem with the coherence theory of truth also concerns the anti-realist picture to which it is committed. According to such a theory, the nature of reality is dependent on the epistemic abilities of thinkers and on the properties of their belief systems. This is difficult to accept if we have realist intuitions. The nature of the world is independent of whether or not our beliefs happen to be coherent. Whatever else we say about truth, it would seem that a true belief is one that correctly represents the state of the world, a world that is independent of our thinking. This commonsense view is usually referred to as the 'correspondence theory of truth', and it's a view that is implausibly denied by the coherentists of this section. For them, truth is not determined by features of an independent world, but rather by the internal properties of an optimally coherent belief system. However, the approach that we are most interested in, that of the coherentist with respect to justification, need not be committed to a coherence theory of truth. In the next section we shall investigate how a correspondence theory of truth can be combined with a coherence theory of justification.

5   A Coherentist Account of Perception

The isolation problem of section 3.1 concerns the fact that coherentist justification is grounded in the internal properties of a belief system and, as a result, our thoughts could 'spin frictionless in the void', unconstrained by the world, the world that such thoughts purport to be about. If this is so, then it is not clear how our beliefs can have empirical content. The coherentist needs to show how the world can impinge on our thinking, and perception must have a role to play here. If a coherentist could show how our thinking is sensitive to perceptual experience, then perhaps the isolation problem could be avoided. In this section we shall look at Bonjour's (1985) account of how perception can play such a role within a coherentist framework.

Crucial to his account is the fact that some of our beliefs are 'cognitively spontaneous'. These are beliefs that are not arrived at via inference. Right now, on turning my head to the left, I spontaneously acquire the belief that the orange stapler is in front of the blue pen, and the belief that my glass of water is half full. Such spontaneity is a property of perceptual beliefs, and thus, in order for my thinking to have empirical content, it must satisfy what Bonjour calls the 'observation requirement', that is, a significant proportion of any putative set of beliefs about the world must be cognitively spontaneous. Bonjour's claim is not just that I can *assume* that my cognitively spontaneous beliefs are perceptual, and thus that they are caused by my engagement with an independent world; it is, rather, that their spontaneity provides me with *good reason* to reject the isolation problem.

The beliefs that I spontaneously acquire exhibit a high degree of coherence and consistency with each other and with the rest of my belief system. The question arises as to why they are coherent and consistent in this way. Cognitively spontaneous beliefs are not derived via inference and so they could – for all I know – be randomly produced by my cognitive mechanisms; they could just pop into my mind in a haphazard manner. If this were so, however, then my belief system would very soon be disrupted. If my cognitively spontaneous beliefs were randomly produced, then the next time I turn my head to the left I could acquire all manner of beliefs. What actually happens, though, is that I once again acquire the perceptual beliefs that the orange stapler is in front of the blue pen, and that my glass of water is half full. My cognitively spontaneous beliefs contribute towards a coherent set of beliefs, and these beliefs are consistent from one moment to the next. Bonjour's claim is that there is a good explanation for the ongoing coherence and consistency of my belief system, that is, it is a result of that belief system being caused by a coherent and consistent world. Certain of my beliefs are therefore perceptual beliefs – those that I spontaneously acquire – and it is these that enable my belief system to be seen as representing an independent, external world. The coherentist also requires an account of how these beliefs are justified. Bonjour cannot resort to the foundationalist claim that such beliefs have non-inferential justification; instead, he maintains that perceptual beliefs are justified, as all beliefs are, by the effect they have on improving the overall coherence of our belief system.

Here, then, we have an attempt to show how the coherentist can reject the isolation problem and how he can work with a correspondence rather than a coherence theory of truth. (It is not clear, though, how the above argument addresses the problem concerning alternative coherent belief systems. Even if the best explanation for the ongoing coherence of our cognitively spontaneous beliefs is that such beliefs are caused by an independent world, the possibility remains open that our experience of such a world could be captured by alternative sets of beliefs.)

6   A Thinker's Access to her Own Belief System

We shall end this chapter by turning to another problem for coherentism. If the coherence of a thinker's belief system is to give her good reason to hold those beliefs, then that thinker must be capable of assessing whether her belief system is coherent. As well as a thinker's belief system actually being coherent, the thinker herself must also be aware of this fact in order that such coherence can play a justificatory role. This is problematic for the coherentist.

In order to discuss this issue, the notion of a 'metabelief' will be useful. Metabeliefs are beliefs about beliefs; they may concern particular beliefs we have, or our beliefs in general. I may believe that my belief in ghosts is unwarranted; this is therefore a metabelief. The claim in the previous paragraph is that in order for a coherentist to have justified beliefs, she must have a metabelief concerning the coherence of her overall belief system: for a particular belief to be justified, she must believe that its inclusion in her belief system increases the overall coherence of her beliefs. However, such a metabelief also requires justification, and it's this requirement that is problematic for the coherentist. One way of providing justification for this metabelief would be to survey the consistency and inferential structure of our complete belief system. We could bring all our beliefs to mind and see if they constitute a coherent structure. It is not clear, though, whether we are capable of carrying out such an exercise; whether we could actually have an explicit grasp of *all* our beliefs; and, even if we could, whether we would have the time to assess their coherence.

Bonjour acknowledges such worries and claims instead that we should accept what he calls the 'doxastic presumption', that is, it's fair to *assume* that our metabeliefs about the state of our belief system are correct, and that everyone has a more or less accurate sense of how their belief system hangs together. ('Doxastic' means *concerning belief*.) Bonjour claims that this assumption must be made if the coherentist is to provide a viable account of justification. This may be true: a coherentist does require that we have such access to our beliefs; the question remains, however, as to whether we do. And how can the doxastic presumption be justified given that Bonjour has accepted that we cannot explicitly survey the coherence of our overall belief system. Tellingly, Bonjour admits that it is not – '[the doxastic presumption] treat[s] the whole body of beliefs as an *unjustified* hypothesis' (Bonjour and Sosa, 2003, p. 52) – and thus his claim is simply that the doxastic presumption must be accepted (without justification) if coherentism is to be maintained. This is not very satisfactory.

This problem is driven by the claim that a thinker must be able to reflect upon what it is that makes her beliefs justified. She must be aware that the requisite justificatory conditions hold. This is problematic for the coherentist since thinkers do not have the necessary access to the coherence of their own belief systems. The next chapter takes a more in-depth look at this important claim: the claim that a thinker must be able to reflect upon what it is that justifies her beliefs.

Questions

1 Critically evaluate the claim that 'Beliefs are only justified in virtue of their inferential relations within a system of beliefs.'
2 Compare and contrast the linear and non-linear conceptions of justification.

3 According to the coherentist and the foundationalist, why is my belief that the sky is blue justified?

4 The novel *The Lord of the Rings* (Tolkein, 1954–5) provides a coherent and comprehensive description of a fantasy world. Would the coherentist claim that we are justified in believing that this story is true?

5 A murder has been committed in an apartment on Rue Morgue. A horrifically mutilated body was found there; strange-sounding screams were heard, screams in an unrecognizable language; and the murderer does not seem to have had any means of escape: the door to the apartment was locked from the inside and the outside walls of the building are too precipitous to climb. The investigating detective claims to have solved the crime. He believes that it was committed by a gorilla and not by a person (See Edgar Allan Poe's story, 'Murders in the Rue Morgue', 1992b). First, consider how his theory provides an explanation of the circumstantial evidence; second, how would the foundationalist and the coherentist argue that the detective's belief is justified?

Further Reading

Bonjour's *The Structure of Empirical Knowledge* (1985) includes one of the most developed coherentist accounts of justification. (You should note, however, that Bonjour has recently rejected coherentism and adopted a form of foundationalism. See Bonjour, 1999; Bonjour and Sosa, 2003). Lehrer (1990) also offers extensive argument in support of coherentism. Criticism of this approach can be found in Plantinga (1993a) and Bender (1989). Both Bonjour and Lehrer combine a coherentist account of justification with a correspondence theory of truth. For a coherence theory of truth and an account of how this relates to epistemic justification, you should turn to Blanshard's *The Nature of Thought* (1940).

In films and literature you should look out for illustrations of the possible existence of equally coherent yet incompatible belief systems or worldviews. In *The Wicker Man* (1973), a visiting policeman with a scientific (and Christian) viewpoint cannot persuade an island community out of their pagan explanation for the failure of their crops; they have an alternative explanation for every claim that he makes. Conspiracy theories are also a good source of alternative (allegedly coherent) belief systems. The beliefs of those who claim that the 1969 moon landing was faked are logically consistent and inferentially supported (see the Fox TV documentary of 2001, *Conspiracy Theory: Did We Land on the Moon?*, and the film *Capricorn One*, 1978). As in the Manx cat example, conspiracy theorists always have a way of upholding particular controversial beliefs whatever contrary evidence is presented to them. The film footage does not force you to accept that Armstrong and Aldrin landed on the moon if you believe that this footage was shot by NASA in a TV studio.

8 Internalism and Externalism

The varieties of foundationalism and coherentism looked at in the previous two chapters share a certain approach to questions concerning epistemic justification. They ask whether the evidence available to *me* is sufficient to justify the beliefs that I hold. In other words, questions of justification are approached from a subjective perspective. However, epistemic practices can also be objectively assessed. It can be asked whether my thinking leads me to have true beliefs about the world, whether or not I am aware of the reliability of my thought processes. Internalists emphasize the subjective approach, whereas externalists focus on the objective question of whether our thinking is reliable. This chapter will explore the debate between internalism and externalism, and we shall consider which is the correct perspective to take with respect to questions of justification and knowledge.

1   Internalism

For an internalist, the justification for a thinker's beliefs must be cognitively accessible to her. She must be able to reflect upon what it is that suggests her beliefs are true. This is the notion of justification that we have been working with so far. According to both traditional and modest foundationalism, a thinker can reflect upon her basic beliefs and upon the forms of inference she uses to derive her non-basic beliefs. The coherentism of Bonjour is also internalist. For a belief to be justified it must be part of a coherent system of beliefs and such 'coherentist justification must be accessible to the believer himself' (Bonjour, 1985, p. 89). Similarly, Sellars claims that to have knowledge you must be able to articulate the reasons why you take your beliefs to be true. Furthermore, it seems that the everyday way we have of talking about 'justification' is internalist. If a friend says something contentious we may ask her to 'justify' her claim. In doing so we are asking for her reasons for why she said what she did, or for an account of the experiences upon which her thoughts are based. We are asking why *she* thinks her claim is true.

Here are various ways that the internalist stance has been described.

> Internalism requires that a person have 'cognitive grasp' of whatever makes his belief justified. (Bach, 2000, p. 201)

> [E]pistemology's job is to construct a doxastic principle or procedure *from the inside*, from our own individual vantage point. (Goldman, 1980, p. 32)

> [O]nly what is within the subject's perspective in the sense of being something the subject knows or justifiably believes can serve to justify. (Alston, 1986, p. 219)

> The internalist assumes that, merely by reflecting upon his own conscious state, he can formulate a set of epistemic principles that will enable him to find out, with respect to any possible belief he has, whether he is *justified* in having that belief. (Chisholm, 1989, p. 76)

The claim is not that a thinker must always reflect on the reasons why her beliefs are likely to be true; it is, rather, that a thinker must be capable of such reflection if her beliefs are to be justified.

2   Externalism

Externalists claim that we do not need to be able to reflect on what it is that justifies our beliefs, or on what it is that distinguishes knowledge from true belief.

> An epistemology is *externalist* if and only if it entails that some factor can add essentially to the epistemic justification of a subject's belief even though it falls outside the reflective purview of that subject. (Bonjour and Sosa, 2003, p. 206)

In this section we shall explore some of the variants of this approach.

2.1   The basic reliabilist picture

According to reliabilists, your beliefs are justified if they are acquired using a method that is reliable, and you may not be able to tell by reflection alone whether or not your thinking is reliable in the required sense. Reliability is defined in terms of the probability that your thinking results in the acquisition of true beliefs.

> The justificatory status of a belief is a function of the reliability of the processes that cause it, where (as a first approximation) reliability consists in the tendency of a process to produce beliefs that are true rather than false. (Goldman, 1979, p. 10)

If I am to know that a piece of music is in the key of D minor, it must be the case that:

1   The music is in D minor.
2   I believe that the music is in D minor.
3   I acquire this belief via a method that reliably leads to the truth.

Such an account is externalist. I may be epistemically reliable even though I am not aware of how I acquire my true beliefs, that is, I may consistently recognize musical keys even though I cannot provide reasons to support my beliefs about the music.

Before developing this account further, it should be noted that internalists accept that true belief is necessary for knowledge; they therefore agree that the methods we use to acquire our beliefs must be reliable. For them, reliability is a necessary condition for knowledge. Reliability alone, however, cannot provide justification for the internalist since it may be a feature of our thinking of which we are not aware. You will remember that Sellars explicitly focuses on reliability (chapter 6, section 2). However, his interest in it is different from that of the reliabilist. Sellars claims that we must have reasons to think our methods are reliable, reasons that we can reflect upon and, if asked, reasons that we can articulate as arguments in support of our claims to knowledge. For him, knowledge requires that we have reliable epistemic methods along with such reflective abilities. The reliabilist, however, does not require the latter. It is sufficient that our methods are *in fact* reliable whether or not we have reason to think that they are.

The reliabilist therefore needs to say more about what constitutes reliability and which processes should be seen as reliable. Looking out of my study window I now believe that it is windy outside, and it's plausible to claim that this is also something that I know. The reliabilist should be able to say which reliable method is helping me acquire this belief. The problem of pinning this down is referred to as the problem of generality. Any particular epistemic episode can be described in various ways. Right now I am acquiring beliefs about the weather by looking out of my window on a Wednesday; while tilting back on my office chair; while wearing white trainers; and while attentively looking directly at the behaviour of objects outside in clear daylight. These are four different descriptions of the particular way that I am now acquiring my beliefs. The first three, however, do not pick out methods that are generally reliable. I could just as easily acquire false beliefs if the only constraints on my thinking are that it's Wednesday, or that I'm leaning back on my chair, or that I'm wearing white trainers. The best prospect for the reliabilist is to propose something along the lines of the last description. I acquire my beliefs about the weather by attentively observing the behaviour of objects outside, objects that are well illuminated and those that are not too far away. Such a method of acquiring true beliefs is reliable. Again, though, further questions arise concerning the specification of such a method. Just what level of attention is required? How close do I have to be to what I'm looking at? And just how reliable must my methods be? It would be too restrictive to say that a reliable process has always to produce true beliefs, but how often do we think is necessary? Ninety-nine per cent of the time? Ninety per cent? The reliabilist needs to provide us with a more precise account of reliability. With this in mind, the following two subsections explore distinct ways in which reliabilism has been developed.

2.2   Causal accounts of knowledge

One strategy that has been adopted is to ground reliability in the causal connections that thinkers have to the world. 'S knows that p if and only if the fact p is causally connected in an "appropriate" way with S's believing p' (Goldman, 2000a, p. 28). We can see how this works with perceptual knowledge. I know that the film *King Kong* is on TV because its presence on the screen causes my belief. Such a causal account can also be applied to cases of testimonial knowledge. I know that Michael Owen scored for England last night because it is true, I believe it to be true, and there is a causal chain connecting my belief to that event. The fact that Owen scored the goal caused the radio commentator to say his name, and it is the commentator's testimony that caused me to believe that Owen had scored. Causal theorists claim that there are such causal connections underlying all cases of empirical knowledge.

2.3   Tracking accounts of knowledge

Robert Nozick (1981, ch. 3) provides a different account of reliability. For him, 'To know that p is to be someone who would believe it if it were true, and who wouldn't believe it if it were false' (p. 178). You only have knowledge if your beliefs 'track' the truth, that is, if your beliefs are sensitive to when p is the case and to when p is not the case. For S to know that p, the following four conditions must be satisfied.

1   p is true.
2   S believes that p.
3   If it were not the case that p, then S would not believe that p.
4   If in different circumstances p were still true, then S would still believe that p.

Let us look at how these conditions are relevant to the distinction between knowledge and mere true belief. Anthony always believes that he has the winning raffle ticket, and at the last Christmas fair he did. However, it could not be said that Anthony knew this because he would have had this belief whatever ticket he held. This is a case that does not satisfy Nozick's third condition for knowledge.

There are also cases in which the first three conditions alone cannot distinguish knowledge from true belief; the fourth condition must also be met. After passing the karaoke pub (chapter 2, section 4), I go home to watch the rest of the game. However, my TV breaks down just as England are about to take a penalty kick. I quickly stick my ear to the wall to listen to next door's TV. I hear a cheer and come to believe that the penalty has been scored. I am right: it is now 2–0. It is also the case that if the goal had not been scored, then I would not have acquired my present belief; this is because a Scottish friend of mine always telephones me to gloat at English misfortune. This is therefore a situation in which Nozick's first three conditions are met. However, I do not *know* the score because luck has played a part in my acquisition of the belief about the penalty. It turns out that my neighbours were not watching the football as they usually do, and the cheer was for a daring escape by James Bond in a movie being shown on a different channel. It was coincidental that my neighbours had forgotten that the match was on, that the film they happened to be watching featured a daring escape at the same time as the penalty kick, and that this escape elicited a cheer from them. Nozick can account for the intuition that this is not a case of knowledge since such a scenario does not satisfy his fourth condition. To know that the goal had been scored, it must be the case that I would have acquired this belief even if the situation had been different in various ways (so long as England had still scored). This, however, is not so; I would not have come to have such a belief if my neighbours had been watching a duller movie, or if they had been out.

Here, though, is an example that does satisfy Nozick's four conditions. I truly believe that I have a pain in my knee. I would not have this belief if my knee were not aching, and, if it does ache, I will always have such a belief however different the particular circumstances may be. My belief tracks the truth – Nozick's four conditions are met – and so I know that I have a painful knee.

We have looked at two ways of thinking about reliability: a reliable method of acquiring beliefs is one that involves our beliefs being caused in the right way, or one that allows our beliefs to track the truth. (Before we move on, it should be noted that there is a question concerning whether the theories above provide an account of the nature of justification, or whether they replace the need for justification. They could be seen as distinguishing between true belief and knowledge, not by adding a justification condition but, *instead*, by simply adding the right sort of causal or tracking relations. Knowledge could be seen as consisting in reliably caused true belief, and not justified true belief. This is a question we shall discuss in chapter 11 when we turn to the naturalistic approach to epistemology.)

3   Arguments for Externalism

3.1   Non-reflective knowledge

It is plausible that we can sometimes know that *p* without being able to give reasons for why we take *p* to be true. First, much of what we know is the result of rote learning, and many facts are simply accumulated without supporting evidence. I know that Oliver Cromwell was born in 1599 without needing to know anything further to justify this claim. Second, there are cases that involve forgotten evidence. I may have been taught at school that Napoleon made a tactical mistake in the Napoleonic Wars, and I can still remember this fact. I cannot, however, remember anything that justifies this claim (I have forgotten that it was because he attacked Russia in the winter). Third, we have certain recognitional abilities: perhaps a detective can know that something has been moved in a room without being able to say how the room looks different, or you can know that someone's appearance has changed without being able to give supporting evidence or reasons for why you think this is so. Some people may be very perceptive in these ways, but they may not be able to articulate just how they come to acquire such true beliefs. These are cases in which we have knowledge even though we are not, as Sellars would say, in the space of reasons. Some also take the cognitive abilities of animals and young children to support this line. Henry the cat knows when his bowl contains food and a child knows when her mother is near, even though neither can offer rational justification for such knowledge. A reliabilist account of knowledge is now tempting. If a thinker has a reliable method for remembering historical facts, or the layout of a room, or for determining the proximity of her mother, then she can acquire knowledge in these ways whether or not she can reflect upon the methods she uses.

3.2   An epistemological cure-all

The strongest motivation for externalism is that an externalist account of knowledge can solve some of our deepest epistemological problems. Externalism purports to have a response to the Gettier cases (chapter 2, section 4), and answers to both the threatened regress of justification (chapter 6, section 1), and to Cartesian scepticism (chapter 9). If externalism's solutions to these problems are persuasive, then this would favour adopting an externalist account of knowledge. Here we shall look again at the first two of these problems.

Let us remind ourselves of the Gettier cases. I seem to have a justified true belief that there is a cow in front of the physics building. However, it is lucky that my belief is true given that I am looking at a disguised shopping trolley, a trolley that obscures the real cow from view. The role of luck here means that this should not be seen as a case of knowledge (even though I seem to have a justified true belief). What would the externalist say about such a scenario? According to a causal theorist, I can only know that there is a cow there if it's a cow that causes my belief. In this case, though, it's a shopping trolley that causes my belief; the facts that cause me to acquire my belief about the cow are distinct from those that make my belief true. Thus, according to a causal theorist, I do not *know* there is a cow there, and this is just what our intuitions say about such a case. Nozick's tracking account also leads to the same conclusion. For my belief about the cow to amount to knowledge it would have to track the truth. In order for this to be so, it must be the case that I would not have had this belief if the cow had not been there. This, however, is not so since the trolley would have caused me to have this belief even if the cow was not there. Again, then, we have an externalist account that matches our intuitions.

On an internalist account, having justified beliefs does not guarantee that those beliefs are true. I could have a justified belief that there is a cow in the quad even if this is not so. It is such a notion of justification that opens up the possibility of Gettier cases: from my perspective I may have good reason to think a certain belief is true, but from the objective standpoint I have been lucky since the source of my justification is distinct from what actually makes that belief true. The externalist rules out the occurrence of such luck. Knowledge is distinguished from true belief by objective relations of causation or tracking; for the externalist, therefore, knowledge has a direct connection to what it is in the world that makes our beliefs true. There is not a gap for a Gettier scenario to exploit between a subjective notion of justification and the objective notion of truth.

In chapter 6 we considered the problem associated with a threatened regress of justification. The traditional foundationalist response to this problem is to ground our thoughts in certain basic beliefs, beliefs that are justified in virtue of the infallible knowledge we have of our non-conceptual perceptual experience (the Given). Many philosophers, however, do not find this satisfying since it is not clear how non-conceptual experience can play a justificatory role. An alternative response to the threatened regress is that of the coherentist. For him, the source of the problem is the linear conception of justification and he argues that we should adopt a holistic account instead, one that does not allow the regress to get started. The externalist, on the other hand, offers a different response, although this response is in some ways foundationalist in nature. The linear conception of justification is accepted, and our belief systems are grounded in certain basic beliefs. However, our basic beliefs need not be justified by our acquaintance with the Given. For our basic beliefs to count as knowledge, all that are required are the right kinds of causal or tracking relations with the world, relations that do not have to be cognitively accessible to the thinker. I can have a basic perceptual belief that there is a red hole punch in front of me because that kind of belief reliably tracks the truth. Such a belief does not have to be inferentially supported by the further belief that I seem to see a red shape over there; the reliability of my perceptual and cognitive mechanisms allows the regress of justification to be halted at my belief about the hole punch.

It would be a big feather in the cap of externalism if the above could be accepted as successful responses to Gettier and to the regress of justification. In the next chapter we shall look at the externalist response to Cartesian scepticism and, if persuasive, this would amount to a very big feather indeed. Let us now, however, turn to arguments against the externalist approach.

4   Arguments against Externalism

We shall look at two kinds of cases in which our beliefs are the product of reliable epistemic processes yet we would not want to say that they amount to knowledge. This would entail that a reliabilist account cannot successfully distinguish knowledge from true belief.

4.1   Knowledge and rationally motivated action

Uri is a reliable clairvoyant although he doesn't know that he is. From time to time certain beliefs pop into Uri's head, beliefs that he thinks are spontaneous and unfounded, yet beliefs that are in fact the result of his clairvoyant powers. (In the film *Ghost* (1990), Oda Mae Brown attempts to fleece the recently bereaved by posing as a medium and pretending to speak to their loved ones again. Oda Mae does not believe that she actually has this ability even though it turns out that she does.) One day Uri wakes up with the unlikely belief that the Pope is shopping at the Bullring in Birmingham. It turns out that he is; and, given Uri's reliable clairvoyant powers, his believing so is no accident. On an externalist account, therefore, Uri knows that the Pope is in town even though he has no reason for believing this to be so. This claim is problematic since such an account does not respect the essential connection between knowledge and rationally motivated action. Your actions should be guided by what you know; this, however, is not so with Uri. We can see this if we consider another belief that Uri has, the belief that the Prime Minister is also in town. He believes this because his friend tells him so, although he is not totally convinced that his friend is right given that at times he is somewhat unreliable; nevertheless, Uri believes him (with reservations). Let us consider what Uri would do if he were forced to bet a substantial sum on one or other of these dignitaries being in Birmingham: who would he bet on? It would be rational for him to bet on the Prime Minister because at least this bet has the (albeit weak) support of his friend's testimony. Even such shaky testimony should incline him not to bet on the Pope given that he has no reason at all to think that he is in town. Now, though, we can see that such a bet has troubling consequences for the externalist. We have claimed that Uri should act on a belief that is only fairly reasonable (that based on his friend's testimony) rather than on something that he knows to be true. In such a case, the externalist does not respect the plausible connection between knowledge and rational action – we should act according to what we know – externalism, therefore, is misguided.

You may have qualms about this example because it involves clairvoyance; we can, though, formulate analogous scenarios involving less contentious epistemic abilities. When watching TV detective dramas such as *Midsomer Murders* or *Columbo*, I always have a hunch who the murderer will be early on in the episode, and my hunch is almost always correct. I am not, however, aware of any good reasons that back up my predictions and thus, if asked, I would not bet on them being correct. Perhaps, though, I am not just lucky; I may be good at unconsciously picking up subtle clues that the director gives the viewer. The murderer may always wear clothes of a certain colour, or be listening to music when he or she is first encountered. If this is the case, then my methods for identifying the guilty party are reliable, and thus the externalist is faced with the problem we noted in the previous paragraph: he would have to accept that it is sometimes rational for me not to bet on things that I know to be true.

4.2   *Lucky yet reliable beliefs*

Reliabilists attempt to explain why the accidental possession of true beliefs does not amount to knowledge. This is because such beliefs are not acquired via reliable methods or processes. Plantinga (1993a), however, discusses several examples that illustrate how luck can play a part even when our beliefs are acquired in reliable ways. Imagine a kind of brain lesion that plays havoc with your belief system, mostly inducing lots of false beliefs. It also has the side-effect of reliably causing you to believe that you have such a lesion. According to the externalist, then, this is something that you know. Plantinga, however, argues that because such a belief is the accidental by-product of the lesion's (mostly disruptive) action, then it cannot amount to knowledge. This is a point we keep coming back to: knowledge cannot be a matter of luck.

Various responses have been made to this argument. First, we could take such an example to show that externalism is flawed and that we must instead adopt an internalist approach. Second, Plantinga's intuition could be denied. Is it really so obvious that such a belief cannot amount to knowledge? (I'll leave this for you to consider.) Third, an externalist could admit that reliability alone is not sufficient for knowledge, and that he needs to say more about what distinguishes it from true belief. This is the line that Plantinga (1993b) takes. In the brain lesion example, certain reliably caused beliefs are the result of some kind of cognitive malfunction. To rule these out, Plantinga claims that the mechanisms which give rise to knowledge must be those that are functioning properly. This notion of 'properly' is cashed out in terms of design: a mechanism is functioning properly if it does what it's designed to do. There are two ways of thinking about the kind of 'designer' involved here. Natural selection could have (metaphorically) designed the mechanisms involved in both our bodily functions and cognition; or an intelligent, omniscient God could have done so (see chapter 15, section 2.1). Plantinga favours the latter option.

5   Two Kinds of Knowledge

There are strong intuitions in favour of both internalism and externalism, and the issue concerning which is the correct epistemological perspective to adopt is one that remains hotly debated. There may, however, be room for a different kind of resolution to this debate. There could simply be two distinct conceptions of knowledge – internalist and externalist – and we do not have to choose between them. If this were so, internalists and externalists would not be providing competing descriptions of the same univocal concept; instead, they would be focusing on two distinct concepts that have different roles within epistemology. Internalists focus on the kind of knowledge that essentially involves a subjective notion of justification. Externalists, on the other hand, focus on the objective grounds that distinguish knowledge from true belief, ones that concern a thinker's causal or tracking relations with the world. These two conceptions of knowledge are appropriate for distinct epistemological questions and projects. If we are considering which methods of enquiry we should use to acquire truths about the world, then reflection upon objective factors will indicate that we should look to science rather than to dice throwing or astrology. If, however, I am interested in whether I have good reason to hold a particular belief, then I should focus on the notion of subjective justification. If it is accepted that there are two such distinct conceptions of knowledge, then the intuitions offered by the internalist and the externalist are not in competition; they simply support the ascription of one or other of these distinct epistemic notions in particular cases. I know that chana puri is not being served this week (on an internalist account; see chapter 6, section 1) *and* I know that Cromwell was born in 1599 (on an externalist account; see section 3.1 of this chapter). There is knowledge that is backed up with reasons, and knowledge that only involves a thinker reliably believing the truth. In both cases, knowledge is distinguished from lucky true belief. The internalist attempts to rule out luck by claiming that we must have good reasons to think that our beliefs are true. The externalist, however, provides objective grounds to explain why certain true beliefs are not lucky, that is, because they are the product of reliable cognitive processes. Language-using thinkers have both kinds of knowledge (although young children and animals may only have the externalist kind). (It should be noted, though, that this is only a suggested resolution; most participants in the debate remain partisan to one side or the other.)

Bonjour accepts that there are two distinct conceptions of justification (Bonjour and Sosa, 2003). He insists, however, that the internalist notion is more fundamental than that of the externalist. Before we can go on to ask objective questions about which of our epistemic practices are reliable, we first need to know whether we have good reason for thinking that any of our beliefs are true. We cannot weigh the reliability of dice throwing against that of science without first having some justified beliefs about such practices. If I am not aware of any reasons for thinking that my beliefs are true, then I have no reason to assume that there are scientists, test tubes, charlatans and dice. Thus the objective questions concerning these epistemic methods simply do not arise. Bonjour's internalist claim is that we must first block such sceptical thinking and show how we can have subjective justification for our beliefs; then, and only then, can we go on to consider questions concerning objective justification.

It is such sceptical concerns that the next part of the book investigates. We will turn to certain important arguments which suggest that our beliefs are not subjectively justified. These arguments are seen by many as the core of epistemology, and we shall look at how both the internalist and externalist react to them.

Questions

1 What is the relationship between reliability and empirical knowledge? (Remember, both internalists and externalists make use of some notion of reliability.)
2 Can you think of any non-reflective knowledge that you might have, knowledge for which you cannot provide rational justification? And how might the internalist respond to such examples?
3 What would the internalist and externalist have to say about the following three scenarios?
    (a) Peter claims to know the birth sign of everyone he first meets, and he almost always gets it right. He does not know how he does this, and neither does anybody else.
    (b) Paul is great with very young children. They never cry when he is looking after them because he always seems to know when they want to watch TV, play or eat. He also offers seemingly good reasons for why this is so. He explains that it is their eyes that give it away. His reasons, however, are unfounded; the look in their eyes is not indicative of their desires. Paul is actually good with children because unconsciously he picks up on certain features of their posture, features which are in fact a sure sign of what a child wants to do. Does Paul *know* when young children want to watch TV?
    (c) Mary has lots of illnesses. However, when she believes that she will recover quickly, she does. There is a reason for this: when she is thinking positively her brain produces chemicals that boost her immune system. Beliefs in a quick recovery are reliably self-fulfilling; but does she *know* that she will recover quickly?

Further Reading

In previous chapters we have considered the work of certain key internalist thinkers such as Descartes and Hume. These are both foundationalists, but the coherentists Bonjour (1985) and Lehrer (1990) are also internalist in their approach. Externalism is a recent development and important work includes Armstrong's *Belief, Truth, and Knowledge* (1973); Dretske's *Knowledge and the Flow of Information* (1981); chapter 3 of Nozick's *Philosophical Explanations* (1981); and Goldman's *Epistemology and Cognition* (1986). Sophisticated debate between internalism and externalism can be found in Plantinga's *Warrant: The Current Debate* (1993a), and in the recent exchange between Bonjour and Sosa (2003). The clairvoyant argument of section 4.1 is taken from Bonjour (1985). Kornblith's edited *Epistemology: Internalism and Externalism* (2001) is also a useful collection of articles, as is Luper-Foy (1987). For the problem of generality see Alston (1995) and Conee and Feldman (1998), and for further discussion of causal theories you could turn to McGinn (1984).

PART IV

SCEPTICISM

9 Scepticism

Sceptics claim that we do not have as many justified beliefs or as much knowledge as we think we do. Some claim that we do not have knowledge of particular kinds of fact: perhaps we cannot know things about the future, whether or not other people have minds, morality, or God. Such scepticism is local – confined to a certain area of knowledge – and in chapters 12 to 15 we shall look at these particular sceptical claims. Here, though, we shall be looking at global scepticism, and the claim that we cannot come to know *anything* about the world at all. The key sceptical thinker in the Western tradition is Descartes, whose ideas on scepticism have driven epistemology for over 300 years. This chapter will focus on his arguments and on the various attempts that have been made to refute them.

1 Cartesian Scepticism

1.1 Dreams and the demon

We are aware that our senses sometimes deceive us. The tower in the distance can appear round when in fact it is square, and the pine nuts frying in the kitchen can smell of bacon. Such errors do not usually concern us because we can check whether our perceptions are accurate. I can observe the tower more carefully by moving closer to it, and I can compare the verdicts of my different senses: I can look in the frying pan and see that there are pine nuts frying and not bacon. Furthermore, most of the time we are confident that our senses are not mistaken in this way. I accept that I could be wrong about the shape of the distant tower, but I am as sure as I can be that right now I am sitting in my study and that my computer monitor is on.

Descartes, however, puts forward two arguments that threaten the veracity of all the beliefs we acquire through perception. The first concerns dreams.

> How often, asleep at night, am I convinced of just such familiar events – that I am here in my dressing-gown, sitting by the fire – when in fact I am lying undressed in bed! Yet at the moment my eyes are certainly wide awake when I look at this piece of paper; I shake my head and it is not asleep; as I stretch out and feel my hand I do so deliberately, and I know what I am doing. All this would not happen with such distinctness to someone asleep. Indeed! As if I did not remember other occasions when

> I have been tricked by exactly similar thoughts while asleep! As I think about this more carefully, I see plainly that there are no sure signs by which being awake can be distinguished from being asleep. The result is that I begin to feel dazed, and this very feeling only reinforces the notion that I may be asleep. (Descartes, 1986, p. 13)

Sometimes all kinds of fantastic events may occur in my dreams and, occasionally, I may be aware that I am dreaming. Many dreams, however, are indistinguishable from waking life. Last week I dreamt that I accidentally knocked a hole through the wall to next door, and I used this opportunity to be nosey and have a look at my neighbour's living room. This dream was so lifelike and vivid that there were times during the day when I was unsure whether or not this had happened, and I actually had occasional pangs of guilt thinking that I had spied on my neighbour's house. The Cartesian worry is that such dreams seem to undermine the justification we take our perceptual beliefs to possess. Descartes's experience of sitting by the fire is indistinguishable from the experience he might have of dreaming that he was doing so. The experience I have of sitting in my study typing is no different from the experience I would be having if I were now asleep and dreaming of work. I cannot therefore tell whether I am awake or dreaming. Note that now it is no use attending more carefully to our perceptions, or using our other senses to verify our beliefs. When we are dreaming, all of our senses are being deceived at once, and most dreams are undetectable as such. The sceptical conclusion is that since I do not know that I am not dreaming, I am not justified in believing that I am presently sitting in my study.

Descartes also claims that an even more corrosive form of doubt can be raised. In our dreams we seem to mix and match components of the various experiences we have had in our waking lives. Dreams may include all kinds of fantastic creatures and storylines, but these are constructed from certain features of our experience of the everyday world. A dream of a unicorn may have its origin in my waking experience of horses, the colour white, and horns. Thus, even though I may not be justified in believing that I am currently sitting in my office chair, I am justified in believing that there is an external world, a world that contains – perhaps in different combinations – features corresponding to my experience. Descartes, though, provides an argument that threatens even this belief. In order to do this, he introduces what has come to be a very influential figure in the history of epistemology: the evil demon, evil genius, or *mal génie*.

> I will suppose . . . some malicious demon of the utmost power and cunning has employed all his energies in order to deceive me. I shall think that the sky, the air, the Earth, colours, shapes, sounds, and all external things are merely the delusions of dreams which he has devised to ensnare my judgment. I shall consider myself as not having hands or eyes, or flesh, or blood or senses, but as falsely believing that I have all these things. (Descartes, 1986, p. 15)

Descartes claims that we cannot know that such a being is not manipulating our experience. Such a demon could deceive us about (almost) *everything*: there may not be an external world at all. Descartes is not crazy: he does not believe that there is such a demon. His point, however, is that *if* there were, our experience would be indistinguishable from the experience we currently take ourselves to be having of the world. We therefore have no justification for believing that we are having veridical perceptions rather than merely demon-induced hallucinations.

Hilary Putnam (1981) presents a modern version of this dilemma, one that can hit home for those who find the demon scenario too fantastic to take seriously. It may not be beyond the capacities of medicine in the future to remove a brain and keep it alive in a vat of nutrients. (Such brains appear in various movies, including *The Man With Two Brains*, 1993, and the French film *La Cité des Enfants Perdus*, 1995.) This brain would not receive sensory input from the world; instead, evil scientists could use computers to feed electrical inputs directly into the brainstem, and thus such a brain could receive sensory input that is the same as my brain is receiving right now. The experience of a brain in a vat could therefore be indistinguishable from the experience I currently take myself to be having of the world. Thus, for all I can tell, all my experiences may have been simulated in my brain by evil scientists, with my brain sitting in a vat in their laboratory. As my brain decides to reach out for the (illusory) coffee with my (illusory) arm, the scientists' computer calculates what changes should be made to my brain's simulated perceptual input. I shall be fed with the visual experience of seeing my arm reach for the cup, and the olfactory experience of smelling the coffee as I (seem to) bring the cup to my lips.

Before considering how we should respond to such scepticism, let us be clear about the structure of the Cartesian argument. Certain sceptical possibilities are suggested. If I cannot know that these possibilities are not realized, then there are various other things that I cannot know as well. If I don't know that I am not dreaming, then I don't know that I am currently sitting in my study. If I don't know that I am not a brain in a vat, then I don't know that I am wearing blue corduroy trousers. In order for me to know such facts about my current situation, I would have to be able to rule out the Cartesian sceptical possibilities, and it is not clear how this can be done. This is because my experience would be just the same if reality were radically different from what I suppose it to be. I have no justification for believing in one scenario rather than another, and so none of my beliefs about the external world are justified.

Descartes questions whether our perceptual beliefs are justified. In chapter 4 we considered two accounts of perception – indirect realism and direct realism – and Cartesian scepticism is a problem for them both. The indirect realist claims that we are only directly aware of mental items or sense data. If you favour this approach, it is easy to feel the pull of Descartes's sceptical thinking since my perceptual experience would be the same whatever the origin of my sense data. The demon could have implanted them in my mind. Note, though, that the direct realist is not immune to such scepticism. The direct realist theory that we focused on was intentionalism, with the claim being that perceptual states have intentional content. Parallels were drawn with beliefs: I currently perceive that *my coffee cup is empty*, and I also believe that this is so. Such a view also allows room for the sceptic. I can have false beliefs and I can have beliefs about things that do not exist. Having thoughts with the intentional content that *p* does not entail that *p* is a feature of the external world. Similarly, I can perceive the world as *p*, yet be mistaken. The Cartesian arguments can therefore bite: it could be that I simply have various mental states and perceptions with intentional content, intentional content that does not pick out existent features of the world.

This is a terrible epistemic situation to be in; we must therefore try and find a satisfying response to such scepticism. Descartes himself thinks that he can provide arguments to show that we are not caught in this predicament. Using a priori reasoning, he attempts to prove that God exists and, since God is good, he would not allow us to be globally deceived in this way. In chapter 15 we shall look at one of his arguments for the existence of God. Descartes's legacy, however, remains a negative one. As we shall see, there are various problems with his positive argument for the existence of God; he does not therefore avoid the sceptical arguments that he himself puts forward. Others, however, have offered more persuasive arguments against scepticism and we shall turn to these in sections 3, 4 and 5 of this chapter. First, though, we shall look at the influence of Cartesian scepticism on cinema.

1.2   Descartes goes to the movies

Throughout our discussions I have noted how the philosophical themes that we have been looking at can be illustrated by the arts, and especially by film. This is particularly so with respect to Cartesian scepticism. This has engaged recent filmmakers and I suspect that many of them were inspired by epistemology classes at college or university. A film from the seventies, *Dark Star* (1974), is explicit in its Cartesian references. An astronaut, Commander Doolittle, tries to convince an intelligent bomb that it's only really aware of its own electronic impulses, and it cannot know whether there is an external world at all. It cannot therefore know whether it has really received the command to blow up.

> Doolittle: Hello Bomb. Are you with me? . . . Are you willing to entertain a few concepts? . . . What concrete evidence do you have that you exist?
>
> Bomb: Um . . . well . . . I think therefore I am.
>
> Doolittle: That's good, that's very good; but how do you know that anything else exists?
>
> Bomb: My sensory apparatus reveals it to me. . . .

Doolittle: Now listen . . . listen: here's the big question. How do you know that the evidence that your sensory apparatus reveals to you is correct? What I'm getting at is this: the only experience that is directly available to you is your sensory data and this sensory data is merely a stream of electrical impulses that stimulates your computing centre.

Bomb: In other words, all I really know about the outside world is relayed to me through my electrical impulses. . . . Why, that would mean that I really don't know what the outside universe is like at all for certain.

Doolittle: Now Bomb, consider this next question very carefully. What is your one purpose in life?

Bomb: To explode of course.

Doolittle: And you can only do it once – right? . . . And you wouldn't want to explode on the basis of false data. Would you?

Bomb: Of course not.

Doolittle: Well then, you've already admitted that you have no real proof of the existence of the outside universe . . . so you have no absolute proof that Sergeant Pinback ordered you to detonate . . . all you are remembering is merely a series of sensory impulses which you now realize have no real definite connection with outside reality . . . So if you detonate you could be doing so on the basis of false data.

Bomb: I must think on this further.

The astronaut's strategy succeeds, and the bomb retreats to the bomb bay to ponder further this philosophical argument.

The Cartesian theme is also evident in *The Matrix* (1999) and its sequels. In the distant future, humans are enslaved by a race of intelligent robots, their bodies used as sources of biochemical energy. They are kept in pods and, as in Putnam's brain in a vat scenario, they are fed a simulated stream of sensory input. They experience the virtual reality world of the Matrix, appearing to live a normal life in a modern industrial city, when they are in fact lying in a pod being tended by spider-like robots. Throughout, we have references to Descartes's arguments, particularly to the one concerning dreams. At one point the rebel leader Morpheus says to the hero of the trilogy: 'Have you ever had a dream, Neo, that you were so sure was real? What if you were unable to wake from that dream? How would you know the difference between the dream world and the real world?' (Incidentally, 'Morpheus' is the name of the Roman God of dreams and sleep.)

The whole genre of films concerning virtual reality is influenced by Descartes. The characters in *eXistenZ* (1999) play a futuristic video game that plugs into the base of the spine. At the end of the film the Cartesian worry is expressed: 'Hey, tell me the truth – are we still in the game?' (this is unresolved). A less technological version of the Cartesian dilemma is presented in *The Truman Show* (1998). Unbeknownst to Truman, he has been born on the set of a reality TV show and he has lived all his life in a TV studio. Thus many of his beliefs about his family, his town and the outside world are false. Some films not only portray characters that are stuck in the Cartesian predicament, but they also try to mislead the audience (at least temporarily). In *The Usual Suspects* (1995) – I recommend skipping to the next paragraph if you have not seen this film and if you do not want the excellent denouement to be spoilt – it is only in the final minutes that we discover that everything which we have seen in flashback is a fabrication (and this amounts to a good proportion of the drama of the film). One of the characters, Keyser Soze, could be seen as a Cartesian demon who creates a logically coherent world that deceives both the characters and the audience.

It is important, though, to note the crucial differences between Descartes's scenario and these cinematic presentations of his ideas. First, Truman is still in touch with the real world – the TV studio – and therefore many of his beliefs are justified. There really are tables and chairs, he has a body, and he has correct beliefs about the laws of nature: gravity causes apples to fall from trees, and water boils at 100°C. None of these beliefs is justified in Descartes's scenario. Second, it is crucial to Descartes's arguments that the dreaming and demon scenarios are indistinguishable from the veridical case. This, however, is not so in some of the films we have mentioned. In *The Truman Show*, part of the studio's lighting rig falls from the sky, an event which the producers of the show have some trouble in explaining away; and in *The Matrix*, Morpheus and Neo can feel that 'there's something wrong with the world. You don't know what it is, but it's there, like a splinter in your mind, driving you mad.' In both films these clues are picked up on and the respective heroes are able to escape their Cartesian predicament.

2   Accepting Cartesian Scepticism

One response to Cartesian scepticism could be that of indifference. So what if I am in a vat, the Matrix or a Truman-type show – all my experiences will be the same regardless – and so why should I be concerned? It is not clear, however, if anyone could really think that it doesn't matter whether or not the whole world is some kind of illusion, and this would certainly be an odd attitude for a philosopher to take, someone who professes to pursue wisdom and truth. There are, however, three less disingenuous responses to this form of scepticism. First, we could accept that our empirical beliefs have no justification and attempt to live in the shadow of such scepticism. Second, we could accept the sceptical arguments and give a psychological explanation of why we are simply incapable of believing their disturbing conclusion. Third, we could refute Descartes's arguments. The third option will be our main focus, and it has been the main preoccupation of the last 300 years of epistemology. First, though, we shall briefly consider the other two options.

2.1 *Withholding belief*

We should only believe what we are justified in believing, and thus, if we are to be epistemically responsible, we should withhold all beliefs concerning the external world. Could we, though, actually adopt such an attitude? We can withhold certain beliefs and in particular cases it is clear what difference this should make to how we should act and live in the world. I may decide that I am not justified in believing in the existence of UFOs. Withholding this belief will have an effect on some of my other thoughts: I may now believe that the strange lights in the sky are the result of meteorological phenomena, and I may lose the desire to go on holiday to Groom Lake, Nevada, the hotbed of UFO sightings. In considering how the withholding of such a belief will affect my behaviour, I take it that many of my other beliefs and desires stand firm. I still believe that something is going on in the sky and that there are other interesting places to go on holiday. These beliefs will cause me to act in certain ways: I may buy a book on meteorology, and go to Paris. It is not clear, though, how you could coherently act if you withheld *all* of your beliefs about the external world. Could you *live* Cartesian scepticism? Think about how you would act and what it would be rational to do if you withheld all your empirical beliefs.

2.2 *Dinner, backgammon and conversation*

Hume's scepticism can come as a surprise. Descartes is often one's introduction to epistemology and, to some, his demon imagery and (interim) sceptical conclusions are rather exasperating. Hume comes along and it all looks more promising. Here we have a down-to-earth Scotsman, a hardcore empiricist who claims that 'armchair philosophy' cannot provide us with philosophical conclusions concerning either the world or our epistemic limitations. Here, though, is the shock: Hume is more sceptical than Descartes. First, his enquiries end with certain sceptical conclusions still standing; Descartes, remember, claims to have refuted his own scepticism. Second, after Descartes has presented his sceptical arguments, he famously claims that there is one thing that he knows for sure – 'I am' – and he knows this on the seemingly undeniable grounds that he is thinking: 'Cogito, ergo sum' ('I think, therefore I am'). I know that *I* exist, that *I* endure through time, and that *I* have certain beliefs about the world, beliefs that, as it happens, are not justified. Hume's extra sceptical mile is that we have no reason to believe in the self: there is no *I*, no Cartesian ego that endures from moment to moment. All that can be claimed is that there are thoughts – thoughts, though, that are not entertained by a particular thinker. There is no justification for believing in the external world or even in the existence of thinking subjects.

We shall not concern ourselves here with Hume's sceptical arguments; instead, we shall consider his strategy for coping with such scepticism. Hume accepts that his sceptical conclusions are correct.

However, it so happens that this doesn't worry us, not because we choose not to be concerned, but because we are psychologically incapable of being sceptics. This is a contingent fact about creatures with minds like ours.

> Most fortunately it happens that since reason is incapable of dispelling these clouds, nature herself suffices to that purpose, and cures me of this philosophical melancholy and delirium, either by relaxing this bent of mind, or by some chimeras. I dine, I play a game of backgammon, I converse, and am merry with my friends; and when after three or four hours' amusement, I would return to these speculations, they appear so cold, and strained, and ridiculous, that I cannot find in my heart to enter into them any farther. (Hume, 1978, p. 269)

(You should note that the presentation of Hume that I have given is somewhat contentious. There are actually two strands to Hume's approach – one sceptical and one naturalistic – and some interpreters stress the latter rather than the former. Such an interpretation will be briefly considered in chapter 11, section 1.1.)

The strategies we have so far looked at accept that we do not have any justified beliefs about the external world. It would, of course, be much more satisfying if we could find good reason to refute the sceptical hypotheses, and it is this line that will be investigated in the rest of the chapter.

3 Contextualism

Throughout the book we have focused on epistemologies that are 'invariantist', that is, they work with a single set of standards, standards that *all* claims to knowledge must meet. A recent response to scepticism has questioned such invariantism, and various writers including Keith De Rose (1995) and David Lewis (2000) have proposed a 'contextualist' approach. The contextualist argues that the standards which beliefs must meet in order to be classified as knowledge differ between contexts. Alvin Goldman was one of the first to suggest such a contextualist approach; he offers the following example (Goldman, 2000a). When driving along a country road you may see the facade of a barn across a field. Thus you correctly come to believe that there is a barn there, and on various accounts this belief would constitute a case of perceptual knowledge. This may, however, be a strange county, one in which many of the local farmers have erected papier-mâché barns. Virtually all of the facades that you see are fake. The one spotted from the road, however, is actually one of the rare authentic barns. In such a county, your true belief does not amount to knowledge since it is lucky that you have encountered the real thing. The same claim to knowledge is correct in one environmental context and not in another. Such contextual relativity is a feature of many of our concepts. The standards that we use to assess whether a surface is flat differ depending on whether we are considering a cricket pitch, the floor of a U-shaped valley, or the face of a diamond.

More recently, contextualists have focused on conversational contexts. In everyday circumstances I can correctly claim to know that the supermarket is still open, that the mountain Bowfell is almost 3,000 feet high, and that Triumph makes motorcycles in the Midlands. In the philosophy seminar, however, all such claims come to be questioned. If Descartes's demon had his way, there would be no supermarket, Bowfell or Triumph motorcycles. The conclusion of the Cartesian arguments is that we cannot know about such things. Here, then, we have contexts constituted not by the distinct physical features of the environment (as in the example involving fake barns), but rather by features of the conversational context, that is, by the types of questions that usually arise in conversations concerning such things as mountains and motorcycles. If asked whether the supermarket is open, I would think about what the time was and whether or not it was Sunday. I would not consider the possibility that the supermarket is the work of an evil demon. Such a possibility can be safely ignored in the everyday context; or, as it is sometimes put, only some of the alternative possibilities are 'relevant'.

> Our definition of knowledge requires a *sotto voce* proviso. S *knows that P* iff [if and only if] *S*'s evidence eliminates every possibility in which not-*P* – Psst! – except for those possibilities that we are properly ignoring. (D. Lewis, 2000, p. 371)

It is certainly true that the standards we actually use to ascribe knowledge do vary between contexts. In most situations, access to Wainwright's *Pictorial Guide to the Lakeland Fells* is all that's required if I am to know that Bowfell is almost 3,000 feet high; this, however, is not enough in the context of Descartes's sceptical arguments. The contextualist claims that this is not merely how we use the concept of KNOWLEDGE; we are also justified in using it in this way. It is right to say that I can have knowledge of Bowfell when discussing my next trip to the Lake District *and* it is also right to say that I cannot have such knowledge when discussing Descartes. Further, there are not simply two distinct epistemological contexts – one with respect to Cartesian scepticism, and a catch-all that includes all others – there is a whole range of contexts, each with its own set of epistemic standards. The possibilities that we count as relevant differ depending on whether we are discussing if anyone knows whose turn it is to buy the next round of drinks; whether the jury knows that the defendant is guilty; or whether Catherine knows that Jim is in love with her.

The context with which we have been most concerned is that of the philosophy seminar. In this rarefied air, all possibilities seem to be open, including those involving deceiving demons and brains in vats: 'you have landed in a context with an enormously rich domain of potential counter-examples to ascriptions of knowledge' (D. Lewis, 2000. p. 377).

Here the standards required for knowledge are very high indeed. We must rule out all such sceptical scenarios, and the Cartesian claim is that this is something we cannot do. Contextualists, then, may accept that in the context of the philosophy seminar we do not have very much knowledge, perhaps none at all concerning the external world. However, when we return to our everyday life we return to our everyday epistemic standards, and here there is much that we do know: in such a context the existence of an evil demon is not relevant to whether the supermarket is open or not. It is therefore epistemically interesting when we switch between different kinds of discourse. Walking into a philosophy seminar becomes a dangerous thing to do, in that our everyday knowledge is threatened by the new alternative possibilities that now become relevant. Conversely, walking out of a seminar is epistemically enriching: you can now know that *King Kong* is on TV tonight, a fact that you could not have known five minutes ago (by Cartesian lights).

> [E]pistemology destroys knowledge. But it does so only temporarily. The pastime of epistemology does not plunge us forevermore into its special context. We can still do a lot of proper ignoring, a lot of knowing, and a lot of true ascribing of knowledge to ourselves and others, the rest of the time. (D. Lewis, 2000, p. 377)

4 Cognitive Externalism

Putnam (1981) puts forward an ingenious argument against the possibility that we could be brains in vats. To see how this argument works, we first need to say something about the position called cognitive externalism and, more generally, about the philosophy of mind. Our thoughts have *content*, that is, they are about certain aspects of the world. The content of one of my current thoughts is that *my computer is on*. (We looked at such an account of the mind when we considered the intentionalist theory of perception in chapter 4, section 4.2.) An important question in the philosophy of mind concerns the nature of such content. Cognitive internalists claim that the content of a particular thought is determined wholly by what is inside the head of the thinker. On various traditional accounts – those of Locke, Descartes and Hume – our thoughts are seen as ideas, ideas conceived of as images, images that are inside our heads. Recent developments in the philosophy of mind have moved away from this picture and concentrated instead on items that can be given a scientific description. Some have claimed that mental states are just physical states of the brain. Others take a computational approach and see the mind as analogous to software, with the brain providing the hardware that enables our programs to run. These modern accounts, however, share one important feature with the traditional picture, that is, such physical or computational states are inside our heads, and it is these that determine the content of our thoughts.

For cognitive externalists, however, the world plays a constitutive role in determining the content of our mental states: 'Cognitive space incorporates the relevant portion of the "external" world' (McDowell, 1986, p. 258). Various arguments have been put forward in favour of this externalist approach; most notable is Putnam's (1975a) Twin Earth thought experiment. We can imagine two physically identical characters, Oscar and Toscar; Oscar lives here and Toscar lives on Twin Earth, a superficially identical planet over on the other side of the universe. Oscar and Toscar are molecule-for-molecule alike, right down to the structure of their brains, and they both have beliefs about the clear stuff that lies in puddles and rains from the sky. On Twin Earth, however, this clear refreshing liquid is in fact XYZ and not H_2O. Toscar is thinking about different stuff from Oscar; their thoughts, therefore, have different content, even though we have specified that everything inside their heads is the same. Thought content is not wholly determined by what's in the head.

Before considering how the adoption of such a philosophy of mind might enable us to refute Cartesian scepticism, it should first be noted how this form of externalism differs from epistemological externalism. The debate between epistemological externalists and internalists concerns whether we are able to reflect upon what it is that distinguishes knowledge from true belief; the question that cognitive externalism addresses, however, is the metaphysical one concerning what it is that determines the content of our thoughts. These are distinct issues. This can be seen by noting that you can be an externalist in one sense and not in the other. For example, you could argue that mental content is wholly determined by the internal computational states of the brain (cognitive internalism), and that knowledge only requires your cognitive mechanisms to track the truth reliably (epistemological externalism). In this section we shall consider the cognitive variety of externalism, and in the next the epistemological variety. Both can be seen as offering a challenge to the sceptic.

Putnam accepts cognitive externalism, and takes it to entail that the claim 'I am a brain in a vat' is self-refuting. One cannot truly claim it, or think it. We can see what 'self-refuting' means by considering the claim 'I do not exist'; if one thinks this, then it is not true. (If you are thinking anything, then you must exist – remember: 'cogito, ergo sum'.) Similarly, Putnam argues that if you think you're a brain in a vat, then you're not. According to the cognitive internalist, a brain in a vat can have the same thoughts as you and I, since what determines the content of our thoughts is wholly within the brain. For the externalist, however, this is not so. I can have thoughts about trees because there are trees in my world, trees that I can causally and perceptually engage with. A brain in a vat, however, cannot think about trees because it does not causally or perceptually engage with such things. And even though such a brain may be sitting in a vat, it does not perceptually or causally engage with such an object; it cannot, therefore, think true thoughts about such a container; nor can it think about itself as a *brain* since brains in vats do not perceptually or causally engage with other brains. The only thing to which a brain in a vat is causally connected is the computer that feeds it simulated sensory information. Thus, according to the cognitive externalist, either brains in vats do not have thoughts at all since they are not causally connected to a world that could determine thought content, or their thoughts must be about the electronic impulses within the scientists' computer. If the former is so, then the sceptical hypothesis cannot be put forward. If a brain in a vat does not have any contentful thoughts, then it cannot think about anything, let alone the possibility of global scepticism.

Let us, however, turn to the second suggestion: the thoughts of a brain in a vat do have content; content, though, that differs from that which we take our own thoughts to possess. The content of the thought 'I am a brain in a vat' would actually be something like 'I am circuit 584' (it is circuit 584 to which such a brain is causally connected and not brains and vats). If, though, I am a brain in a vat, then this is false: I am supposedly a brain in a vat and not a circuit in a computer. I cannot therefore express the true thought that I am a brain in a vat. If I were, I would not have the conceptual resources with which to describe my predicament. Thus I should not take the sceptical claim seriously; I cannot truly think that I am in such a Cartesian scenario. (Do not worry if you find this argument difficult; it is extremely slippery. It would be worth pausing here – consider whether you understand just how the argument runs, and whether you find it convincing.)

One problem with this argument is that it's only applicable to a very specific sceptical scenario, one in which (according to the externalist) a thinker could never have acquired the ability to have contentful thoughts about his own (alleged) predicament. Consider, however, the following scenario. I take it that for most of my life I have been untroubled by demons and evil scientists. I, like everyone else, have lived in the real world surrounded by coffee cups, paper clips, and vats, and I have discussed brains both in biology classes at school and in philosophy seminars at university. I can therefore have thoughts about such things. Yesterday, however, I could have been kidnapped by the evil scientists, my brain could have been removed and placed in a vat, and my experience of the abduction could have been erased from my memory. The Cartesian claim is that in order for me to know anything about the external world, I must be able to rule out this sceptical possibility. This, however, I cannot do given the fact that my envatted experiences would be indistinguishable from those I take myself to have of the world. And, crucially, I do have the conceptual resources to talk about *this* sceptical scenario. My life outside the vat – that up until yesterday – would enable me to acquire the concepts of BRAIN and VAT, and it is these that I can use today to consider the possibility of my Cartesian predicament.

5   The Epistemological Externalist Response to Scepticism

In the preceding section it was argued that we cannot have the requisite thoughts to express some sceptical scenarios. This argument was based on a metaphysical claim concerning the nature of intentional content. In this section we turn to an epistemological argument. Traditionally, to have knowledge we must be able to justify the beliefs that we hold, and such justification must be cognitively accessible to us. If this internalist approach is adopted, then scepticism looms large. Descartes has argued that from our perspective the sceptical scenario is indistinguishable from that of common sense. I cannot therefore have justified thoughts about the world since I cannot provide reasons in support of the claim that there is a world of coffee cups and paper clips rather than simply the sparse world of the demon.

However, according to the epistemological externalist, we do not have to be aware of the cognitive facts that ground knowledge. The basic reliabilist claim is that knowledge is produced by reliable cognitive mechanisms, mechanisms that tend to produce beliefs that are true rather than false. Nozick develops this approach with his tracking account: we know that *p* if we are disposed to believe that *p* when *p* is true, and not to believe that *p* when *p* is false. Importantly, though, from our perspective we may not be able to tell whether our beliefs are caused by such reliable processes, or whether they track the truth in the requisite way. Descartes is right to claim that our experience would be the same whether paper clips and cups of coffee are really out there in the world, or whether these are simply the work of a demon. And if the latter possibility is realized, then we do not have knowledge of the external world since our beliefs about it are false. According to the externalist, however, if the demon does not exist and my beliefs are reliable, then I can have knowledge of the world. The key claim is that the mere possibility of the sceptical hypotheses does not undermine my knowledge of the world. If *in fact* I am a reliable thinker, then I can have such knowledge.

The externalist accepts that we may not be aware – indeed, perhaps cannot be aware – of the reliability of our own thoughts. I do not, therefore, know that I know that my cup of coffee exists. The externalist, however, claims that such second order knowledge is not required, and that a reliabilist account of first order knowledge – that of the coffee cup and the paper clip – is sufficient to refute Cartesian scepticism. Some, though, do not find this a satisfying response to scepticism.

> So even if it is true that you can know something without knowing that you know it, the philosophical theorist of knowledge cannot simply insist on the point and expect to find acceptance of an 'externalist' account of knowledge fully satisfactory. If he could, he would be in a position of someone who says: 'I don't know whether I understand human knowledge or not. If what I believe about it is true and my

beliefs about it are produced in what my theory says is the right way, I do know how human knowledge comes to be, so in that sense I do understand. But if my beliefs are not true, or not arrived at in that way, I do not.' I wonder which it is. I wonder whether I understand human knowledge or not. That is not a satisfactory position to arrive at in one's study of human knowledge – or of anything else. (Stroud, 2000, pp. 321–2)

The externalist accepts that in the face of Cartesian scepticism he has no *reason* to think that his beliefs are reliable; however, it may just turn out that they are and, if so, such beliefs amount to knowledge. I shall leave you to consider this question: is Barry Stroud right to say that this is unsatisfactory, or should the externalist response to Cartesian scepticism be embraced? In chapter 11 we shall further investigate such externalist thinking and its place within a wider naturalistic view of epistemology.

Questions

1 In order to know that there is a book in your hand, do you need to know that you are not a brain in a vat?
2 Could the demon or the evil scientists trick us into falsely thinking that 2+2=5 or that there may be a bachelor who is married?
3 Hume claims that if we were to accept that none of our empirical beliefs were justified, then: 'All discourse, all action would immediately cease; and men [would] remain in a total lethargy, till the necessities of nature, unsatisfied, put an end to their miserable existence' (Hume, 1989, sec. 12.23). Is he right?
4 What is the difference between cognitive externalism and epistemological externalism, and can either provide a satisfying refutation of Cartesian scepticism?
5 In a seminar on Cartesian scepticism, a friend passes you a note asking whether you have your mobile phone with you. You nod to her that you have. On a contextualist account, it seems that you do not know that there's a mobile in your bag (in the context of your spoken conversation concerning Descartes's sceptical arguments) *and* that you do know that there is (in the context of your unspoken communication). You know that *p* and you do not know that *p*. Is this a coherent claim?

Further Reading

The classic presentation of Cartesian scepticism can be found in the first of Descartes's *Meditations* of 1641. Russell (1912, ch. 2) and Ayer (1976, ch. 5) are clear introductions to this topic, and more sophisticated discussion is provided by Stroud's *The Significance of Philosophical Scepticism* (1984), and Hookway's *Scepticism* (1990). The literature on contextualism is rapidly expanding with good starting points being De

Rose (1995), D. Lewis (2000) and Unger (1984). Cognitive externalism is explained in McCulloch (1995) and Rowlands (2003). For the epistemological externalist response to scepticism, you could turn again to the authors that were introduced in chapter 8, particularly Nozick (1981, ch. 3).

As discussed, Cartesian scepticism has captured the imagination of many filmmakers and writers, and various pieces have been written about the Cartesian themes in *The Matrix* (1999). See Irwin's *The Matrix and Philosophy* (2002), and http://whatisthematrix.warnerbros.com (this site includes links to papers by leading philosophers such as Colin McGinn, David Chalmers and James Prior). Other films that explore the virtual reality theme are *Dark City* (1998), *Abre los Ojos* (1997), *Vanilla Sky* (2001), *The Lawnmower Man* (1992), *Total Recall* (1990) and *13th Floor* (1999). These films are heavily influenced by science fiction writers, and similar themes can be found in Philip K. Dick's 'We Can Remember It for You Wholesale' (Dick, 1970; filmed as *Total Recall*, 1990), *The Three Stigmata of Palmer J. Eldridge* (Dick, 1965), and *Time Out of Joint* (Dick, 1959; very influential on *The Truman Show*, 1998); George H. Smith's 'In the Imagicon' (G. Smith, 1970); and Ray Bradbury's *The Martian Chronicles* (1950). An entertaining collection of short stories concerning the distinction between dreams and reality is Knight's *Perchance to Dream* (1972), and a classic 'it was all a dream' scenario is given in Pedro Calderon de la Barca's *La vida es sueño* (Life is a dream) of 1636 (Calderon de la Barca, 2002).

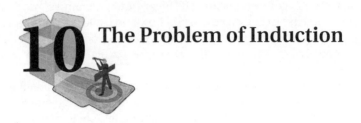

10 The Problem of Induction

1 Inductive Inference

In this chapter we turn to an important form of local scepticism. Its locale, however, is somewhat vast in that it concerns our knowledge of the unobserved (of which there is a lot). This is knowledge that we acquire through inductive inference or induction: past regularities in my experience are taken to justify beliefs about things that I have not experienced. It is important to note that such reasoning is often presented as only concerning our knowledge of the future, but this is not so. Inductive arguments concern the future, present and past. Consider the following arguments:

The Future *Premise*: Every day of my life the sun has risen.
Conclusion: The sun will rise tomorrow.

The Present *Premise*: All the snow that I have ever seen has been white.
Conclusion: All the snow that now exists is white.

The Past *Premise*: All the apples I have eaten have contained pips.
Conclusion: The apple that William Tell shot contained pips.

I do not claim that these conclusions are certain; after all, it is possible that the sun may not rise tomorrow if it prematurely turned supernova or if the Earth were knocked out of its orbit by a large meteorite. Nevertheless, I would like to claim that there is a very good chance that my inductive conclusions will turn out to be true, and that I am therefore justified in accepting them.

We shall look at two arguments which suggest that such reasoning is not valid, arguments to the conclusion that we are not justified in believing that the sun will rise tomorrow, that all snow is white, or that apples had pips in the past. We shall first turn to Hume's argument (Hume, 1978; 1999), and then move on to look at a contemporary version of the problem presented by Nelson Goodman (1953).

2 Hume's Inductive Scepticism

We assume that our limited experience of the world is a reliable guide to the behaviour of the world at other times and places. In order for such an assumption to be justified, we must take it that the world behaves in a regular way, that it will continue to do so, and that our experience helps us to pick up on the nature of this regularity. Such assumptions constitute the 'uniformity principle', and it has been suggested that this principle is a hidden premise in all inductive arguments. A more complete version of one of the arguments above would be as follows:

Premise: All the snow that I have ever seen has been white.
Premise: The Uniformity Principle:
   'instances, of which we have had no experience, must resemble those, of which we have had experience, and that the course of nature continues always uniformly the same' (Hume, 1978, p. 89).
Conclusion: All the snow that now exists is white.

With the inclusion of this premise, such reasoning is deductively **valid** (see **inference**). But is this extra premise justified? There are two ways that I could be justified in believing in the uniformity principle. It could either be an a priori truth, or it could be an empirical claim about the world, one for which we have a posteriori evidence. Hume, however, argues that it cannot be justified in either way. The uniformity principle is not an a priori truth since it is not contradictory to deny it; the world need not have been regular. If the uniformity principle does hold, this is an empirical truth, one for which our experience must provide justification. However, the only evidence we have to go on is our experience of the small slice of space and time that we inhabit. Here the uniformity principle has held, but this principle concerns *all* of space and time, and we do not have experiential evidence that its application is so broad.

We could try and argue along the following lines.

Premise: In my experience the course of nature has always continued uniformly the same.
Conclusion: The course of nature has always *and will always* continue uniformly the same.

This, however, would be using inductive inference to justify the uniformity principle: past regularities in my experience are taken to justify beliefs about the universal occurrence of such regularities. Such reasoning is question begging; if the uniformity principle is to ground induction, we need an independent argument for why we are justified in accepting it. Hume claims that this is something we do not have.

It is important to be aware of the radical nature of Hume's claim. He argues that all inductive reasoning is invalid: we have neither a priori nor empirical reasons to accept beliefs based on inductive inference. We are not justified in believing that the sun will rise tomorrow. Here's the crux: I could claim that the sun will rise tomorrow, whereas my friend may claim that it will turn into a giant fried egg. According to Hume, my belief is no more justified than that of my friend.

Of course I do not really have a friend who believes this, and Hume has an explanation for why this is so. Due to 'custom' or 'habit', we all think along inductive lines. However, such thinking is not justified; it's just a product of certain psychological dispositions that creatures like us possess: 'it is not, therefore, reason, which is the guide of life, but custom' (Hume, *Abstract*, in Hume, 1978). In his *Treatise* of 1739, Hume supports this claim by giving a rudimentary causal explanation of how we have the beliefs that we do (Hume, 1978). (With this emphasis on causal description, his account can be seen as a precursor to the modern naturalistic approach to epistemology, an approach that we shall discuss in the next chapter.) Animals also have such dispositions; they are guided by custom and they expect the regularities that they have experienced to continue. However, as Russell (1912) notes, the chicken that has been fed every morning by the farmer may tomorrow have its neck wrung instead. We are in an analogous position to the chicken: we expect the sun to rise just as the chicken expects its feed, but neither of us has any justification for our beliefs or behaviour.

A common response to this sceptical stance is that we know that the sun will rise tomorrow because we have a scientific explanation for it doing so, one describing the movement of the Earth in relation to the Sun. Here, though, we should note how deep Hume's argument cuts. We have arrived at our scientific story through repeated astronomical observations. Our scientific explanation of the sun rising is therefore inductive, and thus it too is prey to Hume's argument. According to Hume, the scientist cannot justify his belief that gravity will continue to keep the heavenly bodies in the orbits we have so far observed them as following.

3   Responses to Inductive Scepticism

Various commentators have criticized Hume for supposing that all valid reasoning must be deductive; good reasoning must provide us with conclusive reasons for holding our beliefs. In the inductive arguments above – those concerning the sun, snow and apples – the uniformity principle is added so that the conclusions of these arguments deductively follow from the premises. Two attitudes can be taken to this deductivist approach. The first type of response accepts that deduction is the only logically valid form of inference, and it is argued that empirical reasoning is deductive rather than inductive. This is the approach taken by Karl Popper (1959). The second type of response rejects deductivism and argues that inductive reasoning is itself justified.

3.1   Popper's deductive conception of science

Popper claims that scientific methodology is not inductive; it should instead be seen as following a two-stage hypothetico-deductive model. First, we put forward a hypothesis or theory to account for the observable data. Second, we test this theory by trying to find data that it does not explain. The continued observation of inductive regularities does not provide further justification for our theories; observation, rather, is concerned with uncovering cases where proposed regularities break down. We look to 'falsify' our theories. If we succeed in this, then our theories must be wrong and we must think up new ones. The essential difference between the two models is this: following the inductive approach we have an open mind as to the regularities in nature, and the ones we come to believe in are those for which we find inductive evidence. Following the hypothetico-deductive model, we come to the world with preconceptions, with a working hypothesis concerning the nature of the regularities that will be found there. Popper claims that his account has two virtues. First, it gives a better description of the practices of working scientists. Second, the inference used in falsification is deductively valid.

Hypothesis: All swans are white.
Observation: There are non-white swans in Australia (black swans were discovered there).
Conclusion: It is not the case that all swans are white.

If the premises of this argument are true, then the conclusion must follow.

The theories we propose are often those that are suggested by the inductive evidence: it was claimed that all swans are white because all observed swans had been so. This, however, is simply one way we could come up with a hypothesis. There are many others. It could be suggested that the maximum temperature in a given year is the same as the average age of the world's population. For Popper, this hypothesis is not epistemically inferior to one based on past meteorological records (although it would undoubtedly be swiftly falsified).

One problem with Popper's account is that we are no better off with respect to justification and knowledge. We have no reason to claim that our theories are true; they have simply not yet been proved false. Popper's account embraces the sceptical consequences of Hume's argument.

> [W]e must not look upon science as a 'body of knowledge', but rather as a system of hypotheses which in principle cannot be justified, but with which we work as long as they stand up to tests, and of which we are never justified in saying that we know they are 'true' or 'more or less certain' or even 'probable'. (Popper, 1959, p. 317)

We would, however, like to be able to reject the worrying conclusion that we have no justification whatsoever for believing that the sun will rise tomorrow. With this in mind, we shall move on to look at less sceptical responses to Hume's problem.

3.2 Probability

Russell (1912) accepts that induction does not provide us with beliefs about the unobserved that are certain; he claims, however, that there is a high probability that our inductive conclusions are correct. If all the emeralds we have so far examined have been green, then there is a good chance that the next one will also be green. And a conclusion that has a high probability of being correct is one that we can justifiably accept.

However, such an approach faces a problem in that we do not know whether we have examined a representative sample of the kind of thing in question. The first three coins a child spins may land heads up. Following the above reasoning, she would be justified in thinking there is a good chance that the next spin will also be a head (if she has not previously examined the coin). This, however, is not so; it is just as likely that she will not throw a head. It could be the case that our sample is also skewed and that the colours of the emeralds we have looked at so far are just a lucky run, like the child's throwing of three heads.

If I have a bag containing a thousand red sweets and one blue sweet, then it is reasonable for me to believe that I shall pick out a red one since the chances are a thousand to one in my favour. My belief may not be certain, but there is a very good chance that it will turn out to be true. This, however, is not analogous to the Humean predicament. We know the odds with respect to the red and blue sweets because we know what the whole bag contains. This is not the case with our inductive inferences concerning the unobserved. We have only experienced an infinitesimally small fraction of all there is to experience; we cannot therefore know that our sample is a representative one. Perhaps green emeralds are very unusual if we could consider their occurrence throughout all space and time. From our limited experience we cannot tell whether our sample is representative or not; we are not therefore justified in making even probabilistic inferences concerning the unobserved.

The following two responses to the problem of induction are more persuasive. They do, however, rely on two wider theories of epistemic justification, these being reliabilism and coherentism.

3.3 The reliabilist response to the problem of induction

For reliabilists, knowledge is the product of cognitive mechanisms that generally lead to the acquisition of true belief. You do not have to be able to articulate reasons to justify your beliefs, and you do not have to be aware of the kinds of cognitive processes involved in your thinking; the objective connection to truth is all that's required for knowledge. It could therefore be the case that inductive inference is a reliable method of acquiring true beliefs. If there are regularities in the world, then induction would be a good way of identifying them. If this were so, then we would have knowledge of the unobserved. Hume may show that we cannot provide reasoned argument to justify induction, but for a reliabilist this doesn't matter. All that matters is whether or not inductive reasoning is a reliable method of acquiring truths about the world. In assessing this response to Hume, it would be useful to think back to our earlier discussion of reliabilism (chapter 8) and to whether we thought it was a tenable approach to epistemology.

3.4   The coherentist response

It has been claimed that the problem of induction does not bite for those who accept a coherence theory of justification. According to the coherentist, if believing in the uniformity principle leads to a more coherent belief system, then such a belief is justified. It has been argued that this is the case. Let's say that I believe that Laura's emerald is green, that the ones in the British Museum are, and that so too is the emerald owned by my mother. A belief in the uniformity principle and the consequent belief that *all* emeralds are green cannot help but cohere with these particular beliefs. First, none of my beliefs contradict the universal claim. Second, the coherence of my belief system is increased because of the inferential relations of the uniformity principle: beliefs about the colour of particular emeralds can be inferred from my belief that all emeralds are green. According to the coherentist, then, we are justified in accepting the uniformity principle with respect to any regularities that we have found in nature. If we accept coherentism, we can reject the problem of induction. It is important to bear in mind, though, that in chapter 7 we found that there were various difficulties associated with the coherentist theory of justification. These would have to be solved if we were to accept this as a satisfactory response to the Humean predicament.

We have looked at various responses to Hume's disconcerting argument. It has been claimed that: (1) Hume is right: inductive inference cannot provide us with justified beliefs about the unobserved. Science, however, is a deductive discipline. (2) Induction may not provide conclusive justification, but there is a high probability that our inductive beliefs are correct. (3) Whether or not we can provide reasoned argument to justify induction, it is a fact that such a method of inference reliably provides us with true beliefs about regularities in nature. For externalists, this is all that is required for us to have knowledge of the unobserved. (4) Coherentists claim that the uniformity principle increases the coherence of our belief system, and inductive inference is therefore justified.

4   The New Riddle of Induction

Goodman (1953) introduces a distinct argument for inductive scepticism. We have to face up to his argument even if the Humean line is rejected. We may be justified in believing that the world is a regular place, but Goodman claims that there is an open-ended number of ways of describing any observed regularities, and we are no more justi-fied in believing one description than another. Once again, then, we do not have justification for the particular inductive beliefs that we hold.

Goodman defines a new **predicate**, 'grue'. This applies to things that are examined before 2010 and are green, and to things that are exam-ined after that date and are blue. Let's say that Graham uses such a predicate. To him, all my emeralds are grue since his predicate 'grue' applies to them, and there is nothing I can show him to make him change his mind. Even my most prized emerald – that which to me is a dazzling green – is still grue to him. Before spelling out how such a pred-icate causes a problem for induction, we should note the generality of Goodman's line. 'Grue'-like predicates are easy to formulate. Graham may see emeralds as grue, but to others they may be grellow (examined before 2010 and are green/examined after 2010 and are yellow), gred (green/red) or grurple (green/purple). Things that we have classified as square, to others may be squound (examined before 3000 and are square/examined after 3000 and are round) or squangular (square/triangular). Political parties may be socialative: examined before 1997 and are socialist/examined after 1997 and are Conservative!

These predicates are problematic because they enable different inductive conclusions to be drawn from a particular pattern of experi-ence. The colours of the emeralds I have seen can be taken to support the conclusion that the next one I see will also be green; Graham, however, expects the next one to be grue. Goodman claims that there is no reason to prefer one inference over the other, and thus the infer-ences that we actually make can be seen as arbitrary. We again arrive at Hume's conclusion: we cannot justifiably claim that all emeralds are green, or that it's reasonable to expect the next one we see to be green; it is just as likely to be grue or grellow. Incompatible hypotheses are supported by the same evidence, and there is therefore nothing that justifies our belief in one hypothesis rather than another. (Consider how predicates akin to 'grue' would undermine our inductive beliefs of section 1, those concerning the sun, snow and apples.)

It should be noted that the arguments of Hume and Goodman are distinct. This can be shown by reconsidering one of the suggested solu-tions to Hume's problem. The coherentist argues that our inductive generalizations are justified because they result in a more coherent belief system. However, this coherentist line can still fall prey to Goodman's argument. Given that Graham believes that all the emeralds he has seen have been grue, it will follow that the coherence of his belief system will be increased if he adopts the belief that *all* emeralds are grue. His beliefs about emeralds will be consistent, and the inferential relations between his beliefs about grue emeralds are exactly parallel to the inferential relations between my beliefs about green emeralds. Graham's belief system is just as coherent as mine, even though he is committed to a distinct description of reality. So, even if we accept the coherentist response to Hume, the possibility of such alternative coherent belief systems will undermine the justification we take our particular set of inductive beliefs to possess.

Goodman's 'New Riddle' often strikes the reader as bizarre and frivolous. Hume's argument is given credence by the fact that we sometimes discover cases that lead us to reject what we once thought were universal regularities. All swans were considered to be white until black ones were discovered in Australia. We can therefore entertain the possibility of any regularity not continuing to hold. (We must be clear, though, that Hume is not just claiming that we may be mistaken about some of the particular regularities we take there to be in nature; his claim is that we are not justified in taking there to be any regularities at all.) It is harder to engage with Goodman's line since, as it is often put, '"grue" is just made up'. In the following sections this initial response to Goodman's argument will be sharpened up, and we shall try and clarify what it is about his predicates that we find objectionable.

5   Responses to the New Riddle of Induction

5.1   Simplicity

One response that has been made to Goodman's argument is that 'green' is a simpler predicate than 'grue'; grue is more complex because it is defined in terms of the simpler qualities of green and blue. And, given a choice, it is the simpler predicate that we should use in inductive reasoning. This is a strategy that guides science. Take a look at the diagram of experimental data and consider what you would predict the next value of Y to be.

X	1	2	4	6	10
Y	2	4	8	12	?

The answer may seem obvious – the relation between the X and Y values is clear: the Y value is always twice the X value, or, Y=2X. We would therefore predict that the next Y value will be 20. However, there are other relations that hold between the X and Y values. This is another: $Y = 2X + [(X-1)(X-2)(X-4)(X-6)]$. Try it; it does work. This equation, though, leads to a different prediction. Those who see the data as suggesting this relation would expect Y to be 1,748. We have an analogous situation to that suggested by Goodman in that there are various incompatible ways of describing the regularities in a set of data. Here, though, we have a plausible rationale for only accepting one of those descriptions, a rationale that scientists use when choosing which hypothesis to put forward. If this were the only evidence to go on, then a scientist would always predict the next value to be 20 rather than 1,748, and this is because 20 is the value given by the simpler hypothesis. It is also clear that such a methodology is not restricted to scientific investigations. If you were told that one drink costs £2 and that four drinks cost £8, you would take £20 to the bar for a round of ten drinks (and not £1,748).

The first question to be asked about such a response to Goodman is whether this methodology is justified. We are assuming that simple theories are more likely to be true, and it is not clear why this should be the case. Argument is required to back up such a claim. Second, even if we accept that simplicity is a guide to truth, it can be denied that 'green' and 'blue' are simpler predicates than 'grue'. Goodman argues that simplicity is relative to the system of predicates that one happens to use. Graham also uses some other predicates that are strange to us, one of which is 'bleen'. 'Bleen' applies to things that are examined before the year 2010 and are blue, and to things that are examined after that date and are green. To him the sky is now bleen, and Birmingham City Football Club should be called the Bleens and not the Blues. On discovering this oddity in Graham's language, we ask him why he uses such unnecessarily complex predicates and why he refuses to use our simpler ones of green and blue. He looks perplexed: 'Simpler – what do you mean? Your "green" is bizarrely complex. It seems to me that your word "green" applies to things that are grue before 2010 and to things that are bleen thereafter. Why not just stick with my simpler "grue" and "bleen"?' To us, 'grue' is more complex because to apply it we require an understanding of both 'green' and 'blue'. For Graham, however, green is the property possessed by grue things before 2010 and by bleen things after that date. To him, 'green' and 'blue' are the more complex predicates, and so Goodman's riddle cannot be solved by appealing to the notion of simplicity.

5.2   Grue is not a colour

Another suggestion is that 'grue' is not a bona fide predicate because it makes an implicit reference to time. We can see why this is unacceptable by thinking further about Graham and some of his idiosyncrasies. I have two paintings of the Centre Court at Wimbledon: the subject of one of them is John McEnroe winning the Men's Singles tennis title in 1981; the other is a futuristic scene in which an oval-headed alien is making a winning volley in the 2050 Extra-Terrestrial Open. Imagine that I cover up the figures of John McEnroe and the alien so that only the grass court can be seen. To us, of course, this is green in both pictures. Graham, however, cannot describe its colour. If the players were uncovered he would say that McEnroe's court was grue and that the alien's was bleen. (Look back at the definitions of 'grue' and 'bleen' to see if you understand why he would say this.) However, if Graham does not know the date of the picture, then he cannot use his colour predicates since they have an essential temporal component. These two paintings could also be reproduced as line drawings in a colouring book. Graham can only colour the grass grue if clues to the date of the picture are also reproduced. One way of explaining Graham's inabilities is to say that 'grue' does not refer to a colour because it is not usable in the way that colour predicates are. Colours are visually conspicuous: we can identify them simply by looking at them. This is not so with grue. To identify this property we must also know the date. Grue, then, is not a colour.

It is not clear, though, how much comfort we can take from such a response. Goodman could accept that 'grue' is not a *colour* predicate. However, he would then claim that Graham does not see emeralds as having a colour in common, but rather, another type of property, the recognition of which requires that he knows the date. This still leads to a sceptical conclusion since the same evidence supports both my expectation that all emeralds are coloured green, and Graham's expectation that they all have the property grue. It seems that Goodman's line is rather resilient and it is not clear how it can be rejected.

Questions

1 Could you *live* inductive scepticism? What would life be like for a person who did not accept inductive inference?
2 Am I justified in believing that all emeralds are green?
3 Popper's hypothetico-deductive model is not just applicable to science. Consider how both the inductive and hypothetico-deductive models provide different explanations of how we acquire certain non-scientific beliefs. Take as an example the belief that all cyclists in the Tour de France are thin. Which model is the most persuasive?
4 Is the 'New Riddle of Induction' new? Is it distinct from Hume's inductive scepticism?
5 Do we have any reason to prefer the predicates 'green' and 'blue' to 'grue' and 'bleen'?

Further Reading

The classic presentation of inductive scepticism can be found in Hume's *Treatise* (1978, book I, pt III, secs 2–8), the *Abstract* which is appended to this work, and his *Enquiry* (1999, sec. 4). Discussion of the various responses to Hume can be found in *The Justification of Induction* edited by Swinburne (1974), and Skyrms's *Choice and Chance* (1966). Papineau (1987) advocates the reliabilist response. For a rather different interpretation of Hume, one that does not take him as an out and out sceptic, see Stroud's *Hume* (1977, ch. 3), and Noonan's *Hume on Knowledge* (1999, ch. 3). The grue problem first appeared in Goodman's *Fact, Fiction and Forecast* (1953), and a useful collection of articles on grue is *Grue: The New Riddle of Induction* edited by Stalker (1994). This includes an annotated bibliography that describes over 300 significant research papers devoted to Goodman's argument.

 # Naturalized Epistemology

A naturalized approach to epistemology is one that is driven by the findings of empirical science. In this chapter we shall look at various versions of naturalized epistemology, the first being that of Quine. An important aspect of this account is his distinct response to sceptical worries; consideration of this will lead us into a wider discussion of the relationship between science and philosophy.

1   Quine and Epistemology

1.1   The failure of traditional epistemology

Traditional epistemology has focused on the problem of justification. Descartes and Hume consider whether our beliefs about the external world and about the unobserved are justified. They offer certain sceptical arguments, and in the previous two chapters we have looked at various responses to their scepticism, these responses all working within epistemologies that focus on the notion of justification. In this chapter, however, it will be suggested that this whole framework should be abandoned. Quine claims that 'traditional philosophical problems are not meant to be solved' (1985, p. 465). The project of Descartes and Hume has failed and cannot be resuscitated; traditional philosophy should be abandoned and we should undertake an altogether different approach to questions concerning our knowledge of the world. 'The stimulation of his sensory receptors is all the evidence anybody has to go on, ultimately, in arriving at his picture of the world. Why not just see how this construction really proceeds? Why not settle for psychology?' (Quine, 1969a, pp. 75–6).

Quine claims that we should aim to give a scientific account of how we come to have the beliefs that we do. We should not consider whether these beliefs are *justified*. All that is required is a description of the causal nature of our belief-forming mechanisms. This causal story will be informed by the work of cognitive scientists, neurophysiologists, and those working in evolutionary biology. Naturalized epistemologists should be interested in how biological creatures like us come to represent the state of their environment, and what cognitive mechanisms are involved in processes such as belief formation, perception, and memory.

Such a naturalized approach bears certain similarities to Hume's positive account of epistemology. Both Quine and Hume acknowledge that sceptical doubts cannot be refuted by philosophical argument: 'The Humean predicament is the human predicament' (Quine, 1969a, p. 72). And, in the face of such scepticism, Hume also provides a genetic account of how we are caused to have the beliefs that we do. This account involves a rudimentary associative psychology which describes the regular flux of ideas or images in our mind. For both, then, the task of the epistemologist is empirical. We should note the subtitle of Hume's *Treatise* of 1739: 'An Attempt to Introduce the Experimental Method of Reasoning into Moral Subjects'. (Given Quine's basically Humean standpoint, his professed attitude to lecture giving is somewhat uncharitable: 'Determining what Hume thought and imparting it to students was less appealing than determining the truth and imparting that' (Quine, 1985, p. 194).)

1.2   Quine and scepticism

As part of Quine's rejection of traditional epistemology, he claims that we should not be concerned with scepticism. We shall look at two lines of argument to this conclusion. First, we shall consider Quine's claims concerning the scientific origin of sceptical doubt; second, we shall turn to his suggestion that scepticism is ruled out by certain evolutionary considerations.

Quine claims that it is only through a broadly scientific engagement with the world that we can come to realize that we are sometimes prey to illusions and perceptual error, notions that are central to Descartes's sceptical stance. It is empirical observation of the half-submerged stick that introduces us to the idea of non-veridical perception: in reality it is straight even though it appears bent. Cartesian scepticism, then, is seen to develop from empirical investigation: once we acquire the notion of perceptual error, then the possibility of its widespread occurrence is raised. '[S]cepticism is an offshoot of natural science . . . sceptical doubts are scientific doubts' (Quine, 1975, pp. 67–8).

Quine's further claim is that since sceptical doubts arise from within science, then it must be scientific resources that are used to ease them. Cartesian scepticism is an overreaction to the scientific discovery that we can misperceive the world. A developed scientific account of our perception and belief-forming mechanisms will reveal that bent stick cases are not the norm, and that usually we do come to represent the world correctly. Quine provides a diagnosis of why we have such sceptical doubts, and a scientific cure for them.

> A far cry, this, from the old epistemology. Yet it is not a gratuitous change of subject matter, but an enlightened persistence rather in the original epistemological problem. It is enlightened in recognizing that the skeptical challenge springs from science itself, and that in coping with it we are free to use scientific knowledge. The old epistemologist failed to recognize the strength of his position. (Quine, 1974, p. 3)

Quine finds a metaphor of Neurath's instructive.

> I see philosophy not as an a priori groundwork for science, but as continuous with science. I see philosophy and science as in the same boat – a boat which, to revert to Neurath's figure as I so often do, we can rebuild only at sea while staying afloat in it. There is no external vantage point, no first philosophy. (Quine, 1969b, pp. 126–7)

If we are interested in improving our sailing, we do not question the nature of buoyancy. Instead, we look to refine our sailing techniques by finding more and more sophisticated ways of using the equipment on board the boat. Analogously, when empirically investigating the world, we should not question whether the practice of science is justified; instead, we should simply continue to construct more and more sophisticated scientific theories of how the world and our cognition proceed.

However, even if Quine is correct that sceptical thoughts have an empirical origin, it does not follow that science can therefore ease such doubts. George's thoughts of personal inadequacy may have their origin in his poor performance on the sports field; such thoughts, though, may not be eased by more sporting endeavour. It could be that an altogether distinct discipline is required; perhaps psychoanalysis. So too with scepticism: perhaps an altogether distinct discipline is required to ease the doubts that have arisen from within science, and the traditional suggestion here is that this discipline is philosophy. It is just not clear whether a scientific story alone can provide any comfort to those who feel the epistemological problems highlighted by Descartes and Hume.

Quine has a second argument against scepticism, one that is grounded in evolutionary theory. He claims that creatures with true beliefs have a greater chance of survival. Their offspring will therefore inherit the mechanisms that lead to the acquisition of such beliefs. If this is so, then knowledge can be seen as a product of evolution or natural selection; knowledge here is conceived of in externalist terms, as reliably formed true belief. There are, however, two problems with this argument. First, there is the assumption that the scientific theory of evolution is true. It is not clear, though, how this can be straightforwardly accepted in the face of scepticism. The objection is not that evolutionary theory in particular is scientifically controversial, but that given the Cartesian line, no scientific discoveries can be accepted unless we find a way to refute the sceptical arguments. Second, it is not obvious that only true beliefs have survival value. In certain circumstances it could be evolutionarily advantageous to have false beliefs. It is perhaps best to believe that all fungi are poisonous. Communities who think in this way would avoid nasty deaths due to misidentification. It would also seem that so long as we have certain true beliefs about things crucial to our survival – such as the location of food and water – then many of our other beliefs could be false. Survival-wise, if we get enough to eat and drink, then it doesn't matter what we believe about astrology, UFOs or postmodernism.

There are therefore various objections to Quine's claim that science can ease our sceptical concerns. In order, though, to fully appreciate Quine's position we must turn to a further argument of his, one in which he claims to show that there is no distinction between a priori and a posteriori reasoning; if this is so, then there is not a sharp distinction between philosophy and science.

1.3   Quine and the a priori

Traditionally philosophy is seen as an a priori discipline, and epistemology has the role of what has been called 'First Philosophy'. Before we acquire any knowledge of the world, we require a theory of knowledge with which to validate it. This is certainly the Cartesian picture: Descartes provides an a priori proof of the existence of God, a God who ensures that our 'clear and distinct' ideas accurately represent reality. Quine, however, argues that there are no a priori truths; there are only those that are empirical. Traditional philosophy is therefore robbed of its medium and the only kinds of investigations that can be pursued are those that are broadly scientific. If this is correct, then Quine's strategy with respect to scepticism would be vindicated. Philosophy cannot engender a priori doubts about the validity of empirical observation since there is not a legitimate a priori method of inquiry. Quine's key argument for this claim focuses on the holistic nature of our belief systems, and it is an argument that can be introduced by returning to the Manx cat example of chapter 7, section 3.2. On visiting the Isle of Man we discover cats that provide evidence against our belief that all cats have tails. We noted, though, that it may not be obligatory to drop the latter belief; it could be maintained if compensatory changes are made elsewhere in our belief system (perhaps Manx cats are not cats). The claim is that we always have alternatives when faced with empirical evidence that clashes with one of our beliefs. Quine's argument also depends on this claim that there are alternatives open to us; he, though, does not focus on how certain beliefs may always be maintained, but on the claim that there are no beliefs that are immune to revision. In order to help us appreciate his claim, we shall need to look at some examples of the kind of belief change that Quine has in mind.

'All bachelors are unmarried' is a claim that is taken to be a priori. Let us, though, consider a possible future state of affairs. It just so happens that for hundreds of years it is all and only the blond men in a certain community who have been bachelors: in living memory no blond men have been married, and no non-blond men have been single. Thus everyone in this community believes that 'all bachelors are unmarried', and that 'all bachelors are blond'. One day a rare male tourist arrives who has blond hair and wears a wedding ring. The Quinean claim is that this community is now faced with a choice. We may perhaps think that the only option is that of maintaining the first belief and dropping the second: it is the empirical generalization concerning the colour of bachelors' hair that has turned out to be unfounded; the a priori claim cannot be threatened by such empirical evidence. There is, however, another option: the second belief could be maintained and the first could be dropped. This tourist is a bachelor since he is similar in many ways to the bachelors of the community: he is a man with blond hair, one who is flirtatious with the local women, and one who spends a disproportionate amount of his income on hi-tech gadgets. We should therefore keep hold of the belief that 'all bachelors are blond'. This bachelor, though, does not have all the properties usually possessed by bachelors; this one is not single. We should therefore drop the belief that 'all bachelors are unmarried'. Quine's claim is that even seemingly a priori beliefs could come to be abandoned if there are radical enough changes in our experience.

Before the arrival of the tourist, the terms 'bachelor', 'blond' and 'unmarried' applied to the same set of men. We can illustrate this with figure 11.1. The tourist upsets this harmony and the intuitive response is that we should now picture the community as in figure 11.2. Quine, however, argues that we are not obliged to see it in this way. The alternative in figure 11.3 could also be adopted. This would entail dropping the a priori claim that all bachelors are unmarried men.

Here is another example taken from Everitt and Fisher (1995). The following claim seems to be a priori: 'If a woman gives birth to a child, then she is that child's mother.' To know that this is true we do not have to look for empirical evidence in maternity wards; we just have to think about the meanings of the terms 'mother' and 'child'. But what should we say if a child is the result of in vitro fertilization, with the ovum being supplied by another woman? The Quinean suggestion is that we have a choice. We could maintain the above claim, or we could deny that it is always true. It could be allowed that in certain cases a child's mother is not the woman who gives birth to that child. Quine even takes such a line with respect to mathematics and logic (disciplines that are thought to be a priori in their approach). '[N]o statement is immune to revision. Revision even of the logical law of the excluded middle has been proposed as a means of simplifying quantum mechanics [a branch of contemporary physics] . . .' (Quine, 1953b, p. 43). The law of the excluded middle asserts that every statement is either true or false. Quine's claim is that recent advances in physics could lead to this law being rejected even though it is traditionally seen as an a priori truth.

Quine claims that the abandonment of so called a priori truths is no different in kind from the revisions of our conceptual scheme that have accompanied the development of science. We no longer believe that the Earth is flat, and we do not need to be forever tied to the belief that all bachelors are unmarried. Continuing the quote above: 'and what difference is there in principle between such a shift [that involving dropping the law of the excluded middle] and the shift whereby Kepler

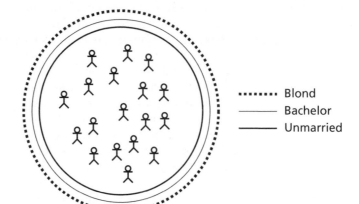

Figure 11.1

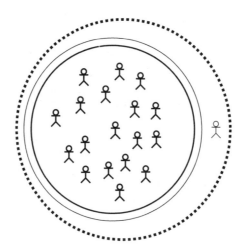

Figure 11.2

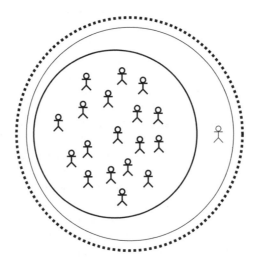

Figure 11.3

superseded Ptolemy, or Einstein Newton, or Darwin Aristotle?' (Quine, 1953b, p. 43). No statements are totally insulated from our ongoing experience of the world; none are sacrosanct; all are revisable.

Without a priori truths there cannot be a First Philosophy, that is, an a priori theory of knowledge to ground our empirical investigations. However, Quine accepts that there is a legitimate discipline of 'philosophy'; it should be thought of, though, as a discipline that is continuous with science, one that considers general empirical questions concerning our belief-forming mechanisms. Philosophers, for example, should consider whether our perceptual mechanisms are generally reliable and whether we successfully come to acquire true beliefs by listening to the utterances of others. These, however, are questions that can only be answered by pursuing empirical investigation. Philosophy does not occupy a perspective outside science from which to assess the latter's methods. Thus we can now see Quine's grounds for the claim that was highlighted above.

> I see philosophy not as an a priori groundwork for science, but as continuous with science. I see philosophy and science as in the same boat – a boat which, to revert to Neurath's figure as I so often do, we can rebuild only at sea while staying afloat in it. There is no external vantage point, no first philosophy. (Quine, 1969b, pp. 126–7)

Quine's claim is that without a priori reasoning, traditional epistemology is deprived of its medium.

It could be claimed, though, that certain epistemologies do not make use of the a priori, or of unrevisable beliefs, in the way exemplified by Descartes. Both coherentists and modest foundationalists can embrace the claim that no empirical beliefs are immune to revision – including such claims as 'This looks red to me' – and they reject the notion that our belief systems have infallible foundations that we can know a priori. Quine's target seems to be the traditional foundationalist accounts of both the rationalist and the empiricist, and not these more modest, contemporary approaches.

2   The Normative Nature of Epistemology

We have considered various objections to the arguments that Quine puts forward in favour of his naturalized approach to epistemology. In this section we shall focus on a crucial feature of Quine's developed position, that is, the claim that the notion of justification should be abandoned. In order to appreciate a potential problem with this claim, we must first turn to the issue of normativity. Epistemology is not simply concerned with what we happen to believe; its main interest is in what we should believe, or what we are entitled to believe. The latter are called 'normative' questions, and Quine seems to acknowledge that these are the kind of questions that epistemologists should attempt to answer.

> Naturalism not only consigns the question of reality to science; it does
> the same for normative epistemology. The normative is naturalized,
> not dropped . . . It is natural science that tells us that our information
> about the world comes only through impacts on our sensory surfaces.
> And it is conspicuously normative, counselling us to mistrust sooth-
> sayers and telepathists. (Quine in Barrett and Gibson, 1990, p. 229)

Through empirical investigation of the world we come to discover that
only some of our methods of acquiring beliefs are reliable. We rightly
conclude that experimental science should be pursued and that sooth-
saying should not.

Within science itself we also have to choose between competing
hypotheses, and Quine and Ullian (1970) suggest various normative
constraints on such theory choice. The theory that we should adopt is
the one that is most conservative (the one that least disrupts our standing belief system); most general (the one that explains the widest range
of phenomena); and the one that is the simplest. Quine therefore seems
to agree that epistemology is a normative discipline, and he also
appears to be concerned with the key issue of whether our beliefs about
the world are justified.

> The relation between the meagre input and the torrential output is a
> relation that we are prompted to study for somewhat the same reasons
> that have always prompted epistemology; namely, in order to see how
> evidence relates to theory, and in what ways one's theory of nature
> transcends any available evidence. (Quine, 1985, p. 465)

This quote suggests that Quine is facing up to Cartesian scepticism. He
is interested in whether the 'torrential output' of our beliefs about the
world can be legitimately derived from the 'meagre input' of our
sensory experience. He encourages 'an enlightened persistence in the
original epistemological problem' (1974, p. 3).

It is not clear, though, whether this is so. Quine's talk of 'normativity'
is somewhat misleading. He claims that we should undertake a descrip-
tive, scientific investigation of cognition, and not one that is concerned
with the issue of justification. He is interested in the causal ancestry of
our beliefs; epistemology, however, is concerned with whether we are
entitled to hold the beliefs that we do. Quine claims to be considering
how 'evidence relates to theory'; such a claim, though, is inconsistent
with his overall view of epistemology. Having 'evidence' for a theory
implies that we have *reason to believe* that it is true, or that the theory is
justified given the evidence in question. Quine, however, has rejected
such notions. He is only concerned with the causal relationship
between two types of physical event: the stimulation of our sensory
apparatus and the particular cognitive states of our brain that, for
Quine, constitute the possession of knowledge. As we have seen: 'The
stimulation of his sensory receptors is all the evidence anybody has to
go on, ultimately, in arriving at his picture of the world. Why not just see
how this construction really proceeds? Why not settle for psychology?'

(Quine, 1969a, pp. 75–6). It could therefore be claimed that Quine is not talking about *epistemic* issues since he is not interested in the relation between knowledge and justification. Quine's conception of psychology is not that of a science which is continuous with epistemology, but rather that of a science that does not engage with certain crucial epistemological issues. In the last section of this chapter we shall further investigate the relation between science and philosophy, and we shall note that some naturalists propose a more measured approach to the incorporation of scientific method into epistemology.

3   Less Radical forms of Naturalism

Certain naturalists do not eschew the philosophical notion of justification; instead, they attempt to give a scientific account of the nature of this epistemic property. Their naturalism does not involve a rejection of traditional philosophy, but rather the claim that scientific practice should feed into the traditional philosophical debate.

> [A] mix of philosophy and psychology is needed to produce acceptable principles of justifiedness. (Goldman, 1994, p. 314)

> [T]he results from the sciences of cognition may be relevant to, and may be legitimately used in the resolution of traditional epistemological problems. (Haack, 1993, p. 118)

Richard Feldman (1999) refers to such an approach as 'methodological naturalism', and Jaegwon Kim's (1988) term is 'epistemological naturalism'. We have already come across such epistemologies in chapter 8; there, however, we referred to them as 'externalist' rather than 'naturalist'. Some externalists explain justification in terms of the causal relations that there are between thinkers and the world. Reliabilists claim that justified beliefs are those that are acquired using a method that tends to produce true beliefs. Justification is described in terms of causation and probability. Such approaches are reductive: justification is reduced to, or explained wholly in terms of, properties that are scientifically respectable. Externalists are therefore naturalistic in their approach. Such accounts may pose their own problems, but they remain within the domain of traditional epistemology.

There is, however, a distinct kind of externalism. Some externalists do not consider the question of whether our beliefs are justified. For David Armstrong: 'What makes . . . a belief a case of knowledge is that there must be a *lawlike connection* between the state of affairs Bap [*a* believes that *p*] and the state of affairs that makes "p" true' (Armstrong, 1973, p. 75). Armstrong calls his account a 'Thermometer Model of Knowledge' since we acquire knowledge of the world just as a thermometer represents the temperature. In both systems there is simply a **lawlike** relation between a property of the world and a property of a representational device (the level of mercury in a thermometer, and the state of certain internal cognitive mechanisms of a thinker). There is no mention here of justification. Such externalists can be called **eliminativists**: they eliminate the notion of justification from their epistemology rather than explain it in other terms. However, such externalists do not have to accept Quine's claim that 'traditional philosophical problems are not meant to be solved'. They can attempt to give philosophical solutions to the problems posed by Gettier, the regress of justification, and scepticism. We can see this by looking at how Nozick engages with these issues in chapter 8, section 3.2, and chapter 9, section 5. Nozick is an eliminativist: knowledge only requires true beliefs with the right kind of tracking relations with the world; *justification* is not necessary. (It should be noted that this distinction between the eliminativist and the reductionist was largely ignored in chapter 8. The tracking account of Nozick was presented as a form of reliabilism, with reliabilism introduced as an approach to justification. Now, though, we can see that this is not quite correct. Nozick eliminates justification from his account of knowledge; he does not explain it in other terms.)

In this chapter we have looked at two broad ways in which science has influenced epistemology. Quine claims that traditional epistemology is redundant. In contrast, certain externalists accept that traditional epistemology poses the right questions; these are questions, though, that must be answered using the resources of science.

Questions

1 'Epistemology is best looked upon . . . as an enterprise within natural science' (Quine, 1975, p. 68). Is it?
2 Consider how Quine might deny the a priori status of the following truths: $7+5=12$; vixens are female foxes; and nothing is red all over and green all over.
3 What do we mean when we say that epistemology is a 'normative' discipline?
4 Explain the distinction between traditional epistemology, naturalized epistemology, and methodological naturalism.

Further Reading

Quine's (1969a) 'Epistemology Naturalized?' sets the agenda for the naturalistic approach, and his arguments against the a priori are given in 'Two Dogmas of Empiricism' (1953b). A clear textbook chapter on Quine's rather difficult arguments can be found in Everitt and Fisher (1995). For criticism of Quine's approach you should turn to Kim (1988), the introduction to Kornblith (1994), and Stroud (1984, ch. 6). For the eliminative form of externalism, see Armstrong (1973), Dretske (1981) and Nozick (1981, ch. 3); for the reductionist, see Kim (1988). Goldman is an interesting case. In his early causal account of knowledge in 1967 (Goldman, 2000a), he took the eliminativist line; more recently, however, he has accepted reductionism, with justified beliefs being those that are produced by reliable cognitive mechanisms (1979; 1986). A good survey of the different aspects of the naturalistic approach is given by Maffie (1990).

PART V

AREAS OF KNOWLEDGE

 **Memory**

In part V of the book we shall focus on certain important areas of knowledge. In doing so, we shall consider how the epistemological notions
introduced in parts I–IV relate to specific beliefs that we have about the
world and each other. Thus, the importance of the various sources of
knowledge will be reassessed, and issues concerning justification and
scepticism will be further investigated. We shall first look at knowledge
that involves the operation of memory. Our knowledge of the past will
therefore be considered, but, as we shall see, memory plays a wider
epistemic role.

1 Memory, Belief and Knowledge

We must first consider what we mean by 'memory', and in order to do
this it will be useful to draw certain distinctions. One such distinction is
between remembering how and remembering that. We all remember
how to do certain things: how to ride a bike, make an omelette, or speak
English. 'Memory' in this sense concerns the retention of skills and the
ability to perform certain tasks. Here, though, we shall be primarily
interested in remembering that, or what is called factual memory.
I remember that the poll tax riots were in 1990, the same year that
Mr Frisk won the Grand National, and I remember that Margaret
Thatcher used to be Prime Minister. Certain factual memories concern
your own life and your own mental states. I can remember that my fifth
birthday party was fun, and that I was depressed last week. Such
memories can be called personal memories. There is, however, a
distinct type of memory that I can have of the events in my life. I can
remember not only that they happened, but also what it was like to
experience them; I can remember them 'from the inside'. This kind of
memory is called 'episodic memory' (or what Norman Malcolm calls
'perceptual memory'). I remember that Puccini composed *Madame
Butterfly* (this is factual memory); that I went to a performance of this
opera last year (this is personal memory); and I also remember what
that particular performance of the 'Tu, tu, piccolo Iddio' aria sounded
like (this is episodic memory).

It is important to note that we do not just remember things about the
past. I remember that pi is approximately 3.14; this is a timeless truth –
it has always been true and it will continue to be so. I can also remember things about the present: I can remember that it's Monday. And I

can even remember things about the future: I have just remembered that I am meeting Martin tomorrow. These memories do not refer to the past, but in such cases I am recalling beliefs that were originally acquired in the past. Memory, then, is not a source of knowledge; it is, rather, a faculty that enables us to recall knowledge that we have previously acquired via perception, testimony or a priori reasoning. Remembering 'is akin not to learning lessons, but to reciting them' (Ryle, 1963, p. 261).

Sometimes, however, memory can be involved in recalling things that we did not previously know. In your 'mind's eye', wander around a house or flat where you used to live and count the number of windows you find there. I have just done that and I now believe that there were fourteen windows in my childhood home (and let's assume that there were). This is something that I have never thought about before, and in such a case memory would seem to be a source of new knowledge. Memory, however, is not a *basic* source of knowledge. A basic source of knowledge is one that does not rely on any other source of belief. For the foundationalist, perception is such a source: perceptual knowledge does not depend on other beliefs that we have acquired via testimony or through a priori reasoning. Perceptual beliefs are justified in virtue of our *perceptual* experience. Reid claims that testimony is also a basic source of knowledge. The transmission of testimonial knowledge may require that our perceptual apparatus is working properly – we must hear what our informants are saying – but, for Reid, such transmission does not rely on the possession of any particular perceptual beliefs (see chapter 5, section 4). The claim here is that memory is not such a basic source of knowledge. In the case above, my coming to know that there are fourteen windows in my childhood home relies on the possession of certain beliefs concerning the layout of that house, beliefs that are derived from perception. To be able to recall my old house in the way that I have just done, I must believe, for example, that my bedroom was a corner room and that it had two windows.

It has previously been noted that 'knowing that' and 'perceiving that' are factive, that is, we can only know that it's Monday if it is indeed Monday; and we can only see that it's raining if it is actually raining. This is also plausibly the case with remembering that. If I remember that I have skated in Central Park, then I must have skated in Central Park. Sometimes, though, the beliefs that we recall are mistaken, and so we must be careful how such cases are described. It should not be said that I have false memories (just as it should not be said that I have false knowledge); it is, rather, that I have certain beliefs that only seem to be memories; in fact they are not. I only seem to remember that the first CD I bought was by the Beatles; it was in fact by the Rolling Stones. I do not therefore have a memory of this purchase.

Intuitions, though, can differ on whether 'remember' is always used factively. One type of case where it seems plausible to speak of false memories is when you are only mistaken about the details of a certain episode – an episode, however, that did occur in generally the way that you remember. To some it is acceptable to say that I remember Sally being at Lucy's graduation even if she was not there, but only if Lucy really did graduate and my memory of that event is mostly correct. What are your intuitions here: should the notion of 'remembering that' always be seen as factive, or is it sometimes acceptable to say that you have false memories?

2 Memory Images

In the previous section we were primarily concerned with factual memory; we shall now turn to episodic memory. Sometimes when we remember the past we seem to relive certain events – experience them again. Here is the film director, Ingmar Bergman, describing this aspect of memory.

> I'm deeply fixated on my childhood. Some impressions are extremely vivid, light, smell and all. There are moments when I can wander through my childhood's landscape, through rooms long ago, remember how they were furnished, where the pictures hung on the walls, the way the light fell. It's like a film – little scraps of film, which I set running and which I can reconstruct to the last detail[.] (Bergman, 1973, p. 84)

It is tempting here to embrace an indirect realist account of memory. We looked at such an approach with respect to perception: the indirect realist claims that we perceive the world via intermediaries or sense data. Similarly, then, in remembering the past we are aware of a mental intermediary or memory image, an image that allows us to see again how things used to be. In remembering my past I must be aware of a mental intermediary since I cannot now be directly aware of my fifth birthday party, an event that is long gone. Such a theory is certainly plausible with respect to episodic memory, and it has also been claimed that such intermediaries are necessary for factual memory. To remember a fact about the past – your own or otherwise – you must bring a certain mental image to mind.

There are, however, various problems with the claim that memory images play such an epistemic role. First, I can remember facts about the past without having any associated images. I remember that my primary school teacher had ginger hair even though I cannot now picture what she looked like; and I remember that my first taste of beer was unpleasant even though I cannot now recall the phenomenological quality of what it tasted like. The claim is not that we never have such images – most of us do – it is just that these are not necessary for knowledge. Stephen, a colleague of mine, is an extreme case: he never has such images. He can tell you lots about his past – that his first bike was a Raleigh Chopper and that its brakes squeaked – but he is not able to visualize this bike or to recall what it was like to hear such sounds.

Second, there are times when we believe that our memory images are not an accurate portrayal of the past. I can now picture my friend's wedding last year. I can see him walking down the aisle, clean-shaven in his new suit . . . but hold on, that's not right, he had a beard last year – my memory image is not correct; it does not correspond to my memory of that event. Our sensitivity to such mistakes suggests that memory itself is independent of our ability to have such mental images.

An alternative theory is that memories are stored in the form of intentional content. In the wedding case, I can compare such content with my memory image of that event. I remember that *the groom had a beard* and that *he had a new suit*. Here, then, we have an analogous theory to the intentionalist account of perception. Mental states represent the world in virtue of intentional content rather than in virtue of inner mental objects such as sense data or memory images. Sometimes, though, we do have such images, but they do not function in the way that the indirect realist claims. They are merely visual accompaniments to memory; they are not necessary features of its operation. In expressing our memories, we do not describe the appearance of an inner gallery of images. It is, rather, that we can only bring such images to mind because we can access the corresponding intentional content. Mental images do sometimes illustrate the independently stored information we have concerning the past; such illustration may be very vivid, and it may at times aid our recollection, but the storage medium itself is not imagistic in nature.

Here, though, a familiar worry arises. Some memories are very detailed: I do not just remember that *Justine wore a red dress to the party*; I can recall the exact colour of her dress, and the phenomenology of such a memory experience does not seem to be capturable in conceptual terms. 'Red' or 'dark crimson' does not fully describe what I can recall; my colour words are not fine-grained enough to represent the detail and shading of the fabric. This was a problem for the intentionalist with respect to perception (see chapter 6, section 3). However, in order to avoid this problem some intentionalists invoke the notion of non-conceptual content, and an analogous strategy could be taken with respect to memory, with the details of certain memories stored in non-conceptual form.

In this section I have argued against an indirect realist account of memory. Memories are not constituted by our awareness of mental images. If indirect realism is untenable, then a direct realist picture is suggested, but this can seem problematic: how can we have direct contact with the past? This would seem to require some kind of extraordinary cognitive or perceptual powers. However, there are only problems here if we remain wedded to the picture in which memory is constituted by a certain kind of experience. In rejecting indirect realism we accept that an awareness of a mental image is not essential to memory, but in retreating from this picture we look for an alternative item that can be experienced, one that is in the past. It is such experiential contact with the past that appears mysterious. The solution here is to jettison this aspect of the indirect realist account as well. Memory is not constituted by a certain type of experience; it involves, rather, the storage of conceptual (and perhaps non-conceptual) information, and the ability to access or recall this information. Such recall is sometimes accompanied by certain experiences, but it is not constituted by them.

3   The Causal Theory of Memory

We saw earlier that my memory of Lucy's graduation may not be entirely correct: Sally may not have been there. (Or – depending on your intuitions – it may be better to say that I only seem to remember Sally being there, rather than that my memory is false.) Our imagination, then, can sometimes embellish our memory. In this section we shall look at how the products of memory can be distinguished from those of the imagination.

Hume suggests that the difference between them is clear.

> 'Tis evident at first sight, that the ideas of the memory are much more lively and strong than those of the imagination, and that the former faculty paints its objects in more distinct colours, than any which are employ'd by the latter. When we remember any past event, the idea of it flows in upon the mind in a forcible manner; whereas in the imagination the perception is faint and languid, and cannot without difficulty be preserv'd by the mind steddy and uniform for any considerable time . . . There is another difference betwixt these two kinds of ideas . . . the imagination is not restrained to the same order and form with the original impressions; while the memory is in a manner tied down in that respect, without any power of variation. (1978, p. 9)

In many cases Hume's criteria successfully pick out memories from what is only imagined: my memory of last weekend in Snowdonia is more 'lively and strong' than my daydream about the summer holiday I have planned for the Alps. It is also clear, however, that there are certain counterexamples to his account. Many of my memories are very faint and their order can be jumbled up and confused, and some people have a very vivid imagination, their flights of fancy striking the mind more forcefully than their memories. Nevertheless, there is something attractive about Hume's approach. There does seem to be something distinctive about the experiences associated with memory, even if this cannot be captured in terms of their liveliness and temporal order. Russell describes it as a 'feeling of familiarity' or as a 'feeling of pastness' (1921, ch. 9). As with Hume, these are phenomenological features of which we can be aware, and both philosophers embrace the picture that was criticized in the last section, where memory is constituted by a certain type of experience. The problem with the Hume–Russell line is that they confuse the metaphysical question concerning what it is that constitutes a memory with the epistemological question concerning how we can tell that certain thoughts are the product of memory rather than imagination. It may be the case that we can sometimes distinguish memories according to the phenomenological features noted by Hume and Russell, but the claim in this section is that memories *themselves* are defined according to their causal origin, an origin that the thinker herself may not be aware of.

When you remember something you have knowledge that you also possessed in the past (although we are ignoring here the 'counting windows' counterexample of section 1). However, such knowledge is not sufficient for memory. I may have relearnt a certain fact, a fact that I once knew but had subsequently forgotten. In addition, then, the right kind of causal connection is required between my current knowledge and my past acquisition of that knowledge. (This is so whether our account of memory is grounded in intentional content or in the possession of mental images.) Let us investigate the nature of this causal connection. Consider the following example. When I was five I knew that I had a blue corduroy hat, and my parents treasured a self-portrait I had drawn of myself wearing it. I had forgotten about this hat until that drawing was recently unearthed. It is not the case that I had simply not thought about the hat for a while, even though the memory of it remained; the claim is that I had completely forgotten about it – it had been wiped from my mind. Now, though, on discovering this old drawing I again know that I had such a hat, and there is a causal chain that connects my current knowledge with that which I had many years ago, a causal chain linking together such events as my wearing of the hat, the afternoon spent creating my masterpiece, the putting of this picture in the drawer, and its retrieval. This, however, is not a case of memory, and it will be useful to consider why not.

One suggestion is that my current knowledge of the hat does not constitute a memory because it involves being prompted by the drawing. We often, though, have memories that are prompted in this kind of way: by perhaps looking at a photograph, reading a diary, or being reminded by a friend. In such cases we can usually go on to remember more about the recalled episode. A note in a diary may remind me that I went to the dentist last year, and this note can lead to my recalling the smell of the surgery, the treatment I had, and perhaps the pain I experienced. However, such extra recollection is not necessary: I may not be able to say anything more about that appointment – nothing else may 'come back' – but I can still be said to remember that I went to the dentist. It is also the case that we sometimes only remember a certain event when we are told all the details of what happened, even if we cannot add anything further to what we are told. Prompting – both partial and full – is compatible with the operation of memory.

The key aspect of the above example – that which indicates that I do not remember the hat – is that I had forgotten about it in the intervening years since the picture was put away in the drawer. As argued, prompting is compatible with memory, and so I do not just mean that I needed reminding of the hat in order to remember it; it hadn't just slipped my mind. There was a period of time when this particular item of knowledge was not present in my mind at all, and thus no amount of prompting could have led to my recalling it. We can now say more about the kind of causal connection that is necessary for memory. There must be a continuous causal chain connecting together my past knowledge and my current knowledge, a causal chain that is internal to my mind, not one that is only maintained by items out in the world such as photographs and diaries. The naturalistic approach is then to investigate the physical nature of this internal component, with cognitive scientists attempting to identify the mechanisms in the brain that store knowledge and that causally connect our current representational states with those we acquired in the past.

Whether or not the requisite causal relations are present is something that cannot be determined from the first person perspective. Seeing my drawing again may be accompanied by the kind of phenomenology characteristic of memory that is noted by Hume and Russell; nevertheless, I may not *remember* the hat because the requisite causal chain has been broken. There could be such features of experience without a thinker being causally connected in the right way to his earlier epistemic states. Thus I may not be able to tell whether I remember a certain episode or whether I only seem to.

4 Scepticism and the Reality of the Past

The fact that I may not be able to tell whether I am remembering a certain event or imagining it leads to an analogue of Cartesian scepticism. Russell asks us to imagine that the world was created five minutes ago, and it was only then that we came into existence along with our (only apparent) memories of the past.

> There is no logical impossibility in the hypothesis that the world sprang into being five minutes ago, exactly as it then was, with a population that 'remembered' a wholly unreal past. There is no logically necessary connection between events at different times; therefore, nothing that is happening now or will happen in the future can disprove the hypothesis that the world began five minutes ago. (Russell, 1921, pp. 159–60)

There are no experiences that we could have that would rule out Russell's sceptical scenario, and thus we are not justified in accepting that our 'memories' are true representations of the past. We are not even justified in believing that there is a past.

Malcolm's (1963b) response to such scepticism is one that has much in common with Coady's Martian argument concerning testimony (chapter 5, section 3.2). Russell's scenario relies on the assumption that if we can be mistaken about any particular 'memory' – which of course we can – then we can be mistaken with respect to all of our 'memories'. We are therefore able to imagine a community of thinkers whose 'memory' reports are never correct; the claim, then, is that we could be members of such a community. However, we can only be said to imagine such a community if we are able – in our imagination – to pick out which of their utterances purport to be memory reports. This is so we can be sure we are imagining a community that only seems to have memories, rather than one that is mistaken about some other kind of mental state or thought. Malcolm, however, argues that we cannot actually imagine such a community. A speaker only understands a certain word if she generally applies it in the correct circumstances. Mary only understands the word 'blue' if she can reliably apply it to blue things. Similarly with 'remember': a thinker only understands this word when she is capable of correctly saying things like 'I remember that p'. In Russell's scenario, however, such utterances are always false. Thus we are imagining people who do not understand the word 'remember'. They may make the sound 'I re-mem-bah', but they cannot mean what we do when we make such an utterance. Such people, therefore, are not offering memory reports at all. The Russellian scenario is a conceptual impossibility: if we are really imagining a community of thinkers with memories – ones who therefore possess the concept of REMEMBERING – then it must be the case that their use of this concept is reliable and that many of their reports concerning the past are correct. Scepticism concerning memory is therefore undermined.

> We have an inclination to imagine the past as *behind* us, *out of sight*, and to think that every proposition we make about it might be false. But in imagining this we assume all along that our propositions do *refer* to the past, are genuinely propositions *about* the past. When we think out what is involved in that *reference to the past*, which we took for granted, we see that it requires that many of those propositions about the past should be true. (Malcolm, 1963b, p. 196)

As said, this response to scepticism is very similar to an argument discussed elsewhere with respect to testimony. If you do not find this line persuasive, then you should think about how the other responses to Cartesian scepticism could be applied to the case of memory (see chapter 9). Consider, for example, how the contextualist and the epistemological externalist might respond to Russell's scenario. For a satisfying response to scepticism, an account is required of how our beliefs about the external world are justified, and of how we can retain such knowledge in the form of memory.

5   The Relation between Perception, Testimony and Memory

In this final section we shall look at some of the epistemic relationships between perception, testimony and memory, and at the importance of memory in our empirical and a priori thinking. There is a certain interplay between the sources of knowledge – perception, testimony and a priori reasoning – and the preservative faculty of memory. Memories can defeat the justification we have for believing what we see or what we are told. If I remember that Kate has gone on holiday, then my belief that I saw her across the other side of the park may not be justified. Testimony can also play such a defeating role. In chapter 4 we looked at cases where testimony can defeat our perceptual beliefs: when playing pool I believe Ronnie when he says that the white ball will pass the red one, even though it doesn't look to me as though it will. It is also sometimes the case that testimony can defeat our (apparent) memories: I seem to remember you being at the party, but if you tell me that you weren't, then my justification for that belief is lost (if, that is, you are usually a reliable reporter (Hume) or there is no reason to think that you are mistaken or insincere on this occasion (Reid)). I shall leave you to think of cases where perceptual belief can undermine memory and the justification we have for the beliefs we acquire via testimony.

Memory not only plays a defeating role with respect to perception and testimony, it can also play a positive role: it can affect what we choose to look at, and what we listen to or read. I may remember that Sylvie Guillem dances beautifully and so watch more of her performances, or I may remember that Ryan rarely tells the truth and so refrain from listening to him. Memory therefore has a causal effect on the acquisition of perceptual and testimonial beliefs. More controversially, as we saw in chapter 6, the knowledge we have may affect the very nature of our perceptual experiences. If I remember my music theory, Bach's cello suites may sound different from how they would sound if I lacked such knowledge.

Memory also has an important role with respect to a priori knowledge. The retention of such knowledge is a particular form of factual memory: in remembering that $e^{-i\pi} + 1 = 0$, I have retained a previously acquired item of a priori knowledge. Also, though, memory is involved in the acquisition of such knowledge. The derivation of certain a priori truths requires long chains of reasoning. This is true in philosophy and in mathematics. Descartes's cosmological proof for the existence of God requires many steps, as does the derivation of Pythagoras' theorem. Memory is necessary in order that we can work through these arguments. Our earlier conclusions need to be taken forward and used as later premises in our reasoning. We must therefore remember these earlier conclusions. It is important to note, though, that memory does not provide the justification for the beliefs that we acquire in this way; it is, rather, a necessary condition for the derivation of such truths, a cognitive mechanism that must be in operation if we are to acquire such a priori knowledge. (This is analogous to the role that perception plays in Reid's account of testimony. Perception does not provide justification for our testimonial beliefs, but our perceptual mechanisms must be working properly if we are to acquire any beliefs via the testimonial route.)

Last, let us briefly consider the importance of memory to our very existence as thinking individuals. Consider what your life would be like if you had no memory. I would never finish typing these words because I would not remember what I wanted to say next, what a keyboard is for, or that I am writing a book. I would not enjoy music because I would not be able to experience the melody developing: I would only hear the current pulse of sound. It is not clear how I could coherently continue to act since I would not remember that I plan to work until 1 a.m. this morning, that reading and writing philosophy is the kind of work that I do here, or that this is my study. More worrying still, it is not clear whether I would have any sense of myself at all. How I conceive of myself is partly constituted by my memory of the things that I have done and of my plans for the future. Without memory, though, these would be lost to me: I would not be able to recall that I have enjoyed this week, or that I intend to improve my badminton this year. I would not be able to think of myself as a thirty-something, a philosopher, or even as a mortal being. As we saw in chapter 3, Descartes's method of doubt comes to rest with the *cogito*, with the certain knowledge that one is a thinking thing. The suggestion here is that without memory one couldn't even be sure of this, or rather, that the sense one has of one's self is only coherent in relation to one's past and future, both of which we have claimed require the operation of memory.

Questions

1 How should we conceive of the epistemic role of memory?
2 Can you tell whether you are remembering an event or merely imagining it?
3 It has been claimed that memory involves the retention of previously acquired knowledge. How, then, should we respond to cases where it seems that we remember a certain event even though we do not know or believe that it happened? Here are two examples where this appears to be so.
   (a) When I was a child I believed that I had a hallucination of a lion in the back garden, and I still remember what this experience was like. (This is true; I called the lion Arrowroot!) I was not frightened of Arrowroot because I did not believe that he existed; I thought that I was seeing things. Perhaps, though, I wasn't; it may have been that a lion had escaped from a safari park. If so, I remember a lion being there even though at the time I did not believe that this was the case. Is this how such a scenario should be described?
   (b) How can I account for the fact that I have only just remembered that I was dreaming last night, even though at the time I did not believe or know that I was doing so?
4 Let us consider another science fiction scenario. Imagine that our memory could be improved by adding silicon circuit boards to our brains. There is a limit, though, to what can fit inside the skull and thus our brains could be connected by remote to extra hardware that

is housed elsewhere. Would we say that we remember information that was stored in this way? If so, how could we maintain the earlier claim that memory requires a continuous causal chain that is *internal to the brain*? Also, if such external storage is allowed, then why should the physical constitution of the storage medium matter? Could we not allow other media apart from circuit boards to legitimately house our acquired knowledge, with diaries and photograph albums being literally extensions of our memory?

Further Reading

One of the few books devoted to the epistemology of memory is Don Locke (1971). Ayer (1956, ch. 4) discusses various relevant issues including the role of imagery in memory; Landesman (1962) also covers this, along with the claim that memory is not a source of knowledge. Martin and Deutscher (1966) are particularly good on the causal theory of memory and prompting. Shoemaker (1984b) supports the kind of response to scepticism that is offered by Malcolm (1963b). The latter also discusses the role of causality, and the various distinctions we have looked at concerning factual and personal memory. He also considers the closing suggestion of this chapter; he claims that without memory we would not be recognizably human.

Such thoughts are also explored in the film *Memento* (2000). Leonard Shelby has an extreme form of amnesia. In order to operate in the world and to track down the killer of his wife, he plants various notes and photographs in his pockets, and tattoos on his skin certain important facts such as his name. He does, however, forget he has done this; throughout the film he is surprised to discover these useful mementos. Questions that the film raises include: Does Leonard have any knowledge of the past? (After all, he has certain true beliefs about it.) And, more fundamentally, should Leonard be considered a person? Other films relevant to our discussion include *Brainstorm* (1983), which involves the kind of external storage device suggested in question 4; and *Total Recall* (1990) and *The Eternal Sunshine of the Spotless Mind* (2004), which focus on the issue of scepticism with respect to memory.

 **Other Minds**

In this chapter I shall consider whether I can come to have knowledge of what other people are thinking; more generally, whether I can come to know that others have minds at all; and assuming I can, I shall investigate what it is that provides justification for such knowledge.

1 First Person Authority

Many philosophers have seen the mind as a 'Cartesian theatre'. We have direct access to our own private theatres where we can turn our introspective spotlight on the thoughts and mental states that take centre stage. We perceive the external world, and we can 'introspect' our inner world (with our 'mind's eye'). Moreover, it has been claimed that we are infallible about the contents of our own minds. If I believe that I'm in pain, then I am; if I believe that I like ice-cream, then I do. I have what is called 'first person authority'. We have come across such a picture before. According to the indirect realist, I am not directly aware of the external world; it is sense data that I directly perceive (chapter 3) – sense data that populate my Cartesian theatre – and, according to traditional foundationalism, I am infallible with respect to the nature of these items. We shall briefly look at some problems with this picture of the mind. However, the main purpose of this section is to introduce this Cartesian conception of the mind because it is this that underlies an important sceptical problem – 'the problem of other minds' – the main focus of this chapter.

As we saw in chapter 6, some have questioned the traditional foundationalist claim that we are infallible about our own experience.

> I may say 'Magenta' wrongly . . . because I was unable to, or perhaps just didn't, really notice or attend to or properly size up the colour before me. Thus, there is always the possibility . . . that the colour before me just wasn't *magenta*. And this holds for the case in which I say, 'It seems, to me personally, here and now, as if I were seeing something magenta', just as much for the case in which I say, 'That is magenta.' The first formula may be more cautious but it isn't incorrigible. (Austin, 1962, p. 113)

There are various kinds of circumstance in which it is plausible that we could be mistaken about our own mental states. You could try this: blindfold a friend and tell him you are going to put a hot stone in his hand. Instead, put an ice cube there and ask him whether he has a sensation of heat. Or – in your imagination – picture a nonagon, a nine-sided polygon. Now consider whether you are sure that you are imagining that particular type of shape. Does it definitely have nine sides, or does it perhaps have eight or ten? These are cases where it is suggested that the epistemic access we have to our own minds is not as good as we think it is. There are also times when we may deceive ourselves, when, for one reason or another, we manage to avoid becoming aware of the true nature of some of our thoughts. Harry prides himself on not being the jealous type; it's fine if his wife goes out with male friends after work. It's clear, though, that he is jealous: he rings her mobile more often when she is out with men than when she is out with women friends, and he is far more interested to hear the details of her evening. He is deceiving himself that he is not jealous since he would rather be the kind of person who isn't like that. Similarly, I *do* like whisky; I really do . . . Or, do I just want to be the kind of person who drinks whisky? Conrad wrote in *Lord Jim* that 'no man ever understands quite his own artful dodges to escape from the grim shadow of self-knowledge' (Conrad, 1957, p. 102). It is therefore questionable whether we have infallible access to our own minds. Having said that, it seems clear that we have some level of privileged access to them. This would be something that the modest foundationalist would be happy with. We have prima facie justification for believing that the introspective access we have to our own minds is accurate, unless, that is, we are aware of defeating factors.

In the rest of this chapter we shall not be concerned with whether we have infallible access to our own minds. What will concern us is how we can come to know what others are thinking. And the key aspect of the Cartesian picture that we shall continue to focus on is the claim that we have direct access to our own mental states, yet not to those of others. We therefore have to infer what others are thinking by observing their behaviour.

2   The Problem of Other Minds and Solipsism

Everyone is sceptical to some degree about the extent of our knowledge of what others are thinking. We often say things like: 'what does she really think about that?', 'he's so inscrutable', and 'I just can't work him out'. A more extreme scepticism is expressed by Paul in the film *Last Tango in Paris* (1972) when he is talking to the embalmed body of his dead wife who has committed suicide: 'Even if the husband lives two hundred [. . .] years, he's never going to be able to discover his wife's real nature. I mean, I . . . I might be able to comprehend the universe, but . . . I'll never discover the truth about you. Never.' The problem that we shall look at, however, is deeper still. The question is whether I am justified in believing that others have minds at all. This is known as the 'problem of other minds'.

In the previous section it was claimed that I have direct access to my own thoughts and mental states. I do not, though, have such access to the minds of others. To work out what you are thinking, I have to observe your actions and listen to what you say. In doing so I am only directly apprehending your behaviour. The possibility arises, then, that your behaviour is not driven by thoughts and mental states, but that you are simply a mindless automaton. '[I]f I look out of the window and see men crossing the square, as I just happen to have done, I normally say that I see men themselves . . . Yet do I see any more than hats and coats which could conceal automatons?' (Descartes, 1986, p. 21). This is an analogue of Cartesian scepticism with respect to the external world. The experiences I would have of perceiving minded actions and of perceiving the movements of a mindless robot are indistinguishable, and so I have no justification for believing that your behaviour is of the former kind. The sceptical conclusion is that I have no reason to think that there are any other minds in existence apart from my own. Such a view is called solipsism, and in this chapter we shall look at various responses to this sceptical threat. (Solipsism may also have wider sceptical consequences: consider how testimonial knowledge would be affected if we have no justification for believing in other minds.)

3   The Argument from Analogy

Mill (1889) and Russell (1948) argue that we come to have knowledge of other minds through inference. To do so we must reason in the following way.

> *Premise*: I know that my behaviour is caused by my mental states.
> *Premise*: I observe similar behaviour in others.
> *Conclusion*: Their behaviour is caused by their mental states.

And so, in a particular case:

> *Premise*: Headaches always cause me to moan and rub my temples.
> *Premise*: Roy is moaning and rubbing his temples.
> *Conclusion*: Roy has a headache.

There are, however, problems with this approach; one concerns the kind of reasoning involved. A general conclusion is drawn from limited experiential evidence: because my behaviour is caused by my mental states, it is argued that this is true of everyone. This form of argument is inductive and, in chapter 10, we explored the general problem of induction; a solution must be found to this if inductive inference is to provide us with justified empirical beliefs. The argument from analogy also therefore depends on such a solution. Importantly, though, this particular type of inductive argument has a problem of its own. In the argument from analogy a general conclusion is drawn from just *one* particular case: I conclude that everyone has a mind from the fact that I do.

The argument relies on very weak inductive evidence: we only have one positive case – our own – and we go on to infer that *all* creatures with relevantly similar behaviour are thinkers like us. I could provide an analogous argument for the claim that everyone has a green living room because I do; this, of course, would not be a justified conclusion to draw.

Throughout this chapter we shall be considering what it is actually like to engage with others and to see them as having minds. I can pick up on the fine nuances of your voice and of your smile; your posture may be indicative of the nature of your thoughts, and the movement of your eyes may be illuminating. We are all adept at identifying such subtle behavioural clues. According to the argument from analogy, however, we can only take such behaviour as indicative of the mental states of others if we have previously found such behaviour to be associated with our own mental states. It would seem, though, that we just do not have the relevant knowledge of our own behaviour. Perhaps an incredibly vain person – one who is always looking in a mirror – has more of an idea; but most of us do not know exactly how we stand, how our eyes move, how our lips curl, or how our voice modulates when we express our thoughts. This seems clear given our surprise (and perhaps horror) when we hear a recording of our own voice or see a video of ourselves. There is therefore a problem with the first premise of the argument from analogy. We do not know – in enough detail – the nature of our own behaviour: I am not aware of certain subtle features of my own behaviour, the kind of features that I am capable of discerning in the behaviour of others, those that enable me to ascribe mental states to them.

Furthermore, when I come to see others as having minds, it does not seem as though I go through the kind of reasoning suggested by the argument from analogy. When I see you rubbing your temples, I do not consciously think 'I behave like you are behaving right now when I have a headache, and thus I believe that you have a headache'. I seem to acquire my belief more directly. This alone, perhaps, does not entail that the argument from analogy is flawed. It could be that we perform the inference very quickly (or even unconsciously); or it may be that in most cases we do not reason in this way, but it is our ability to be able to reason thus that provides our beliefs with justification. Nevertheless, the apparent non-inferential nature of our engagement with others does suggest a different model for the knowledge we have of other minds, one that is more direct, and it is to such a model that we turn next.

4   Seeing Minds

Let us think about how people appear to us when we engage with them. Wittgenstein suggests that 'The human body is the best picture of the human soul' (1953, p. 178); that 'Consciousness is as clear in his face and behaviour as in myself' (1967, §221); and he says, 'It is possible to say "I read timidity in this face" but at all events the timidity does not seem to be merely associated, outwardly connected, with the face; but fear is there, alive, in the features' (1953, §537). This is what he seems to mean: I do not arrive at the conclusion that you have a mind by observing features of your behaviour that are usually associated with particular mental states. It seems, rather, that I directly observe your mind. Certain kinds of glance bring this phenomenon into sharper focus. In catching someone's eye, their desire or anger can be immediately recognizable; you, in an instance, see her as a person with a mind, and as desiring you, or as being angry with you. 'The glance of desire concentrates into itself the whole life of the human being' (Scruton, 1986, p. 24). You do not *infer* that she has a mind; you *see* that she does. Glances of desire and anger can often be highly charged, but this phenomenon is evident in all our interactions with each other. When cycling to work I am always aware that a car could pull out on me from a side road. To avoid this, I stare at car drivers who are waiting to pull out, only taking my hands off the brake levers when I catch their attention. In catching their eye I come to see car drivers as having minds, and as having seen me (and, presumably, as having seen that I have a mind). Only after such reciprocal recognition has taken place do I feel I can safely cycle past.

Dylan, a young child of a friend of mine, really likes chocolate and when I visit I usually take him a bar or two. Sometimes, though, I forget and he is disappointed; this disappointment is clear in his face: his face 'drops'. It seems wrong to say that I work out what he is feeling by making an inference based on the beliefs I have about the changing contours of his face. A better description would be that I simply *see* him – directly and unmediated – move from expectancy to disappointment.

These observations may capture the character of our human interactions, but it is not clear whether they constitute an argument against the solipsist. Perhaps I cannot help but believe that others have minds; the solipsistic claim, however, is that these beliefs are not true: the fact that I see people as minded does not entail that they are. A sexist male driver claims to just see that women have a bad driving technique; he is, however, wrong. Some claim to see the hand of God operative in nature, but this alone does not provide sufficient justification for believing in such intervention (although, for a contrasting view, see chapter 15, section 3). The key question is whether we are justified in claiming to perceive that others have minds, and thus whether we have good reason to reject solipsism. In order to answer this question we shall first turn to an argument that threatens the Cartesian picture of the mind, that in which we have direct access to our own private mental states whereas only indirect access to the mental states of others. It is this conception of the mind that drives the argument for solipsism. In section 6 more substance will be given to the claim that we can directly apprehend the minds of other people in their behaviour.

5   The Private Language Argument Revisited

According to the Cartesian account of the mind, I learn to understand the meaning of words referring to mental states from my own case. Pains are those particular sensations which I am aware of from time to time, and the desire for chocolate is that specific kind of urge that I often have. The picture is that a young child has a certain sensation, belief or desire, and by attending to what it is like to have that mental state, he learns to pick it out on future occasions. 'The individual words of this language are to refer to what can only be known to the person speaking; to his immediate private sensations' (Wittgenstein, 1953, §243). *This* feeling is a pain, and *this* one is a desire for chocolate. Such learning episodes are private, performed inside one's own Cartesian theatre, a theatre to which others do not have access. Others only see the billboards outside – one's behaviour – and not the performances on the stage (one's actual mental states).

Wittgenstein, however, argues that this is not how we come to have knowledge of our own minds. If this were the only kind of access we have to our mind, then we could not tell whether we are correctly applying our mental state terms or not; how would we know that we are not applying them haphazardly? The only way that we can be sure our usage is consistent is if there are some objective criteria of correctness. Our own opinion on what amounts to the same kind of sensation or mental state is not objective in the required sense. '[I]n the present case I have no criteria of correctness. One would like to say: whatever is going to seem right to me is right. And that only means that here we can't talk about "right" ' (Wittgenstein, 1953, §258).

We can, though, talk about and identify our own mental states and this is because there are objective criteria for the application of mental state terms, and these criteria are behavioural. The Wittgensteinian claim is that you only come to understand what 'pain' means when you grasp that there is certain behaviour characteristic of that sensation, behaviour such as groaning and moaning. This is also the case with respect to our other mental states: you only understand what it is to have a desire for chocolate if you know that such a desire causes you to consume such confectionery. There is a conceptual connection between observable behaviour and the possession of a mind. In the next section a theory of mind that embraces this conclusion will be sketched. (You should note, though, that Wittgenstein himself is not generally held as endorsing this particular theory.)

6   Behaviourism

Behaviourists claim that the mind is not hidden inside the head, but rather that the mind simply consists in the movements of the body and the sounds that it makes. Mentality is nothing more than behaviour. I can therefore directly see and hear your mind. 'Overt intelligent performances are not clues to the workings of minds; they are those workings. Boswell described Johnson's mind when he described how he wrote, talked, ate, fidgeted and fumed' (Ryle, 1963, p. 57). The examples we looked at above – Dylan, a glance of desire, and catching the eye of a car driver – all make this approach to the mind attractive. To paraphrase Wittgenstein: it does seem as though consciousness is as clear in people's faces and behaviour as it is in myself.

Behaviourism was popular in the first half of the last century. It was largely motivated by the **logical positivist** emphasis on scientific method. The logical positivists claimed that statements which could not be verified were meaningless and, for them, a statement could only be verified if it could be tested by observation or scientific experiment. Behaviourism was an attractive position since, according to such a theory, the mind could be scientifically investigated. The mind was not some kind of shadowy spirit, essentially hidden from view – as dualists had thought – it was out in the open for all to see. For the behaviourist, then, it is my perceptual experience of the behaviour of others that justifies my belief in their possession of mental states. In observing your behaviour, I observe your mind.

Behaviourism, however, is beset with problems. It should first be made clear that the behaviourist does not claim that I must actually be groaning, say, if I'm in pain; I am, however, *disposed* to groan. This notion of a behavioural disposition plays a key role in the behaviourist's account. I may suppress my groans in order to impress my peers, but I am nevertheless disposed or inclined to groan, and this is what I would do if no one else were around. Even though I desire ice-cream, I may not walk to the ice-cream van because I do not have enough money to buy one; nevertheless, I would satisfy my desire if such a constraint did not prevent me from doing so. For the behaviourist, a particular mental state is identified with a set of behavioural dispositions. It is not clear, though, whether a definitive description of such a set can be provided. If I have the desire for ice-cream, then I may be disposed to walk to the ice-cream van; but, depending on what other beliefs I have, I could actually be disposed to behave in any way at all. If I believe that the god of ice-cream favoured those who whistled 'Dixie', then I may whistle 'Dixie'. If I believe that someone has buried a tub of Ben & Jerry's in the garden, then I may dig up the flower bed. All kinds of behaviour could be manifested by someone with a desire for ice-cream, and thus the behaviourist cannot provide an account of mental states in terms of behavioural dispositions. Another problem for behaviourists is that they have been accused of 'feigning anaesthesia', that is, of ignoring the experiential quality of what it is like to have certain mental states. I may groan when in pain, but being in pain also *feels* a certain way, and the behaviourist does not give any account of this feature of what it is like to possess a mind.

Today, behaviourism has few supporters, and in the last fifty or so years various alternative accounts of the mind have been put forward.

The details of these accounts need not concern us here, but their general approach may be of epistemological importance. Many working in the philosophy of mind claim that our understanding of the mind is theoretical. In the next section it will be explained what this means and we shall consider whether such an approach can provide an account of our knowledge of other minds.

7   Theoretical Knowledge of the Mind

When a flame is put under a pan of water, the water heats up and eventually comes to the boil; if a tea bag is then added, the water will gradually turn brown. But why do these things happen? We cannot tell just by observing the contents of the pan; we do, though, have a theory that explains these phenomena. This theory involves a description of certain unobserved entities such as molecules of H_2O that are weakly bound together. Applying heat energy to the pan causes these molecules to move about more and more violently until, at boiling point, some of them fly off into the atmosphere as steam. The remaining fast-moving molecules diffuse in and out of the porous tea bag, dissolving certain coloured compounds on their way, compounds that are found in tea leaves. We believe this description because it provides an explanation of what we see and, importantly, this theory can be used to make predictions, predictions that can then be tested. When tea bags are added to water of different temperatures, hot water should turn brown in a shorter amount of time than cold water (this is because fast-moving molecules have a higher rate of diffusion). This is indeed the case, and we therefore have a successful prediction that supports our molecular theory.

In this section we shall look at the claim that the ascription of mental states is also theoretical. I cannot directly observe what it is that causes you to behave in the way that you do; I can, though, have a theoretical explanation of your behaviour. This theory is called 'folk psychology'. It is so called because it does not involve the kinds of entities that are only at home in a scientific context, such as the molecules above. Folk psychology posits the existence of such everyday mental states as beliefs, desires, pains, hopes and fears, and it is these mental states that provide an explanation for people's actions. These are, however, theoretical states because they are not directly observable (unless you're a behaviourist). Just as physical science posits laws concerning the behaviour of its theoretical entities, so does folk psychology. Folk psychology includes such generalizations as that those in pain tend to cry out, and that people will go to the fridge if they are hungry and believe that it is stocked with food. We can therefore use such generalizations to work out what someone is thinking or feeling: if Kramer is sidling towards the fridge, we can infer that he is hungry. I am justified in believing that others have minds in the same way that I am justified in believing that water consists of H_2O molecules. Molecules can be used to explain and predict the action of water, and folk psychological categories can be used to explain and predict the actions of people. The kind of reasoning applied here is what is variously called 'abductive inference', 'ampliative reasoning', or 'inference to the best explanation'. If there is a theory that explains the occurrence of certain phenomena better than any alternative theory, then you are justified in believing that theory.

It may appear that such a theoretical account is at odds with our earlier observation that we seem to directly engage with the minds of others. There is a distinction between the phenomena that we directly perceive and the theoretical entities that explain such appearances. The physical properties of H_2O molecules explain why water boils, and it is folk psychological states that explain our behaviour. In both cases, the theoretical entities of chemistry and folk psychology are not observed; they are simply taken to exist in order to explain that which is observable. And, as said, this appears to be at odds with the claim that we 'see minds'. Perhaps, though, a theoretical account can make good sense of this aspect of our experience.

When first learning to use an ultrasound machine, a nurse observes various shapes on the screen, and it is a theory that allows her to inter-pret the pattern: 'if there is a shadow there and a darker region just to the left, then the baby is a boy.' With practice, however, and as the nurse becomes adept at interpreting what she sees, she does not have to reason in this way; she simply comes to *see* that the baby is a boy. The following is another example of such non-inferential interpretation. Over the years my bicycles have made all sorts of noises as they have aged. When first hearing a certain noise I try to work out its source. To do this, I consider whether it is a regular noise, whether it sounds like metal on metal, and whether it occurs in all weathers. The answers to such questions help me to develop a theory to explain why that noise is occurring. If it is a regular noise, and one that does not involve metal on metal, then it is likely to be caused by the wheel rim rubbing on the brake pads. Again, as I become adept at applying my theory, I do not have to go through such reasoning; I simply *hear* a certain noise as brake rub. Perhaps, then, such a line could be taken by folk psychologists. As we become adept at applying our folk theory, we do not have to reason in the following way: 'Ludwig is writhing on the floor, and so he must be in pain'; rather, we can simply *see* that Ludwig is in pain. A theoretical account therefore offers a solution to the problem of other minds. The explanatory and predictive success of our folk psychological theory provides justification for our beliefs concerning the minds of others, and if we accept the above, then we can also accommodate the persua-sive claim that we see the mental states of others operative in their actions and that we do not merely come to infer that they are involved.

No one is really a solipsist – no one can *live* that kind of scepticism – but do we have justification for our belief in the existence of other thinkers? We have looked at three broad approaches to this question.

First, I could infer that you have a mind from the fact that you behave like me. Second, I can directly perceive your mind because your behaviour should not be seen as merely evidence that you are minded; it is, rather, constitutive of your mind. Third, the best explanation for your behaviour is that it is driven by your internal mental states.

Questions

1 Think honestly about yourself: do you deceive yourself in any way about your own mental states? (Or do others that you know?) How does your answer relate to the issue of whether we have first person authority with respect to our own minds?
2 Does the following quote by the actor Laurence Olivier support any of the suggested solutions to the problem of other minds? He is discussing how he learns to act a particular part.

> I sometimes on the top of a bus see a man. I begin to wonder about him. I see him do something, make a gesture. Why does he do it like that? Because he must be like *this*. And if he is like this, he would do – in a certain situation – that. (Harris, 1971, p. 84)

3 In trying to ascertain whether you have a mind, it seems the only evidence I have to go on is your observable behaviour. Is this enough to justify my belief that you are minded?
4 The justification provided by the argument from analogy, behaviourism and folk psychology is internalist in character, that is, we can reflect upon what it is that provides justification for our belief in other minds. In contrast, how could an externalist account for such alleged knowledge?
5 There is a philosophical joke concerning two behaviourists. After making love, one asks the other: 'it was great for you, how was it for me?' What problem does this highlight for the behaviourist account of the mind? (And why is it funny?)

Further Reading

Issues concerning self-knowledge and self-deception are often raised in the context of love and obsession. Right from the start of Shakespeare's play *Much Ado About Nothing*, it is plausible that Benedick and Beatrice are in love, even though they claim they are not interested in each other. Also see the films *Play Misty for Me* (1971) and *A la Folie . . . Pas du Tout* (2002); these could be interpreted as involving cases of self-deception in which thinkers attempt to suppress the belief that they are not loved. (10cc's song 'I'm Not in Love' is also relevant to the issue of self-deception!) The solipsistic fear that you might be the only mind in existence is explored in a short story by Robert Heinlein (1964a) entitled 'They'. Various films also focus on this paranoid solipsistic suspicion, and it is a useful exercise to consider just how radical the scepticism is that such films express. Often the suggestion is that certain creatures do not have emotional responses in the way we do, although they are to some extent conscious. *The Invasion of the Body Snatchers* (1978) and *Blade Runner* (1982) take this line. The latter is interesting in that when we first meet Rachael, a robot, she does not know that she is not human. She takes others to have thoughts like her; actually, though, they don't: the thoughts of others are emotionally richer than she believes. Other films suggest a more extreme scepticism in which certain groups of apparently human characters are automata with no conscious thought at all. This is the kind of scenario in *The Stepford Wives* (1975) and *Westworld* (1973).

Film can also highlight the nuances of behaviour that reveal our mindedness, those that perhaps enable us to *see* minds. Directors often focus the camera on those everyday touches, shrugs and facial expressions that say so much about what we are thinking and feeling. Dickens writes in *Bleak House*: 'She stands looking at him . . . and only her fluttering hands give utterance to her emotions. But they are very eloquent; very, very eloquent' (Dickens, 1993, p. 615). Watch how Hubbell ties Katie's shoelace in *The Way We Were* (1973); how Terry Malloy pushes away his brother's gun in the back of a taxi in *On the Waterfront* (1954); and how Jill's expression changes in *Once upon a Time in the West* (1968) when she discovers that a certain man (not to give it away) has survived a gunfight, and then as she hears him say that he must leave town (and, of course, her).

A recent defence of the argument from analogy can be found in Goldman (2000b), and Pargetter (1984) favours a theoretical account of other minds. Buford (1970) is a useful collection of papers on the various approaches to the problem. For an introduction to the philosophy of mind, you could turn to Kirk's (2003) textbook *Mind and Body*, and Maslin (2001) is good on behaviourism.

Moral Knowledge

As well as simply observing what people do, we also place value on their actions: we see some of them as good, laudable or praiseworthy; and others as bad, evil or wretched. Further, we feel it is the former that we should strive to perform and the latter we should avoid. There are some very clear-cut examples: premeditated murder is evil, and the relief of pain is good. Whatever we may think about certain more contentious cases – Is it right to kill animals? Is abortion wrong? – it is undeniable that we all see the actions of people in such moral or ethical terms. (I shall use 'morality' and 'ethics' interchangeably.) The main purpose of this chapter is to illustrate and illuminate the key epistemological notions that we have been discussing throughout the book. Necessarily, then, this chapter can only serve as an introduction to moral philosophy. In sections 1 and 2 we shall discuss two highly influential approaches to ethics; one claims that our ethical beliefs have empirical justification, the other claims that they have a priori support. Section 3 will consider whether we can acquire justified ethical beliefs via testimony. And last, in section 4, we shall turn to the issue of scepticism with respect to morality, and to the claim that we cannot have moral knowledge.

1 An Empirical Approach to Morality

1.1 Utilitarianism

Utilitarians such as John Stuart Mill argue that ethical thought always involves at least an implicit consideration of the pleasure or pain experienced by the people affected by a particular action: 'actions are right in proportion as they tend to promote happiness, wrong as they tend to produce the reverse of happiness' (Mill, 1998, p. 7). We should not, though, simply be concerned with the immediate pleasure or pain that may be the result of a certain action. Childbirth may be excruciatingly painful, yet the rewards – in terms of the lifelong pleasure of being a parent, and the future happiness of the child – entail that the job of a midwife is morally worthy. Pain in the present may result in increased pleasure in the future, and this must be taken into account when making our utilitarian calculation as to whether an action is good or bad. Also, we are not simply talking about the pleasure or pain of the person who is deciding what to do. If I make a substantial donation to charity, then I may have a less pleasurable lifestyle since I will not be able to afford as much champagne and caviar; however, the medical research that my donation funds leads to an increase in the happiness of many others. A good action is therefore one that leads to an increase in the overall pleasure experienced by a certain community, and an action is wrong if it leads to a reduction in pleasure or to an increase in pain. There are certain forms of utilitarianism that distinguish between higher and lower pleasures (Mill, 1998) – between, say, drinking beer and reading poetry – and those that emphasize goals other than the experience of pleasure (Moore, 1903). In this chapter, though, we shall focus on the basic form of utilitarianism that sees happiness as simply the experience of (undifferentiated) pleasure, and as the only morally relevant goal.

Utilitarianism is empiricist in its approach. The calculations that must be performed to determine the moral worth of an action are those that involve empirical evidence: you must have a posteriori knowledge that a full stomach leads to happiness and that pain does not. However, such calculations would appear to be highly problematic: can we really quantify and compare the pleasure and pain caused by our actions? 'How can you measure the weight of a tear against the weight of a drop of blood?' (De Beauvoir, 1965, pp. 588–9). One of the founders of utilitarianism, Jeremy Bentham, suggested that we can; to do so we must apply the hedonic calculus (the root of 'hedonic' being 'hedone', the Greek word for pleasure). Numeric values could be assigned to our pleasures and pains according to such factors as how intense they are and how long they last. Such values can then be used to work out how we should act. Should I spend fifty pounds on a slap-up meal or should I give it to a Third World charity? The first option would lead to me having an experience of pleasure 10 on the hedonic calculus. The second, however, would provide a meal for 100 people, each of these people experiencing pleasure 1. The respective pleasure resulting from the two actions is 10 and 100; I should therefore give my money to charity. This example is of course extremely crude, but it does give an idea of the kind of calculation that a utilitarian thinks should be performed. (And this is not just a theoretical stance: the utilitarian philosopher Peter Singer gives a fifth of his income to Oxfam.)

Let us be clear on what provides the justification for our ethical beliefs according to the utilitarian. Goodness is a natural property that exists in the world; it simply consists in happiness or pleasure. Our beliefs about such a property are justified in the same way that our beliefs about other natural properties are justified. I believe that adding logs to the fire will increase the temperature of my living room. This belief is justified on inductive grounds: whenever I have added logs in the past, the temperature has risen. My beliefs about ethical matters are justified in a similar manner. I have inductive grounds for believing that hitting children for no reason is a bad thing to do because I have seen that such actions in the past have led to there being less happiness in the world. Moral knowledge is therefore a species of a posteriori, empirical knowledge.

1.2   Problems for utilitarianism

One way to attack utilitarianism is to think of scenarios in which the verdicts given by utilitarian thinking differ from our ethical intuitions. Such intuitions consist of our commonsense ethical opinions. We may be able to think of cases where a clearly evil act is counted as good in utilitarian terms, or vice versa. This would suggest that our ethical thinking is not utilitarian. Here is an example from Dostoyevsky's *The Brothers Karamazov*:

> 'Tell me yourself, I challenge you – answer. Imagine that you are creating a fabric of human destiny with the object of making men happy in the end, giving them peace and rest at last, but that it was essential and inevitable to torture to death only one tiny creature – the baby beating its breast with its fist, for instance – and to found that edifice on its unavenged tears, would you consent to be the architect of those conditions? Tell me, and tell the truth'. 'No, I wouldn't consent,' said Aloysha softly. (Dostoyevsky, 1993, p. 282)

Aloysha, then, is not a utilitarian. The happiness of humankind would easily outweigh the pain experienced by one tortured baby; nevertheless, such torture is not morally defensible. William James agrees:

> If the hypothesis were offered us of a world in which . . . millions [are] kept permanently happy on the simple condition that a certain lost soul on the far-off edge of things should lead a life of lonely torment . . . how hideous a thing would be its enjoyment when deliberately accepted as the fruit of such a bargain. (1897c, p. 68)

Such examples could be taken to show that utilitarianism is unacceptable.

There are, however, two possible utilitarian responses to this kind of objection. First, a distinct kind of utilitarianism has been suggested, one which claims that certain moral rules must be upheld, rules such as that murder or torture are always wrong. In particular circumstances it may be the case that such acts would lead to a net increase in pleasure; in general, though, torture and murder lead to an increase in pain and that is why there should be a utilitarian prohibition against them. This approach is called 'rule utilitarianism' as opposed to 'act utilitarianism' because it applies utilitarian principles to the assessment of whether certain rules are ethically sound, rather than to the consequences of particular acts. There is a useful analogy here with games or sports. These are played for fun or pleasure. With this in mind, it may seem sensible to play fast and loose with the rules of a particular game; if rent is ignored in *Monopoly*, or extra money given for passing 'Go', then players could continue to play for longer without becoming bankrupt and would therefore have more fun. This is akin to the act utilitarian line: rules can be broken if those rules limit the possible pleasure that certain actions can bring. The rule utilitarian, however, observes that the point of competitive games would be lost if such an attitude is taken to the rules of the game, and in the long run more fun is had if the rules are strictly enforced.

Second, you could bite the bullet and accept the unintuitive utilitarian conclusions. It may be unpalatable in certain respects, but in such an unusual situation – one in which the happiness of mankind can be secured by the torture of a baby – then the ethically right thing to do would be to perform such an act. This is a line adopted by J. C. C. Smart (1973). He claims that our ethical intuitions have been wrong at various times in the past, and this torture scenario may be just such a case. We used misguidedly to think that slavery was ethically permissible; we now think that we should never torture babies – again, though, we may be wrong.

We could also attack utilitarianism by questioning whether pleasure should play such a central role within ethics. Nozick (1981, ch. 5) suggests a scenario in which you can be plugged into an experience machine that feeds you pleasurable experiences. (One is reminded here of *The Matrix* (1999), and of the orgasmatron in Woody Allen's *Sleeper* (1973).) If you are a utilitarian, then the ultimately good act would be to plug everyone into a bank of these machines. This, however, does not seem to be right. Would we really want this for ourselves, and would it be a good thing if it could be realized? I shall leave you to consider these questions. (Of relevance here, I think, is the answer that Miles Davis the jazz trumpeter gave when he was asked, on one of his later tours, why he did not play ballads anymore. He said, 'Because I like playing ballads too much.') Pleasure is not all we desire, and pleasure should not be our only ethical goal. With respect to morality, it would seem that various other concepts are of central importance; concepts such as rights, justice, duty and obligation; these, however, are not considered by the utilitarian. We should not torture the child – whatever the beneficial consequences of doing so – because that is unjust: he has done nothing to deserve such treatment.

2   An A Priori Approach to Morality

In this section we shall turn to a radically different approach to ethics, one that does not depend on empirical evidence like utilitarianism, and one that is a priori in its approach.

2.1   Kant and the categorical imperative

Kant argues that there are absolute moral rules that forbid certain actions whatever the consequences. These can be derived a priori using the 'universalisability test'. In order to act morally we have to check whether our actions accord with a rule that we would wish to be universally adopted. Let us work through a particular example of how a moral rule can be derived using this test. Let's say that someone asks you a rather personal question that you do not wish to answer. You could be tempted here to lie; giving, perhaps, an innocuous reply or one that they expect to hear. You do not do this to gain anything; you simply do not think it is any of their business. In lying, however, you are implicitly accepting the rule that 'it's OK to lie'. Kant's claim, though, is that you would not want everybody to adopt this rule. If they did, then the assumption that people generally speak the truth would have to be discarded and the whole practice of communication would be endangered. Acting according to such a principle would be self-defeating. When you lie, you want others to think that you are telling the truth. However, in a community where it is considered acceptable to lie, people will not assume that you are telling the truth and so the whole point of lying is lost. It is simply not logical to want everybody to abide by such a rule: if they did, then the very practice that you wish the rule to countenance would be threatened. (There are echoes here of being reprimanded with the phrase 'what if everybody acted in that way'.) So, if it's not OK to lie, we should live by the rule: 'Do not lie.' Such a rule is an example of the synthetic a priori: it is derived using reasoning alone rather than from perceptual experience of the world, and it constitutes a substantive claim about morality, a claim that does not simply follow from the meaning of what it is to lie.

Kant calls the principles that can be derived in this way, 'categorical imperatives'. Hypothetical imperatives prescribe actions that we ought to perform *if* we want to achieve a certain goal or satisfy a certain desire. I ought to revise for my exams if I want to pass. Categorical imperatives, however, prescribe ways we should behave irrespective of what goals or desires we happen to have. One such categorical imperative is 'Do not lie', another is 'Do not commit murder'. I abide by such rules not just so that people trust me, or to avoid going to jail; I abide by them simply because that is how one should act. Similarly, I should not steal someone else's rightful property, humiliate them, or cause them unnecessary emotional or physical pain. (It would be useful here to consider how the universalisability test could be used to derive these categorical imperatives.)

Kant also formulates his moral theory in terms of how we should respect the autonomy of individuals. We should not use other people simply as a means of acquiring things we desire: 'act so that you treat humanity, whether in your own person or in that of another, always as an end and never as a means only' (Kant, 1997, sec. 2). If we lie, this principle is contravened. Let's say that you lie about your age in order to get into a certain club. In doing so, you treat the doorman simply as a means of gaining entry to somewhere desirable. You should, however, treat him as an autonomous agent, one whom you trust to make an informed decision concerning your age. Perhaps he'll let you in because he can see that you will not cause any trouble, or perhaps he is right that you are too young for such places; this, however, is a decision that should be left in his hands.

In section 1.2 we saw that the rule utilitarian also accepts that there are absolute moral principles; for him, though, empirical evidence is required in order to show that there is a correlation between lying, say, and the amount of unhappiness in a community. For Kant, however, such ethical principles can be worked out a priori. Moral knowledge is a priori knowledge: the categorical imperatives can be derived just by thinking about whether it is coherent to want certain rules to be adopted by everybody, and whether particular actions respect the autonomy of individuals.

The difference between Kantian ethics and utilitarianism is illustrated by the film *Saving Private Ryan* (1998). In the Second World War, Ryan is trapped behind enemy lines. Since he is the last surviving son of a mother who has lost her other three sons in the war, a decision is made to send a unit of men to go and get him back. Some of these men are concerned about the mission and express utilitarian thoughts: 'This Private Ryan better . . . cure cancer or invent a light bulb that never . . . burns out, or a car that runs on water'; 'Well, sir, strictly just talking arithmetic here, what's the sense, the strategy, in risking eight lives to save one?' Utilitarianism is only concerned with the consequences of our actions and is thus referred to as a 'consequentialist' theory. It only makes ethical sense to risk eight lives in this way if the one saved life is likely to bring more pleasure to the world than the pain caused by the number of casualties that the mission is likely to sustain. The film, however, can be seen as recommending a Kantian approach. Crucial for Kant is the motivation behind our actions; the consequences that an action may have should not be weighed up when considering its moral worth. This mission is the right one – whatever the risks – because it is motivated by loyalty, comradeship and compassion (motives that everyone should live by).

2.2   Problems for Kant's moral theory

Kant's moral theory also clashes with some of our ethical intuitions. There are cases where his absolute prohibition of certain actions does not seem right. Lying is a good example of this. Surely it is sometimes not only permissible to lie, but it is also the right thing to do. In the film *Amélie*, the eponymous heroine spends most of her time plotting random acts of kindness to strangers. One of these involves forging a letter to a grieving woman, Madeleine, who cannot get over the fact that her husband ran away with his lover and that he is now deceased. The letter purports to be from the husband, and it tells Madeleine that he loves her and that he is returning home. Amélie's plan involves the further deception of claiming that the letter has only recently been found by a team of climbers after a fatal plane crash on Mont Blanc many years before. Madeleine can now have closure and she is once again able to get on with her life. The letter, however, contains lies and thus, according to Kant, Amélie's act is morally wrong. It would seem, though, that the consequences of Amélie's actions allow them to be seen as morally praiseworthy. Here, then, Kant's moral theory is not in line with our moral intuitions.

A further problem for Kant is that there could be scenarios in which you are called to uphold more than one moral rule; rules, however, that may clash. Imagine you bump into a mad axeman in the street, blood dripping from his axe; he asks you where your friend lives and says that he intends to go and kill him. What should you do? As we have seen, Kant claims that you should *never* lie; you should therefore obey the axeman's request. First, this is clearly counter to our ethical intuitions: surely the right thing to do here would be to lie. Second, even if you accept Kant's total prohibition on lying, you will nevertheless contravene another categorical imperative, that being: do not willingly endanger the life of another person. You can either protect your friend and lie, or not lie and endanger his life. Whatever you do, you will have to break one moral rule; Kant's theory is therefore unworkable.

It is easy to be pulled in opposite directions by the two ethical theories that we have looked at and by the scenarios that are put forward in support of them. It does seem right that the motivation behind our actions is morally important, and that there are certain actions that are reprehensible whatever the consequences. There is, however, 'a point . . . at which purism becomes moral frivolity' (B. Williams, 1995, p. 554): if enough lives are saved as a result of certain unpalatable actions, then utilitarian principles start to look more attractive. If you really could put an end to world starvation and poverty by slapping an innocent child, then what should you do? According to Kant, you should never punish an innocent person. That would be treating her as a means of attaining a certain goal; she should, however, be treated as an end in herself, and *she* does not deserve such punishment. In such a situation, though, Kantianism is hard to sustain: it is not hard to see how you could be tempted to act in such a way, and how it could also be claimed that this is the right thing to do.

We have looked at two ethical theories, one involving empirical justification, and one that can be derived a priori. Let us now turn to the other key source of knowledge – testimony – and consider how this might be related to moral knowledge.

3 Moral Testimony

As with empirical matters, the acquisition of moral beliefs very often involves testimony. This is so for particular ethical claims – Ken can tell me that Rita's new husband is a bad man; and also for more general ethical principles – the Church Council can argue that the cloning of human embryos is wrong. We do not just accept what anybody says about such matters. Concerning the former, we would have to believe that Ken was a good judge of moral character, and with the latter we would perhaps demand more: our informants would need to have a certain amount of expertise in the relevant empirical issues and have devoted a fair amount of time to the consideration of their moral dimension. That we acquire moral beliefs in this way is undeniable; the key question, however, is whether such beliefs are justified. Here we are not concerned with cases where we are prompted to think for ourselves about Rita's husband or cloning, but rather cases where we simply come to accept someone else's word. Can I have justified moral beliefs simply in virtue of acquiring them from someone else who has moral knowledge of these matters?

In chapter 4 it was accepted that testimony provides justification for our empirical beliefs, and the debate on which we focused concerned just how this was so. We considered two accounts, those of Hume and Reid. With respect to moral testimony, the Humean line would be that we are justified in accepting someone's word on moral matters if we have evidence that they have been a reliable moral judge in the past. Those, however, who favour Reid's approach would claim that we have a prima facie right to accept moral testimony unless we are aware of factors that defeat such justification, such as past episodes in which the moral verdicts of a certain thinker have been suspect. We shall not revisit this debate here; the question that shall concern us is whether there is any special reason to think that testimony cannot provide the requisite justification for moral knowledge.

Bernard Williams (1972) claims that it is intuitively obvious that we cannot justifiably accept someone's word on a moral matter without reasoning the issue through for ourselves (whether that reasoning is based on Kantian or utilitarian principles). This is in some ways persuasive; I shall claim, however, that the grounds on which Williams's intuition is based do not give us any *epistemic* reason to doubt that we can acquire justified ethical beliefs via testimony. I shall first criticize an argument that could be seen as supporting Williams's claim; second, I shall look at an important consideration in favour of moral testimony; and third, following Robert Hopkins (2004), I shall consider the claim that there are moral and not epistemic reasons lying behind the intuition that there is something wrong with accepting someone's word on a moral issue.

First, then, let us look at a line of argument that specifically applies to a priori moral theories such as that of Kant. Perhaps there is a general problem with testimony concerning the a priori; in order to acquire a priori knowledge we may be obliged to work through the reasoning behind such truths ourselves. Williams claims that this is so for the a priori discipline of mathematics: if you are to have a justified mathematical belief about a certain formula, you have to be able to show how that formula is derived or how it can be proved. On reflection, however, such a constraint seems far too strong. This can be shown by looking at a variety of cases. First, I would like to say that I know that Pythagoras' Theorem is true; after all, I can use this theorem to work out the length of wood I shall need to make a brace for my shelf. I do not, however, know the proof for this theorem or how it can be derived. Second, even such claims as $2+2=4$ are derived from simpler mathematical truths – Peano's axioms; not many of us, though, know how this is done, yet surely we are justified in believing that such sums are correct. Third, the proofs for certain mathematical truths cannot be performed by anybody. This is true of the four-colour theorem which states that it is possible for any map to be coloured in using only four colours, with no adjacent shapes having the same colour. This conjecture has been proved by a computer using algorithms that are beyond the abilities of both the layman and the mathematician. If Williams's claim is correct, then it would follow that no one has a justified belief about this theorem. To say that we do not have justified beliefs in these three kinds of cases is highly unintuitive and – to answer question 3 of chapter 5 – it seems right to say that we can acquire (at least some) a priori knowledge via testimony, and thus the (alleged) fact that ethics is an a priori discipline cannot be seen as a reason to be sceptical about the justificatory role of moral testimony.

There is also an area of moral discourse where it would be hard to deny that we are justified in accepting moral testimony, and that is moral education. From an early age we are taught what is right and wrong. Furthermore, at such an age we do not have the resources to think it through for ourselves whether kicking the cat is a bad thing to do, or whether we should thank Grandma for her Christmas present. Early moral education can be a piecemeal affair, and it is not until later that we can be said to grasp the principles or reasoning behind our moral beliefs. It would be implausible to claim that a child cannot come to know that it is wrong to steal until she can work out why this is so for herself (using, perhaps, Kant's categorical imperative or the hedonic calculus). It would seem that when we first acquire moral beliefs, we are justified in simply accepting what others say, others, that is, who have moral knowledge themselves. If this is so, then we have all at some time acquired moral knowledge via testimony.

We haven't therefore found any epistemic reasons why we cannot justifiably accept moral testimony. There is, however, another way of accounting for the intuitive force behind the claim that all ethical verdicts must be thought through for oneself. Perhaps there is some *moral* failing in not doing so: I have acted unethically if I simply accept what Ken says about the moral standing of Rita's new husband. This claim is somewhat plausible if I consider my reaction to someone who asks me why I have this particular ethical belief. I would feel some kind of embarrassment if I could only say that I believe he is bad because Ken told me. Have I not done something wrong here – something ethically wrong – since I have neglected my moral duty to work out rationally the moral standing of this individual for myself? Let us, then, leave this section with this rather tentative conclusion: we have not found any epistemic grounds on which to question the justificatory status of moral testimony; nevertheless, there may be something morally suspect in simply accepting what others say on such matters.

4 Moral Scepticism

So far in this chapter we have been looking at how our ethical beliefs might be justified. Some, however, have a nagging doubt that there is something insubstantial about moral issues. We shall look at two kinds of approach that take this line. First, that of the relativist, who claims that morality is not an objective matter. Second, we shall consider emotivism; this is a form of moral scepticism which claims that we do not have beliefs concerning moral matters, and that we do not therefore have moral knowledge.

4.1 Relativism

Objective truths are those that do not depend on what individuals say or think about the matter. The number of craters on the dark side of the moon is objective in this way. There is a determinate answer to this question whether or not anyone ever works out what it is. When statements are subjective, however, their truth does depend on the thoughts and reactions of particular individuals or communities. I may think that baked beans taste fantastic. This, however, is simply a subjective fact about my taste and not an objective fact about the world. Statements can also be subjective with respect to the views of a community or culture. The comedy series *Seinfeld* (1989–98) is funny; this, however, is because we all think so and not because of any objective fact that is independent of our tastes and reactions to the world. In this section we shall consider the claim that ethical statements and beliefs are subjective in this way.

One line of argument to this conclusion follows from the fact that different cultures appear to have different values. The French eat horses; the English, however, think this is ethically dubious. In Utah, Mormon men are allowed to have more than one wife; in New York, though, this is not considered right. The bigoted response to such cultural differences is to claim that *our* ways are right and that everyone else is wrong. A more enlightened approach, however, is to allow such variety to breed tolerance for the ethical viewpoints of other cultures. Who am I to say that the French and the Mormons are wrong. A consequence of this seemingly enlightened stance is that we are accepting that ethical matters are not objective. There are actions that are right for those in Utah, and those that are right in New York: the truth of ethical beliefs is relative to the views of the particular culture in question.

However, this argument for relativism is invalid. The claim is that there are no objective ethical truths because different cultures have different ethical values. We can see that this is a bad argument by looking at other areas of inquiry. Different cultures do not agree on the existence of God, or on the causes of the weather, but this does not entail that there are no objective facts about such matters. Relativism does not follow from cultural diversity. There may, however, be other reasons to doubt the objectivity of ethics. With respect to the weather, we have some idea about how we might resolve disputes over the causes of meteorological phenomena. We could perhaps persuade a primitive tribe that our scientific explanation of the weather is better than their explanation involving demons and spirits; we could do this by demonstrating that our account provides better forecasts, ones that give more accurate predictions. (We shall consider disputes concerning the existence of God in the next chapter.) With respect to ethics, however, it is not clear how we could persuade someone that our ethical view is the correct one or how we might try to arrive at ethical agreement. Even when it has been explained why we think a certain action is wrong, the option appears to be open for those of a different culture to say 'Now we understand why you see it that way, but we simply disagree; that's not how we look at things here.'

It was suggested that an attractive feature of relativism is that it encourages a tolerant attitude towards other cultures. We must be careful to note, though, that a relativist cannot say that this is an objectively good thing, or that it is an attitude that all cultures should adopt towards one another. If you are a relativist, tolerance is no more objectively correct than jeering at another culture, or trying to convert them to your ways. The relativist cannot be allowed to claim that his view has certain virtues – such as an objectively correct tolerant attitude towards others – that, by his own lights, cannot be possessed. More worrying, however, is that relativists cannot criticize other cultures, however extreme they may be. According to relativism, the Nazi persecution of the Jews cannot be seen as objectively wrong: to us it was, but to the Nazi it was right, and there is no higher court of appeal, no objective moral verdict on their actions. Such relativism strikes us as not only epistemically wrong, but also as morally suspect. We do not think that Nazism is just averse *to us*; tolerance – in this case – has lost its ethical appeal.

A distinct way of attacking moral relativism is to claim that there is not as much cultural diversity as may first appear, and that there are certain values shared by all communities. Cultures do differ in some of their ethical beliefs, but this may be due to differences in the empirical beliefs that they have, rather than to differences in their ethical principles. The Nazis may have shared our view that it is wrong to exterminate innocent people; to support their actions, however, they claimed that their victims were subhuman and that they should not be seen as people. Such a claim is of course abhorrent, but it is not in itself an ethical view; it is simply an empirical belief about those who are Jewish. We can also see how such a line could be taken with respect to the apparently distinct ethical views held by the opposing sides in the debate over abortion. Everyone agrees it is wrong to kill a child. Some, however – the pro-abortionists – do not think that the foetus has such a status; it is simply an unconscious bundle of cells, not yet developed enough to be considered a person. Perhaps, then, there are certain universal values common to all cultures, values that should not be seen as merely relative to the practices and beliefs of a particular community.

4.2   Emotivism

According to the relativist, we do have ethical beliefs that represent certain acts as wrong and others as right. Such beliefs may not concern objective moral truths, but they represent the moral status that particular cultures take actions to have. Ways of thinking that are representational are called 'cognitive'. Some, however, have claimed that ethical thought is not representational; it is non-cognitive. In talking of such matters we are not reporting our beliefs; our moral discourse has a different purpose – it expresses our emotions. In saying that murder is wrong, we are merely expressing our disapproval; a hiss or a boo would have sufficed. In saying that famine relief is good, we are merely expressing our approval; a cheer would have said as much. Praising an action as morally worthy is akin to sighing as you eat a peach, rather than to articulating your belief that the peach is delicious. Such an approach to ethics is called 'emotivism', 'expressivism' or the 'boo-hooray theory'. It is a sceptical approach since moral 'judgements' are not descriptions of the world at all; they are simply emotional reactions we have to our fellows, and we do not therefore have moral beliefs or moral knowledge.

As well as seeing the actions of people in moral terms, we also regularly engage in ethical debate. You may attempt to convince someone that your position on animal welfare is the right one, or that Rita's husband is not as bad as everyone takes him to be. Such discussion is also carried out on a larger scale. The British government recently attempted to convince the British people that going to war in Iraq was the ethically right thing to do; indeed, that it was our duty. On both the personal and national level, arguments are put forward to persuade others of the legitimacy and objective truth of a certain moral stance. According to emotivism, however, arguments to the effect that Saddam Hussein was an evil dictator are no such thing; they are merely an appeal to the emotional distaste we may have for this man. Arguments in favour of pre-emptive action are merely cheers in favour of war. Ethical arguments amount to mere clashes of feeling. This, however, does not seem right; rather, 'the traditional moral concepts of the ordinary man as well as of the main line of Western philosophers are concepts of objective value' (Mackie, 1977, p. 35), and it is the possession of such value that is the focus of dispute in ethical debate.

There are therefore problems with the broadly sceptical views we have looked at in this section. Perhaps, then, we should try to resolve our competing intuitions concerning the moral theories of the utilitarian and Kant. Theirs are both non-sceptical approaches, approaches that provide objective criteria for our ethical beliefs. According to utilitarianism, ethics is grounded in naturalistic facts concerning pleasure and pain; according to Kant, we can come to agree on a moral issue through a priori reasoning. The following questions may help clarify your views on which of these ethical theories, if any, is the most persuasive.

Questions

1 It has been claimed that Winston Churchill knew in advance that the Luftwaffe were about to bomb Coventry in the Second World War. This fact was not revealed because, if it had been, the Germans would have known that we had cracked the Enigma Code and this would have resulted in them gaining a strategic advantage on the Western Front and possibly victory. Discuss whether Churchill's decision was ethically correct.
2 Devise a screenplay for a film that would illustrate the moral theory you find most satisfying.
3 What is the source of moral knowledge?
4 Formulate a utilitarian and a Kantian argument against abortion. What do your conclusions tell you about abortion and about moral knowledge? (Repeat this question but with reference to another moral dilemma that is currently in the news.)
5 How could it be argued that we do not have moral knowledge? Are the arguments persuasive?

Further Reading

The classic utilitarian and Kantian approaches to ethics can be found in Mill (1998), Bentham (1970), and Kant (1997). Blackburn's (2001) *Being Good* is an interesting introduction to ethics, and useful textbooks include Scarre (1996) on utilitarianism, Sullivan (1994) on Kant, and Rachels (1986) and Singer (1993) on ethics in general. Smart and Williams (1973) provide an engaging dialogue for and against utilitarianism. Ayer (1990) forcibly argues for emotivism, and sophisticated critiques of this approach can be found in Smith (1984) and Miller (2003). Ladd (1973) contains a good collection of articles on ethical relativism. Lawrence Hinman's 'EthicsUpdates' website is excellent: it includes streamed videos on utilitarianism and Kant, and links to e-texts and further relevant websites (http://ethics.acusd.edu).

A version of Dostoyevsky's torture scenario can be found in Ursula Le Guin's (2000a) 'The Ones Who Walk Away from Omelas'. The success and harmony of the city Omelas depend on an innocent baby being confined in a squalid room. Implicit criticism of utilitarianism is given when some of the city dwellers walk away from their comfortable life. Utilitarian themes can also be found in Huxley's *Brave New World* (1932), Gunn's *The Joy Makers* (1984), and the films *The Life of David Gale* (2003) and *Run Lola Run* (1998). *Extreme Measures* (1996) explores the debate between utilitarianism and Kantianism. The Kantian claim that the motivation behind an action is paramount underlies the actions of Marshall Kane in the Western *High Noon* (1952). He knows it is his moral duty to wait for the return of the outlaws even though there is a good chance this will result in his own death. Card's science fiction novel *Speaker for the Dead* (1994) illustrates ethical relativism: the distinctive biology of a community of aliens entails that they have an ethical system that differs from ours, yet it is one that can plausibly be defended. Singer and Singer (2005) is an excellent anthology of fiction, drama and poetry relevant to various ethical issues.

# 15 God

Today and throughout the ages many millions of people have believed in some kind of supernatural being who created the universe. The philosophy of religion is (in part) concerned with whether such a belief is justified. However, before turning to issues of justification, we should clarify just what we mean by 'God'. For the purposes of this chapter we shall be talking about the kind of God that is worshipped by the monotheistic religions of Judaism, Christianity, and Islam. This is an intelligent God, one who is able to suspend the laws of nature, and who can intervene from time to time in human affairs. Such an entity is omnipotent (able to do anything), omniscient (knows everything), perfectly good, and eternal. Various arguments or proofs have been put forward for the existence of God; in section 1 we shall consider an a priori argument, and in section 2, two that are empirical.

1 An A Priori Proof for the Existence of God: The Ontological Argument

The ontological argument dates back to St Anselm in the eleventh century, and has had many incarnations since. We shall look at Descartes's version. His argument starts from the premise that we have an idea of God. That's not to say that we necessarily believe that He exists; the claim is simply that we have thoughts about such an entity. If we examine these thoughts we find that we think of God as a perfect being, or as a being who possesses all the perfections. We think of God as infinitely powerful, absolutely good, and as having complete knowledge. Now, to actually exist in reality is better – it is more perfect – than to be simply an object of thought, and thus, if God is all perfect, He must actually exist. Since God has all the perfections:

> existence can no more be separated from the essence of God than the fact that its three angles equal two right angles can be separated from the essence of a triangle, or than the idea of a mountain can be separated from the idea of a valley . . . From the fact that I cannot think of God except as existing, it follows that existence is inseparable from God, and hence that he really exists. (Descartes, 1986, p. 46)

Using a priori reasoning, Descartes claims to have shown that God necessarily exists. This is an example of the synthetic a priori (chapter 3, section 3), a substantive conclusion about the nature of reality arrived at using reasoning alone. (Descartes actually provides two arguments for the existence of God, but it is only the ontological argument that we shall look at here.)

Before turning to the problems with this argument, we should remind ourselves of its place in Descartes's overall epistemology. Although the kind of global scepticism we looked at in chapter 9 is called 'Cartesian', Descartes himself is not a sceptic. As we have just seen, Descartes claims that he can prove that God exists; and, since God is good, He would not allow man to be deceived by the demon, or, for that matter, by evil scientists and their vats. We do therefore have empirical knowledge of the world. (Hume, 1999, sec. 12, wryly comments on the unintuitive order of knowledge here: 'To have recourse to the veracity of the supreme Being, in order to prove the veracity of our senses, is surely making a very unexpected circuit.')

Let us consider whether the ontological argument is sound. For most, it is tempting to agree with John Mackie that '[e]ven a would-be **theist** will feel that this is too good to be true' (1982, p. 42). Some kind of conjuring trick seems to have been performed. An objection was put forward by Gaunilo to St Anselm's original argument, and it is an objection that cuts equally against Descartes's version. Gaunilo suggests that we could have an idea of a perfect island (perhaps one with perfect beaches, perfect bars, and a perfect climate). As with the theistic argument, the claim is not that we must believe in the existence of such an island; it's merely that we are able to imagine such a place. However, it is better – more perfect – for an island to exist than not to exist, and so, a perfect island must in fact exist. According to Gaunilo, though, someone who reasoned thus would be a 'fool', and, as the ontological argument has the same structure, such a route to God would also be foolish. If this is so, we must try to uncover where Descartes's reasoning has gone wrong.

A key objection to the ontological argument concerns Kant's claim that 'existence' is not a predicate (Kant, 1998). 'Is hot' and 'is yellow' are predicates, that is, they ascribe properties to things. My coffee has the property of being hot, and my cup has the property of being yellow. Kant claims that the phrase 'exists' does not play such a role; it does not ascribe a property to anything; it only seems to. When we say that 'God exists', we are not providing further information about God in the way that we would be if we were to say that 'God is wise'. What we are actually saying is that there is an entity in the world, an entity that corresponds to the idea we have of God. Existence is not a property of God; it is, rather, that which is necessary if God is to possess all the properties we think of Him as having. Thus, if existence is not a property, it should not be seen as one of the perfections that must be ascribed to God. The ontological argument cannot therefore be run.

Kant's argument has two parts. First, he claims that existence is not a predicate; second, he gives an alternative account of how we should understand the assertion that 'God exists'. It is the second claim that provides the clearest attack on the ontological argument. Kant's first claim does not seem to be correct. 'Exists' can provide us with further information about the subject in question. When watching the credits at the end of the film *Serpico* (1973), we come to know more about the character Frank: we are told that the story is based on fact, and thus that this policeman really exists. It is therefore plausible that existence is a property-ascribing predicate. Kant's second suggestion is more promising. We should accept an alternative reading of what we mean by 'God exists'. This statement should be taken, not as one about God Himself, but as one about the concept GOD. 'Frank Serpico exists' means that the concept FRANK SERPICO has one instance: there is an ex-policeman who attempted to fight corruption in the New York Police Department. 'God exists' means that the concept GOD is instantiated: there is an entity that is all perfect. Existence is not a predicate that applies to God, one that can be added to His list of perfections – a claim that is essential to Descartes's argument – but rather it is a predicate that provides further information about our concept of GOD. The theological question is whether we are entitled to make such a claim about this concept. Are we justified in claiming that there is something in the world that corresponds to GOD? In the following section we shall move on to some empirical arguments that claim we are justified.

2   Empirical Justification for Religious Belief

The ontological argument is a rationalist argument *par excellence*: from the comfort of our armchairs we can prove that there exists in the world an all-powerful God. In this section, however, we shall look at two empiricist arguments. The first claims that God should be seen as the best explanation for certain observable features of reality. The second concerns testimony, and the claim is that religious beliefs are justified by reported cases of miracles.

2.1   The argument from design

Imagine walking in the park and discovering a complex metal object. It is made of many intricate cogs and springs and these move in various regular ways. You would take it that someone had designed this artefact for some purpose and that it had not just fallen together by chance. Now:

> Look round the world: Contemplate the whole and every part of it: you will find it to be nothing but one great machine, subdivided into an infinite number of lesser machines . . . All these various machines, and even their minute parts, are adjusted to each other with an accuracy, which ravishes into admiration all men, who have ever contemplated them. The curious adapting of means to ends, throughout all nature, resembles exactly, though it much exceeds, the production of human contrivance; of human design, thought, wisdom, and intelligence.

> Since therefore the effects resemble each other, we are led to infer, by all the rules of analogy, that the causes also resemble; and that the author of Nature is somewhat similar to the mind of man; though possessed of much larger faculties, proportioned to the grandeur of the work, which he has executed. By this argument, a posteriori . . . do we prove at once the existence of a deity, and his similarity to human mind and intelligence. (Hume, 1998, pt II, p. 15. Note, however, that Hume goes on to criticize this argument.)

The best explanation for the order and complexity of nature is that it was designed to be this way. Regularities in nature are analogous to regularities in the works of man; nature, therefore, must also have been created by an intelligent designer.

Early formulations of this argument focused on biological structures. The human eye and the leaves of trees are perfectly designed for the purposes of vision and photosynthesis; thus they are part of the design plan of the creator. It would be incredible if they were simply the product of chance. Hume, however, suggests that: 'Thought, design, intelligence, such as we discover in men and other animals, is no more than one of the springs and principles of the universe' (Hume, 1998, pt II, p. 19). There may be another source for the order we find in nature. And, a century after Hume, Charles Darwin (1859) shows us what this is: the blind forces of natural selection. It is the Darwinian theory of evolution through natural selection that explains the 'curious adapting of means to ends'. There is a blueprint of the structure of our bodies coded in our DNA. Occasionally certain random mutations in this genetic material lead to structural abnormalities, abnormalities that are usually either of no consequence or detrimental to survival. Sometimes, however, such mutations prove to be useful to an organism and the DNA that codes for them is then passed on through reproduction to the next generation. Gradually, then, advantageous structural features become established in a population. Such features as the human eye are the result of a long chain of such random yet advantageous mutations. Evolution by natural selection provides an explanation for the order and complexity of biology that does not appeal to the foresight of an intelligent designer.

There is, however, an order in nature that cannot be explained by Darwinian evolution, and that is the cosmic order. Richard Swinburne (1968; 1991) appeals to this in his version of the argument from design. The universe has a spatio-temporal order: the various kinds of galaxy contain regular arrangements of astronomical bodies, and all bodies – both large and small – continue to behave according to the laws of nature. Always and everywhere, bodies are attracted to each other through gravitational forces; electric currents produce magnetic fields; and, at atmospheric pressure, water boils at 100°C. Swinburne allows that much of this order can be given a deeper scientific explanation. The spatial order of the universe – that is, the arrangement of the galaxies – can be explained by appealing to the law of gravity. Similarly, some of the laws of nature can be derived from more fundamental laws. The fact that water boils at 100°C can be explained by appealing to physical laws concerning the bonding of H_2O molecules. There are, though, certain laws that cannot be explained in terms of other scientific regularities; these are the fundamental laws of nature. There is some debate within physics concerning which laws these might be, but it is plausible that laws concerning gravity and electromagnetism have such a status. There is a choice with respect to such regularities. It can either be accepted that there is no explanation for why the universe is regular in these ways – it is simply a brute fact about nature – or it can be insisted that there must be some explanation for this order. Swinburne argues that the latter strategy is more satisfying and that the best explanation for the cosmic order is that it was put in place by God.

Opponents of this line claim that it is not clear why such a hypothesis should be seen as more likely than simply the brute existence of regularity. Any explanation will have to leave something unexplained. Swinburne accepts that there is no explanation for the order and complexity of God's mind – *that* is brute. If he is allowed to make such a claim, then that should also be an option for those who would like to offer a scientific explanation all the way down, with the fundamental laws of nature being left as brute (rather than God's mind). The claim would be that 'the solution [to the order found in nature] lies in laws, not in ingenuity' (Mackie, 1982, p. 139).

2.2   The argument from miracles

In part II of this book, a key source of knowledge was found to be testimony, and many see this as providing justification for our religious beliefs. One particularly important form of testimony in this regard is that concerning miracles. Let us first look at what we mean by a 'miracle'. It could be said that it was 'miraculous' that the Apollo 13 mission returned safely to Earth, and that Manchester United scored in the last minute of the 1999 Champions League Final. Such events, though, are not miraculous in the sense in which we shall be interested. They are simply coincidental, highly unlikely, or fortuitous in some way. We shall be concerned with events that are scientifically inexplicable. Miracles, in this sense, are violations of the laws of nature. There are reports of such events in the traditions of many of the major religions of the world. It has been claimed that Hindu statues have cried milk; that Moses parted the Red Sea; and that Jesus walked on water and raised Lazarus from the dead. The claim is that we have good testimonial evidence that such events occurred, and thus good reason to think that at times there has been supernatural intervention in the usually regular course of nature.

2.3   Hume on miracles

Hume argues that there has never been a persuasive report of a miracle. In order to show this, he first turns to the notion of testimony in general and considers how we should go about deciding whether we should believe a particular testimonial report. We should always weigh up the chance of a report being false against the chance of the event actually happening. If the former outweighs the latter, then we should not believe the report; if the latter outweighs the former, then we should accept that the event happened; and if they are as likely as each other, then we should suspend our judgement. This certainly seems plausible. I would not be justified in believing a usually deceitful acquaintance who tells me he has won the lottery; I would, however, be justified in believing my mother if she tells me she went to a concert last night. Note that Hume is working with his reductive account of testimonial justification, although this is a more sophisticated version than the one we looked at in chapter 3. There it was only the past record of the reporter that was taken into consideration; here, though, this is weighed against the objective likelihood of the particular event in question occurring.

Hume applies this decision-making procedure to the special case of testimony concerning miracles. Miracles are events that are counter to the laws of nature; they are therefore as unlikely as any event could be since all our experience has suggested that the laws of nature are universal: the dead have always remained dead, and water has always boiled at 100°C. Importantly, a believer in miracles also has to concede that such events are highly unlikely; it is precisely this fact which indicates that their source must be a supernatural being such as God. In a particular case, then, we must compare this very small chance of the miraculous event actually happening with the chance of the report being false. Hume claims that we would only be justified in believing in the occurrence of a miracle if the latter probability was less than the former, that is, if false testimony is less likely than the violation of a law of nature.

Let us, for example, consider whether or not we should believe that Jesus raised Lazarus from the dead. This is a miraculous event since it is counter to the law of nature that the dead stay dead. It is therefore a highly unlikely event because we have never had experience of this law of nature being contravened. We must weigh this very small probability against the chance that the biblical testimony is false. The latter may be unlikely because the writers of the Gospels were known to be honest and reliable, but we do know of cases where reliable onlookers have been tricked by a clever illusionist, and cases in which usually honest people have lied. This is not to accuse the protagonists in this case; the claim is only that such deceit is not as unlikely as a law of nature being broken. There is at least some precedent for deceit, but none for resurrection.

Hume then goes on to suggest that there are various empirical reasons why testimony concerning miracles is likely to be false. People are often titillated by the fantastic and seemingly inexplicable; they are therefore only too open to the belief that there must be a supernatural explanation for certain phenomena. For various reasons, people often desire that God exists and such a desire can induce them to believe even if the evidence in favour is not good. Hume also claims (controversially) that reports of miracles are usually only heard in 'ignorant and barbarous nations'. Given these kinds of considerations, there is always more chance of a particular testimonial report being mistaken than of the miraculous event actually happening. After all, miracles are as unlikely as any event can be, and however reliable your witnesses may seem, the chance that they are mistaken cannot be as unlikely as this. Hume suggests that his argument should be seen as an 'everlasting check on all kinds of superstition and delusion', and, rather pointedly (and with irony), that some people actually do have evidence for miraculous happenings: 'whoever is moved by *faith* to assent to [the Christian religion], is conscious of a continued miracle in his own person, which subverts all the principles of his understanding' (1999, sec. 10.41). For Hume, those who believe in God simply because they have faith in His existence – and not because they have good reason to – are prey to a defect in their thinking, a defect that leads them astray from their usually reliable, everyday canons of proper reasoning. Hume jokes that thinking in this way is miraculous since it is such a bizarre, out of character and unusual thing to do (although, of course, it is not miraculous in the sense of being counter to the laws of nature).

3 Perceiving God

Plantinga (2000) and William Alston (1991) argue that belief in God can be justified by religious or mystical experiences. In the empirical arguments above, certain evidence is presented, evidence from which we can infer God's existence using reasoned argument. Such evidence consists in the observable order of nature, and in testimonial reports of miracles. Here, though, we shall be interested in the kinds of experience where it is claimed that thinkers have a direct, non-inferential acquaintance with God. Such experiences do not figure as premises in arguments. 'The ordinary religious believer . . . professes, not to have inferred that there is a God, but that God as a living being has entered into his own experience' (Hick, 1966, p. 95).

I have never had such an experience, but many claim that they have. Here is a description of one recorded by William James:

> all at once I . . . felt the presence of God – I tell of the thing just as I was conscious of it – as if his power were penetrating me altogether . . . I think it well to add that in this ecstasy of mine God had neither form, color, odor, nor taste; moreover, that the feeling of his presence was accompanied by no determinate localization . . . At bottom the

expression most apt to render what I felt is this: God was present, though invisible; he fell under no one of my senses, yet my consciousness perceived him. (1999, pp. 67–8)

According to Plantinga and Alston, certain religious beliefs should be seen as basic in the foundationalist sense. They are non-inferentially justified; justified not through the possession of reasons that can be articulated, but through their grounding in religious experience. Let us remind ourselves of the foundationalist approach to justification. Traditional foundationalists claim that our basic beliefs are infallible, and that they concern such immediate experiences as that 'I now seem to be seeing a red shape'. Religious beliefs, however, should not be seen as basic in this sense; they are not infallible. Instead, a position akin to modest foundationalism is adopted. Our basic religious beliefs have prima facie justification: they are justified unless we are aware of evidence to suggest that they are not true. Thus: 'a claim to be perceiving God is prima facie acceptable just on its own merits, pending any sufficient reasons to the contrary' (Alston, 1991, p. 67). We have called such an approach 'modest foundationalism'; Plantinga calls it 'reformed epistemology'. According to traditional foundationalism, our religious beliefs are not basic and they must therefore be justified via inference, with their justification ultimately grounded in our basic (non-religious) perceptual experience. However, according to reformed epistemology, religious beliefs can be seen as properly basic. They are grounded in experience – our mystical, religious experience – just as our basic perceptual beliefs are grounded in perceptual experience. Swinburne (1991) supports such a view. He advocates the principle of credulity: we should accept that both our sensory experience and our religious experience are veridical unless we have reasons to doubt them. The burden of proof is on the sceptic to show that there are such reasons.

From time to time people do have such (seemingly) religious experiences, and sometimes these lead to the acquisition of religious belief. However, it can be claimed that there is a better explanation for such experiences than one that cites our direct acquaintance with a supernatural being. The claim is that they have a perfectly naturalistic, psychological explanation. Research into near-death experiences can provide support for such a suggestion. There have been many reports of those close to death having the experience of moving down a tunnel towards a bright light. According to the principle of credulity, such people have prima facie justification for their belief that they are experiencing the gateway to the afterlife. There is, however, an alternative explanation that defeats such justification. Empirical research has shown that the physical state of hypoxaemia leads to feelings of euphoria and tunnel vision, experiences that perfectly match the reported 'religious' ones. Hypoxaemia is caused by low concentrations of oxygen in the blood, and can be suffered by those close to death.

Also consider the following description of a religious experience.

> I could feel the impression, like a wave of electricity, going through
> and through me. Indeed, it seemed to come in waves and waves of
> liquid love; for I could not express it in any other way. (James, 1999,
> p. 250)

The reformed epistemologist would claim that this experience should
be taken to provide prima facie justification for the belief that such a
thinker has a direct acquaintance with the love of God. However, such a
description is strikingly similar to those given by people who have
taken the drug Ecstasy or MDMA. There is therefore a plausible alternative explanation for such an experience, that is, that it is caused by
chemical happenings in the brain akin to those experienced by takers
of Ecstasy. Such psychological explanations could be seen as better
explanations since no appeal is made to mystical processes and
entities; a naturalistic account of physical mechanisms will suffice.
Alston, however, is unmoved by such a suggestion. He maintains that
we have a sixth sense, one that is sensitive to the perceptible properties
of God, the operation of which is accompanied by the phenomenology
characteristic of mystical, religious experience. 'Why suppose that the
possibilities of experiential givenness, for human beings or otherwise,
are exhausted by the powers of *our* five senses?' (Alston, 1991, p. 17).

4　Pascal's Wager

In sections 1 and 2 of this chapter the burden of proof was taken to be
on the believer: it is up to the theist to provide arguments to persuade
the non-believer to adopt his position. Arguments are required because
'it is wrong, always, everywhere, and for anyone to believe anything
upon insufficient evidence' (Clifford, 2003, p. 518). In section 3, an
opposing position was considered: it was suggested that religious
beliefs are justified even in the absence of such argument. In this
section, however, we shall look at a rather different kind of consideration; it will be argued that there are pragmatic or prudential reasons to
believe in God even though there may not be good epistemic grounds
for such a belief.

Writing in 1660 Blaise Pascal claims that acquiring belief in God is
akin to a gamble, and that in order to decide whether you should
believe in Him, you should perform a cost-benefit analysis. Believing in
God brings with it some minor inconveniences: you must go to church
on Sunday and sing more hymns than you are used to. If this belief in
God is misguided, then such activity has been a waste of time and you
could have perhaps filled your Sundays more profitably. However, if this
belief is true – if there is a God – then the pay-off is enormous: an everlasting life in paradise. '[I]f you win you win everything; if you lose you
lose nothing. Do not hesitate then; wager that he does exist' (Pascal,
1966, §418). Pascal claims that a rational gambler should bet on there

being a God. He admits that you cannot simply choose to believe in God, with or without any supporting evidence. You can, however, choose courses of action that may help you to cultivate your religious beliefs. You should avoid books on the Philosophy of Religion written by known non-believers; you should attend religious services performed in the most impressive, inspiring cathedrals or mosques; and you should seek to find intelligent and interesting friends who are believers. If you act in these ways, then you may find yourself acquiring religious belief. There may only be a small chance that God exists, but the rewards available to those who believe in Him outweigh the unlikeliness of those beliefs being true. The situation is akin to the following. Before Wimbledon you are asked to bet one penny on the Ladies Singles tennis tournament. If you bet on the favourite, Venus Williams, and she wins, then your stake is returned. If you bet on the British outsider and she wins, then you receive 1 million pounds. Any sensible gambler should bet on the long shot.

There are, however, problems with this approach. It is not clear that God would favour those who took Pascal's wager since they do not have the right kind of virtues. Surely God will be looking for the pious believer and the one who is not concerned with the long-term benefits of his beliefs, rather than for the clever gambler who is only concerned with the jackpot prize. It would also be strange for such a gambler to be favoured over the good and virtuous non-believer, one who has simply not found any persuasive evidence for the existence of God. A more fundamental problem with Pascal's strategy concerns the kind of justification it involves. There is a sense in which such a believer would be justified: a pragmatic sense. However, this kind of justification does not have an *epistemic* role. The claim is merely that we shall benefit if our religious beliefs turn out to be true, not that we have good reason to think that they are. If this is the only kind of justification that our religious beliefs can have, then even though they may be true, we shall not have *knowledge* of God.

5   Scepticism, Atheism and Agnosticism

Those who are sceptical about whether we can have knowledge of God are called 'atheists'; their claim is that religious beliefs are false and unjustified. Another type of thinker who is often discussed in relation to religious belief is the agnostic. Agnostics agree with the atheist that we do not have justification for our beliefs concerning God; they also, however, stress that we cannot prove that God does not exist. We should therefore be non-committal and suspend our judgement. It is not clear, though, whether such a position is stable, or, as a student of mine nicely put it: 'agnosticism is a bit lame'. We have many beliefs that we cannot *prove* are correct; nevertheless, we have accepted a fallibilist conception of justification: one approach at which we have looked claims that our beliefs are justified if they provide the best explanation for the phenomena in question (see chapter 13, section 7). Perhaps, then, atheism should be assessed accordingly. We may not be able to prove that God doesn't exist, but a Godless universe may provide the best explanation of our experience. The atheist advocates a wholly naturalistic worldview, and he claims that he needs to be given good reasons to supplement his ontology with the supernatural, or to weaken his view to that of the agnostic. The atheist's position should be seen as the default and the onus is on the theist and the agnostic to persuade him otherwise. When asked what he would do if his atheistic beliefs were wrong and he were face to face with his creator at Judgment Day, the trenchant atheist, Bertrand Russell said, 'I would say, Lord, you should have given us more evidence.'

In chapter 9 we discussed whether it was possible to *live* Cartesian scepticism, that is, to accept that our empirical beliefs are not justified and to live a coherent life in the shadow of this. It has been claimed that there is also a problem here for the atheist – can atheism be *lived*? – and many great works of art and literature have focused on those who struggle with this question. It has firstly been suggested that 'If God is dead, then everything is permitted' (this is one of the themes of Dostoyevsky's *Crime and Punishment*); without God there can be no morality. This, however, is far too quick a conclusion. In the previous chapter we looked at various attempts to show that our ethical views are justified, none of which made reference to God. Even more fundamentally, though, others have thought that without God their life can have no meaning, and that a life simply followed by death is paralysingly empty. This view is expressed in a scene from Bergman's *The Seventh Seal* (1957) in which a medieval knight talks to the hooded figure of Death.

> Knight: I want knowledge! Not faith, not assumptions, but knowledge. I want God to stretch out His hand, uncover His face and speak to me.
> Death: But He remains silent.
> Knight: I call out to Him in the darkness. But it's as if no one was there.
> Death: Perhaps there isn't anyone.
> Knight: Then life is a preposterous horror. No man can live faced with death, knowing everything's nothingness.

Questions concerning the meaning of life, and whether one can be found in the absence of God, are beyond the scope of this book, but to finish I shall leave you with some rather more optimistic thoughts from the philosophers (and long-term companions) Jean-Paul Sartre and Simone de Beauvoir. Sartre near the end of his life claimed:

> [Atheism] has strengthened my freedom and made it sounder . . . I don't need God to love my neighbour. It's a direct relation between men and man . . . my acts have made up my life, my life, which is going to end . . . This life owes nothing to God; it was what I wanted it to be . . . and when now I reflect on it, it satisfies me; and I do not need to refer to God for that . . . The true relation with oneself is with that

> which we really are, and not with that self we have formed roughly in our own shape . . . You [de Beauvoir] and I . . . have lived without paying attention to [God] . . . And yet we've lived; we feel that we've taken an interest in our world and that we've tried to see and understand it. (De Beauvoir, 1981, pp. 444–5)

And, after Sartre's death, de Beauvoir wrote:

> His death does separate us. My death will not bring us together again. It is in itself splendid that we were able to live in harmony for so long. (1981, p. 127)

Questions

1 Assess the following claim made by Michael Dummett, a leading philosopher of language:

> I'm not saying that pursuit of these ideas about . . . [the philosophy of language] would lead to atheistic conclusions, but if they were to do so, although it would be uncomfortable for me, I don't think it would matter very much. My religious belief would tell me I must have made a mistake somewhere. (Pyle, 1999, p. 6)

2 Does Hume think that miracles are impossible?
3 What reasons might we have for doubting someone's testimony concerning miracles?
4 Your theology teacher is an atheist, yet he teaches you the ontological and the design argument for the existence of God. If your teacher's own beliefs are false, and God does exist, can his testimony lead to you acquiring knowledge of God? (See chapter 4, question 5.)
5 In a Catholic Mass, a friend of mine heard a beautiful high-pitched voice accompanying a hymn, but on looking around could see no one there with this voice. Later she was told by the priest that others have heard such a voice (although he never had). Should such an experience be taken as providing justification for my friend's religious beliefs?
6 Can you *live* atheism? Can life really be splendid if there is no God?

Further Reading

The original ontological argument appears in St Anselm's *Proslogion* of 1077–8 (Anselm, 1979); Descartes's is in his *Meditations* of 1641 (1986: 'Fifth Meditation'); and a contemporary version is given in Plantinga's *The Nature of Necessity* (1974). Oppy (1995) provides a good survey of the various versions of the argument. The classic presentation of the argument from design can be found in William Paley's *Natural Theology* of 1800 (Paley, 1826a). Objections to both the ontological argument and the design argument are discussed in Hume's *Dialogues Concerning Natural Religion* of 1779, and he considers miracles in his *Enquiry* of 1748 (sec. 10). This latter discussion has prompted much interest: Earman (2000) and Johnson (1999) find fault with his argument, and Fogelin (2003) endorses it. The best collection of reported religious experiences is James's *The Varieties of Religious Experience* of 1902. A good introductory overview of the various arguments for God is given by Hick (1964); and some excellent textbooks include Mackie's *The Miracle of Theism* (1982), Everitt's *The Non-Existence of God* (2004), and Swinburne's *The Existence of God* (1991) (Swinburne is a believer; Mackie and Everitt are not). A useful web resource is www.philosophyofreligion.info/.

Various movies intersect with some of the topics we have covered. Bergman's loose trilogy of *Through a Glass Darkly* (1961), *Winter Light* (1963) and *The Silence* (1963) concerns faith and religious experience; in the first of the trilogy, Karin claims to have an experience of God, a God who takes the form of a spider (the alternative explanation is that this is a schizophrenic hallucination). *Agnes of God* (1985) considers testimony concerning miracles. An episode of *The Simpsons* is also relevant to our discussion (episode 908: 'Lisa the Skeptic', 1997). The children of Springfield Elementary School discover a strange winged skeleton which they believe is that of an angel. Lisa, however, tries to convince the town otherwise, although even she becomes a little unsure when the 'angel' speaks. I'll leave you to track down the episode if you would like to find out whether Lisa was right to be sceptical.

Glossary

anti-realist Realists about things and properties claim that their existence is independent of the existence of minds or thinkers. I am a realist with respect to the sun because I think that it would still be there whether or not thinking creatures had evolved on this planet or anywhere else in the universe. Anti-realists, however, claim that certain kinds of things or properties do depend on the existence of thinkers. It has been claimed by some anti-realists that morality depends on our emotional responses (see chapter 14, section 4.2), and that all 'physical' objects depend on the perceptual experiences of thinkers (see chapter 4, section 3).

begging the question or 'question begging' To beg the question is to assume what you are trying to prove. In philosophical discussion this phrase does not mean pose, raise or invite the question.

concepts To possess a concept is to be able to think about a certain aspect of the world. I can think of the stuff outside my window as grass, as green, as wet, and as alive; to think in these ways I require the concepts GRASSS, GREEN, WET, and ALIVE. (I have adopted the convention of putting the names of concepts in small capitals.) Possessing the concept GREEN enables me to recognize green things and to distinguish green from other colours; this concept is also necessary for various kinds of thought, e.g. the concept GREEN enables me to *believe* that green is my favourite colour, to *desire* that green shirt, and to *hope* that my gooseberries will soon turn green.

conditionals A conditional is a statement of the form 'if A, then B', e.g. 'if Scotland win, then I will eat my hat'.

counterfactual Counterfactual situations are ways the world would have been if things had been different from how they are. There are counterfactual scenarios in which I am the England cricket captain, and you are the king of France.

deductive reasoning see **inference**

disposition A disposition is a tendency to act in a certain way or to be affected in a certain way by your experience. On passing a fish and chip shop I am disposed to buy a potato scallop. This is only a *tendency* because I only act in this way if certain other conditions are satisfied, e.g. I must not be on a diet.

dualism   Dualism or substance dualism is a philosophy of mind which claims that humans are made up of two distinct kinds of thing: mind and matter. Minds are non-physical; they cannot be described or investigated by the physical sciences. Descartes is a dualist and his argument for this position can be found in his 6th *Meditation* of 1641.

eliminativists   Eliminativists claim that certain things or properties do not exist and that our theorizing need take no account of them. The term usually refers to a certain kind of philosopher of mind. Eliminativists in the philosophy of mind claim that we do not have beliefs and desires, and that a complete account of the mind need only make reference to neurophysiological properties of the brain. I shall use the term to talk about epistemologists who eliminate the notion of justification from their theory of knowledge.

incorrigible   A belief is incorrigible if no one else can make you correct or change that belief. It is plausible that beliefs about your own sensations are incorrigible: I would still believe that I'm in pain even if my doctor says that there's nothing wrong with me.

indubitable   A belief is indubitable if it cannot be doubted. Incorrigible and indubitable beliefs are not necessarily infallible. A Cartesian sceptic may argue that his beliefs about the external world are false (they are not infallible) yet it could be argued that he cannot come to doubt that he is sitting in his chair (indubitability), and he cannot be made to correct his belief that he is reading a book (incorrigibility).

infallible   A belief is infallible if it cannot be false. All claims of infallibility are controversial, although it is very plausible that my belief that 'I exist' is something that I cannot be wrong about.

inference   Inference or argument is used to derive further beliefs from other beliefs that you already possess. From certain *premises* I can draw *conclusions*. There are various forms of inference, the most important being deduction and induction. Deductive arguments are those that follow from logic alone. If the philosopher Socrates is Brazilian (first premise), and all Brazilians are good at football (second premise), then the philosopher Socrates is good at football (conclusion). This argument is valid, that is, the conclusion logically follows from the premises (if it doesn't, the argument is invalid). In this case, however, the conclusion is not true, and this is because both premises are false. Such an argument may be valid but it is not sound. A sound argument is one in which a true conclusion is derived from true premises.

Inductive arguments are arguments from experience: experiential evidence is taken to lead to conclusions about what we have not experienced. I inductively infer that there are beans in this tin because every similar tin that I have opened has contained beans. In chapter 10 we consider whether such arguments are valid.

lawlike   Laws or lawlike statements describe universal regularities, regularities that have always occurred and ones that will continue to do so. To say that gravity is a law of nature is to say that large bodies have always attracted small bodies and that this will always be so.

logical positivist   Logical positivism is an approach to philosophy popular in the early twentieth century. Logical positivists were driven by science, and they were hostile to many of the traditional concerns of philosophy such as ethics, religion and metaphysics. Ayer's *Language, Truth and Logic* is a forthright presentation of this approach (Ayer, 1990).

necessary and sufficient conditions   If *B* is a necessary condition for *A*, then you can only have *A* if you have *B*. Being male is a necessary condition for being the Pope. You cannot be Pope unless you are a man. Being male, however, is not a sufficient condition for Popehood. Other conditions also need to be satisfied, such as, you must be a Roman Catholic. When the sufficient conditions for *A* are met, then it follows that you definitely have *A*. Thus the necessary and sufficient conditions for *A* are those conditions that must each be satisfied, and those that together guarantee that you have *A*. In the case of Popehood, the necessary and sufficient conditions are being male, being a Roman Catholic, and being elected by the College of Cardinals.

predicate   A predicate is a phrase that tells us something about the subject of a sentence. The subject of 'The Kraken wakes' is the Kraken, and the predicate is 'wakes'; the predicate is telling us that the Kraken is waking up.

prima facie   This Latin phrase means 'at first sight' or 'what would seem to be'. Prima facie justification is that which a belief seems to have before factors are considered that may defeat such justification, factors that may entail that this belief is not actually justified.

proposition   A proposition is what a sentence or phrase says about the world. Sentences of different languages can express the same proposition. Both 'snow is white' and 'la neige est blanche' are saying that snow is white.

reductive   Reductionists about a certain kind of thing claim that it can be completely described in terms of other kinds of thing. I am a reductionist about orange juice because I think a complete description can be given of it in terms of the chemicals of which it is made. Orange juice is *nothing but* a mixture of citric acid, sugar, and all the other chemicals that make it up. I therefore have a reductive account of orange juice. This is uncontroversial, but there are various highly contentious reductions: some claim that the mind is nothing but the brain; that biology just amounts to physics; and that good actions are simply those that lead to increased happiness in the world (see chapter 14, section 1). There are therefore reductionists with respect to certain things, theories and properties.

sound   see **inference**

theist   A theist is someone who believes in a God or gods, and theism is the belief in such supernatural entities.

valid   see **inference**

References

Adler, J. (1994) 'Testimony, Trust, Knowing', *Journal of Philosophy*, 91, pp. 264–75.

Alcoff, L. (ed.) (1998) *Epistemology: The Big Questions*. Blackwell, Oxford.

Aldis, B. and Harrison, H. (eds) (1970) *Nebula Awards Two* (1966). Panther, London.

Alston, W. (1976) 'Two Types of Foundationalism', *Journal of Philosophy*, 85, pp. 165–85.

Alston, W. (1986) 'Internalism and Externalism in Epistemology', *Philosophical Topics*, 14, pp. 179–221.

Alston, W. (1988) 'An Internalist Externalism', *Synthese*, 74, no. 3, pp. 265–83. Repr. in Bernecker and Dretske (2000), pp. 214–28.

Alston, W. (1989) *Epistemic Justification*. Cornell University Press, Ithaca.

Alston, W. (1991) *Perceiving God*. Cornell University Press, Ithaca.

Alston, W. (1995) 'How to Think about Reliability', *Philosophical Topics*, 23, no. 1, pp. 1–29.

Anselm, Saint (1979) *St Anselm's Proslogion* (1077–8), trans. M. Charlesworth. University of Notre Dame Press, Notre Dame.

Armstrong, D. (1961) *Perception and the Physical World*. Routledge and Kegan Paul, London.

Armstrong, D. (1969–70) 'Does Knowledge Entail Belief?' *Proceedings of the Aristotelian Society*, 70, pp. 21–36.

Armstrong, D. (1973) *Belief, Truth and Knowledge*. Cambridge University Press, Cambridge.

Asimov, I. (1968a) *I, Robot* (1950). Panther, London, 1968.

Asimov, I. (1968b) 'Reason', in Asimov (1968a).

Audi, R. (1998) *Epistemology: A Contemporary Introduction to the Theory of Knowledge*. Routledge, London.

Audi, R. (2003) 'Contemporary Modest Foundationalism', in Pojman (2003), pp. 174–82.

Augustine, Saint (1942) *Against the Academicians* (AD 386), ed. and trans. Sister M. Garvey. Marquette University Press, Milwaukee.

Austin, J. (1962) *Sense and Sensibilia*. Clarendon Press, Oxford.

Ayer, A. (1940) *Foundations of Empirical Knowledge*. Macmillan, London.

Ayer, A. (1956) *The Problem of Knowledge*. Pelican, Harmondsworth.

Ayer, A. (1976) *The Central Questions of Philosophy*. Penguin, Harmondsworth.

Ayer, A. (1990) *Language, Truth, and Logic* (1936). Penguin, Harmondsworth.

Bach, K. (2000) 'A Rationale for Reliabilism' (1985), in Bernecker and Dretske (2000), pp. 199–213. Originally in *The Monist*, 68, 1985, no. 2, pp. 246–63.

Baehr, J. (2003) 'A Priori and A Posteriori', in *The Internet Encyclopedia of Philosophy*, ed. J. Feiser and B. Dowden. At www.iep.utm.edu/ (accessed 14 Feb. 2005).

Barnes, J. (1980) 'Socrates and the Jury', *Proceedings of the Aristotelian Society*, suppl., 54, pp. 193–206.

Barrett, R. and Gibson, R. (eds) (1990) *Perspectives on Quine*. Blackwell, Oxford.

Bender, J. (ed.) (1989) *The Current State of the Coherence Theory: Critical Essays on the Epistemic Theories of Keith Lehrer and Lawrence Bonjour*. Kluwer, Dordrecht.

Bentham, J. (1970) *An Introduction to the Principles of Morals and Legislation* (1780), ed. J. Burns and H. Hart. Athlone Press, London.

Bergman, I. (1973) *Bergman on Bergman.* Secker and Warburg, London.

Berkeley, G. (1998) *A Treatise Concerning the Principles of Human Knowledge* (1710), ed. J. Dancy. Oxford University Press, Oxford.

Bernecker, S. and Dretske, F. (eds) (2000) *Knowledge: Readings in Contemporary Epistemology.* Blackwell, Oxford.

Bird, A. (2000) *Thomas Kuhn.* Princeton University Press, Princeton.

Blackburn, S. (2001) *Being Good: A Short Introduction to Ethics.* Oxford University Press, Oxford.

Blanshard, B. (1940) *The Nature of Thought.* Allen and Unwin, London.

Block, N., Flanagan, O. and Guzeldere, G. (eds) (1997) *The Nature of Consciousness.* MIT Press, Cambridge, Mass.

Bonjour, L. (1978) 'Can Empirical Belief Have a Foundation?' *American Philosophical Quarterly*, 15, pp. 1–13.

Bonjour, L. (1985) *The Structure of Empirical Knowledge.* Harvard University Press, Cambridge, Mass.

Bonjour, L. (1998) *In Defense of Pure Reason.* Cambridge University Press, London.

Bonjour, L. (1999) 'The Dialectic of Foundationalism and Coherentism', in Greco and Sosa (1999).

Bonjour, L. (2005) 'In Defense of the *A Priori*', in Steup and Sosa (2005), pp. 98–105.

Bonjour, L. and Sosa, E. (2003) *Epistemic Justification: Internalism vs. Externalism, Foundationalism vs. Virtues.* Blackwell, Oxford.

Bradbury, R. (1950) *The Martian Chronicles.* Doubleday, New York.

Buford, S. (ed.) (1970) *Essays on Other Minds.* University of Illinois Press, Urbana.

Burge, T. (1993) 'Content Preservation', *Philosophical Review*, 102, pp. 457–88.

Calderon de la Barca, P. (2002) *La vida es sueño* (1636). Dover, New York.

Card, O. (1994) *Speaker for the Dead.* Tor Books, New York.

Chisholm, R. (1948) 'The Problem of Empiricism', *Journal of Philosophy*, 45, pp. 512–17.

Chisholm, R. (1977) *The Theory of Knowledge*, 2nd edn. Prentice-Hall, Englewood Cliffs.

Chisholm, R. (1989) *The Theory of Knowledge*, 3rd edn. Prentice-Hall, Englewood Cliffs.

Chomsky, N. (1972) *Language and Mind.* Harcourt, Brace, Jovanovich, New York.

Churchland, P. (1979) *Scientific Realism and the Plasticity of Mind.* Cambridge University Press, Cambridge.

Clifford, W. (2003) 'The Ethics of Belief' (1877), in Pojman (2003), pp. 515–18.

Coady, A. (1973) 'Testimony and Observation', *American Philosophical Quarterly*, 10, pp. 149–55.

Coady, A. (1992) *Testimony: A Philosophical Study.* Oxford University Press, Oxford.

Conee, E. and Feldman, R. (1998) 'The Generality Problem for Reliabilism', *Philosophical Studies*, 89, pp. 1–29.

Conrad, J. (1957) *Lord Jim* (1900). Penguin, Harmondsworth.

Cottingham, J. (1986) *Descartes.* Blackwell, Oxford.

Crane, T. (ed.) (1992) *The Contents of Experience: Essays on Perception.* Cambridge University Press, Cambridge.

Dancy, J. (1985) *Introduction to Contemporary Epistemology.* Blackwell, Oxford.

Dancy, J. (ed.) (1988) *Perceptual Knowledge.* Oxford University Press, Oxford.

Dancy, J. (1995) 'Arguments from Illusion', *Philosophical Quarterly*, 45, pp. 421–38.

Dancy, J. and Sosa, E. (eds) (1992) *A Companion to Epistemology.* Blackwell, Oxford.

Darwin, C. (1859) *The Origin of Species by Means of Natural Selection.* John Murray, London.

De Beauvoir, S. (1965) *The Prime of Life* (1960), trans. P. Green. Penguin, Harmondsworth.

De Beauvoir, S. (1981) *Adieux: A Farewell to Sartre*, trans. P. O'Brien. Penguin, Harmondsworth.

Dennett, D. (1991) *Consciousness Explained*. Little, Brown, Boston.

De Rose, K. (1995) 'Solving the Sceptical Problem', *Philosophical Review*, 104, pp. 1–52.

Descartes, R. (1986) *Meditations on First Philosophy*, ed. J. Cottingham. Cambridge University Press, Cambridge.

Dick, P. (1959) *Time Out of Joint*. Lippincott, Philadelphia.

Dick, P. (1965) *The Three Stigmata of Palmer J. Eldridge*. Doubleday, New York.

Dick, P. (1970) 'We Can Remember It For You Wholesale', in Aldis and Harrison (1970).

Dickens, C. (1993) *Bleak House* (1853). Wordsworth, Ware.

Dostoyevsky, F. (1968) *Crime and Punishment* (1886), trans. S. Monas. New American Library, New York.

Dostoyevsky, F. (1993) *The Brothers Karamazov* (1880), trans. D. McDuff. Penguin, Harmondsworth.

Drake, S and O'Malley, C. (eds) (1960) *Controversy on the Comets of 1618*. University of Pennsylvania Press, Philadelphia.

Dretske, F. (1969) *Seeing and Knowing*. Routledge and Kegan Paul, London.

Dretske, F. (1981) *Knowledge and the Flow of Information*. MIT Press, Cambridge, Mass.

Earman, J. (2000) *Hume's Abject Failure: The Argument against Miracles*. Oxford University Press, Oxford.

Everitt, N. (2004) *The Non-Existence of God*. Routledge, London.

Everitt, N. and Fisher, A. (1995) *Modern Epistemology: A New Introduction*. McGraw-Hill, New York.

Faulkner, P. (2000) 'The Social Character of Testimonial Knowledge', *Journal of Philosophy*, 97, pp. 581–601.

Feldman, R. (1974) 'An Alleged Defect in Gettier Counter-examples', *Australasian Journal of Philosophy*, 52, pp. 68–9.

Feldman, R. (1999) 'Methodological Naturalism in Epistemology', in Greco and Sosa (1999).

Feyerabend, P. (1988) *Against Method* (1975), rev. edn. Verso Press, New York.

Fodor, J. (1984) 'Observation Reconsidered', *Philosophy of Science*, 51, pp. 23–43.

Fodor, J. (1987) *Psychosemantics: The Problem of Meaning in the Philosophy of Mind*. Bradford Books/MIT Press, Cambridge, Mass.

Fodor, J. (1992) 'The Big Idea: Can There be a Science of the Mind?' *Times Literary Supplement*, 3 July 1992, pp. 5–7.

Fogelin, R. (2003) *A Defense of Hume on Miracles*. Princeton University Press, Princeton.

Foley, R. (2001) *Intellectual Trust in Oneself and Others*. Cambridge University Press, Cambridge.

Foster, J. (2000) *The Nature of Perception*. Oxford University Press, Oxford.

Fricker, E. (1995) 'Telling and Trusting: Reductionism and Anti-reductionism in the Epistemology of Testimony' (critical notice of Coady (1992)), *Mind*, 104, pp. 393–411.

Galileo, G. (1960) *Il Saggiatore* (1623), in Drake and O'Malley (1960).

Gettier, E. (1963) 'Is Justified True Belief Knowledge?' *Analysis*, 23, pp. 121–3.

Goldman, A. (1976) 'Discrimination and Perceptual Knowledge', *Journal of Philosophy*, 73, pp. 771–91.

Goldman, A. (1979) 'What is Justified Belief?', in Pappas (1979), pp. 1–23.

Goldman, A. (1980) 'The Internalist Conception of Justification', *Midwest Studies in Philosophy*, 5, pp. 27–51.

Goldman, A. (1986) *Epistemology and Cognition.* Harvard University Press, Cambridge, Mass.

Goldman, A. (1994) 'Epistemic Folkways and Scientific Epistemology' (1993), in Kornblith (1994), pp. 291–315. Originally in *Philosophical Issues*, 3, 1993, pp. 271–84.

Goldman, A. (2000a) 'A Causal Theory of Knowing' (1967), in Bernecker and Dretske (2000), pp. 18–30. Originally in *Journal of Philosophy*, 71, 1967, pp. 771–91.

Goldman, A. (2000b) 'Can Science Know When You're Conscious? Epistemological Foundations', *Journal of Consciousness Studies*, 7, no. 5, pp. 3–22.

Goodman, N. (1953) *Fact, Fiction and Forecast.* Bobbs-Merrill, Indianapolis.

Grayling, A. (ed.) (1995) *Philosophy: A Guide through the Subject.* Oxford University Press, Oxford.

Greco, J. and Sosa, E. (eds) (1999) *The Blackwell Guide to Epistemology.* Blackwell, Oxford.

Grice, H. (1961) 'The Causal Theory of Perception', *Proceedings of the Aristotelian Society*, suppl., 35, pp. 121–52.

Gunn, J. (1984) *The Joy Makers.* Crown, New York.

Guttenplan, S. (ed.) (1975) *Mind and Language.* Clarendon Press, Oxford.

Haack, S. (1993) *Evidence and Inquiry: Towards Reconstruction in Epistemology.* Blackwell, Oxford.

Hanson, N. (1965) *Patterns of Discovery* (1961). Cambridge University Press, Cambridge.

Hanson, N. (2004) 'From Patterns of Discovery' (1988), in Schwartz (2004), pp. 292–305.

Harman, G. (1997) 'The Intrinsic Quality of Experience', in Block, Flanagan and Guzeldere (1997).

Harris, K. (1971) *Kenneth Harris Talking To.* Weidenfeld and Nicolson, London.

Heinlein, R. (1964a) 'They', in Heinlein (1964b).

Heinlein, R. (1964b) *The Unpleasant Profession of Jonathan Hoag.* Dennis Dobson, London.

Hick, J. (1964) *The Existence of God.* Macmillan, New York.

Hick, J. (1966) *Faith and Knowledge.* Cornell University Press, Ithaca.

Hookway, C. (1990) *Scepticism.* Routledge, London.

Hopkins, R. (2004) 'The Epistemology of Moral Testimony', MS.

Hume, D. (1978) *A Treatise of Human Nature* (1739), ed. L. Selby-Bigge. Oxford University Press, Oxford.

Hume, D. (1998) *Dialogues Concerning Natural Religion* (1779). Hackett, Indianapolis, 1998.

Hume, D. (1999) *An Enquiry Concerning Human Understanding* (1748), ed. T. Beauchamp. Oxford University Press, Oxford.

Huxley, A. (1932) *Brave New World.* Chatto and Windus/Doubleday, New York.

Irwin, W. (ed.) (2002) *The Matrix and Philosophy.* Open Court, Illinois.

Ishiguro, K. (1989) *The Remains of the Day.* Faber and Faber, London.

Jackson, F. (1977) *Perception: A Representative Theory.* Cambridge University Press, Cambridge.

James, W. (1897a) *Essays in Pragmatism.* Hafner, New York.

James, W. (1897b) 'The Moral Philosopher and the Moral Life' (1891), in James (1897a).

James, W. (1897c) 'The Will to Believe', in James (1897a).

James, W. (1999) *The Varieties of Religious Experience* (1902). Penguin, Harmondsworth.

Johnson, D. (1999) *Hume, Holism and Miracles.* Cornell University Press, Ithaca.

Kant, I. (1997) *Groundwork of the Metaphysics of Morals* (1785), ed. and trans. M. Gregor. Cambridge University Press, Cambridge.

Kant, I. (1998) *The Critique of Pure Reason*, ed. P. Guyer and A. Wood. Cambridge University Press, Cambridge.

Kim, J. (1988) 'What is "Naturalized Epistemology"?' in Tomberlin (1988), pp. 381–405.

Kirk, R. (2003) *Mind and Body.* Acumen, Chesham.

Kitcher, P. (1980) 'A Priori Knowledge', *Philosophical Review*, 89, pp. 3–23.

Knight, D. (ed.) (1972) *Perchance to Dream.* Doubleday, New York.

Kolbel, M. (2002) *Truth without Objectivity.* Routledge, London.

Kornblith, H. (ed.) (1994) *Naturalizing Epistemology* (1985), 2nd edn. Bradford Books/MIT Press, Cambridge, Mass.

Kornblith, H. (ed.) (2001) *Epistemology: Internalism and Externalism.* Blackwell, Oxford.

Kuhn, T. (1970) *The Structure of Scientific Revolutions* (1962), 2nd edn. University of Chicago Press, Chicago.

Lackey, J. (1999) 'Testimonial Knowledge and Transmission', *Philosophical Quarterly*, 49, pp. 471–90.

Lackey, J. and Sosa, E. (eds) (2006) *The Epistemology of Testimony.* Oxford University Press, Oxford.

Ladd, J. (ed.) (1973) *Ethical Relativism.* Wadsworth, Belmont.

Landesman, C. (1962) 'Philosophical Problems of Memory', *Journal of Philosophy*, 59, no. 3, pp. 57–65.

Le Guin, U. (2000a) 'The Ones Who Walk Away from Omelas' (1973), in Le Guin (2000b).

Le Guin, U. (2000b) *The Wind's Twelve Quarters*, Orion, London.

Lehrer, K. (1990) *The Theory of Knowledge.* Westview Press, Boulder.

Lehrer, K. and Paxson, T. (1969) 'Knowledge: Undefeated Justified True Belief', *Journal of Philosophy*, 66, pp. 225–37.

Leibniz, G. (1981) *New Essays on Human Understanding* (1705), ed. P. Remnant and J. Bennett. Cambridge University Press, Cambridge.

Lewis, C. (1929) *Mind and the World Order.* C. Scribner's Sons, New York.

Lewis, C. (1946) *An Analysis of Knowledge and Evaluation.* Open Court, La Salle.

Lewis, D. (2000) 'Elusive Knowledge' (1996), in Bernecker and Dretske (2000), pp. 365–84. Originally in *Australasian Journal of Philosophy*, 74, 1996, pp. 549–67.

Locke, D. (1971) *Memory.* Macmillan, London.

Locke, J. (1975) *An Essay Concerning Human Understanding* (1689), ed. P. Nidditch. Clarendon Press, Oxford.

Lowe, E. (1995) *Locke on Human Understanding.* Routledge, London.

Luper-Foy, S. (ed.) (1987) *The Possibility of Knowledge: Nozick and his Critics.* Rowman and Littlefield, Totowa.

Mackie, J. (1977) *Ethics.* Penguin, Harmondsworth.

Mackie, J. (1982) *The Miracle of Theism.* Oxford University Press, Oxford.

Maffie, J. (1990) 'Recent Work on Naturalized Epistemology', *American Philosophical Quarterly*, 27, no. 4, pp. 281–93.

Malcolm, N. (1963a) *Knowledge and Certainty.* Prentice-Hall, Englewood Cliffs.

Malcolm, N. (1963b) 'Three Lectures on Memory', in Malcolm (1963a), pp. 187–240.

Martin, C. and Deutscher, M. (1966) 'Remembering', *Philosophical Review*, 75, pp. 161–95.

Maslin, K. (2001) *An Introduction to the Philosophy of Mind.* Polity, Cambridge.

Matilal, B. and Chakrabarti, A. (eds) (1994) *Knowing from Words.* Kluwer, Dordrecht.

McCulloch, G. (1995) *The Mind and its World.* Routledge, London.

McDowell, J. (1986) 'Singular Thought and the Extent of Inner Space', in McDowell and Pettit (1986), pp. 137–168.

McDowell, J. (1994) *Mind and World*. Harvard University Press, Cambridge, Mass.

McDowell, J. and Pettit, P. (eds) (1986) *Subject, Thought and Content*. Clarendon Press, Oxford.

McGinn, C. (1984) 'The Concept of Knowledge', *Midwest Studies in Philosophy*, 9.

McGinn, C. (1997) 'Consciousness and Content' (1988), in Block, Flanagan and Guzeldere (1997), pp. 295–307. Originally in *Proceedings of the British Academy*, 74, 1988, pp. 219–39.

Mill, J. S. (1884) *A System of Logic* (1843). Longman, London.

Mill, J. S. (1889) *An Examination of William Hamilton's Philosophy*. Longman, London.

Mill, J. S. (1998) *Utilitarianism* (1861), ed. R. Crisp. Oxford University Press, Oxford.

Miller, A. (2003) *An Introduction to Contemporary Metaethics*, Polity, Cambridge.

Moore, G. (1903) *Principia Ethica*. Cambridge University Press, Cambridge.

Morton, A. (1977) *A Guide through the Theory of Knowledge*. Blackwell, Oxford.

Moser, P. (ed.) (1987) *A Priori Knowledge*. Oxford University Press, Oxford.

Moser, P. (1989) *Knowledge and Evidence*. Cambridge University Press, Cambridge.

Nagel, T. (1974) 'What It Is Like to Be a Bat', *Philosophical Review*, 83, pp. 435–50.

Noonan, H. (1999) *Hume on Knowledge*. Routledge, London.

Nozick, R. (1981) *Philosophical Explanations*. Cambridge, Mass.

Oppy, G. (1995) *Ontological arguments and Belief in God*. Cambridge University Press, Cambridge.

Paley, W. (1826a) *Natural Theology* (1800). Repr. in Paley (1826b).

Paley, W. (1826b) *The Works of William Paley in One Volume*. Peter Brown and T. W. Nelson, Edinburgh.

Papineau, D. (1987) *Reality and Representation*. Blackwell, Oxford.

Pappas, G. (ed.) (1979) *Justification and Knowledge: New Studies in Epistemology*. Reidel, Dordrecht.

Pargetter, R. (1984) 'The Scientific Inference to Other Minds', *Australasian Journal of Philosophy*, 62, pp. 158–63.

Pascal, B. (1966) *Pensées* (1660), trans. A. Krailsheimer. Penguin Books, Harmondsworth.

Peacocke, C. (1992) *A Study of Concepts*. MIT Press, Cambridge, Mass.

Peirce, C. (1965a) *Collected Papers*, vol. 5. Harvard University Press, Cambridge, Mass.

Peirce, C. (1965b) 'How to Make Our Ideas Clear' (1878), *Popular Science Monthly*, 12, pp. 286–302. Repr. in Peirce (1965a).

Plantinga, A. (1974) *The Nature of Necessity*. Clarendon Press, Oxford.

Plantinga, A. (1993a) *Warrant: The Current Debate*. Oxford University Press, Oxford.

Plantinga, A. (1993b) *Warrant and Proper Function*. Oxford University Press, Oxford.

Plantinga, A. (2000) *Warranted Christian Belief*. Oxford University Press, Oxford.

Plantinga, A. and Wolterstorff, N. (eds) (1983) *Faith and Rationality*. University of Notre Dame Press, Notre Dame.

Plato (1987) *Theaetetus*, trans. R. Waterfield. Penguin, Harmondsworth.

Poe, E. (1992a) *Complete Tales and Poems*. Random House, New York.

Poe, E. (1992b) 'Murders in the Rue Morgue' (1841), in Poe (1992a).

Pojman, L. (ed.) (2003) *The Theory of Knowledge: Classical and Contemporary Readings*, 3rd edn. Wadsworth, Belmont.

Popper, K. (1959) *The Logic of Scientific Discovery*. Hutchinson, London.

Price, H. (1932) *Perception*. Oxford University Press, Oxford.

Pritchard, D. (2005) *Epistemic Luck*. Oxford University Press, Oxford.

Putnam, H. (1975a) 'The meaning of "meaning" ', in Putnam (1975b), pp. 251–71.

Putnam, H. (1975b) *Philosophical Papers, Volume 2.* Cambridge University Press, Cambridge.

Putnam, H. (1981) *Reason, Truth and History.* Cambridge University Press, Cambridge.

Pyle, A. (1999) *Key Philosophers in Conversation: The Cogito Interviews.* Routledge, London.

Quine, W. (1953a) *From a Logical Point of View.* Harvard University Press, Cambridge, Mass.

Quine, W. (1953b) 'Two Dogmas of Empiricism', in Quine (1953a), pp. 20–46.

Quine, W. (1969a) 'Epistemology Naturalized?', in Quine (1969c), pp. 69–90.

Quine, W. (1969b) 'Natural Kinds', in Quine (1969c), pp. 114–38.

Quine, W. (1969c) *Ontological Relativity and Other Essays.* Columbia University Press, New York.

Quine, W. (1974) *The Roots of Reference.* Open Court, La Salle.

Quine, W. (1975) 'The Nature of Natural Knowledge', in Guttenplan (1975).

Quine, W. (1985) *The Time of my Life.* Bradford Books/MIT Press, Cambridge, Mass.

Quine, W. and Ullian, J. (1970) *The Web of Belief.* Random House, New York.

Rachels, J. (1986) *The Elements of Moral Philosophy.* McGraw-Hill, New York.

Radford, C. (1966) 'Knowledge – By Examples', *Analysis,* 27, pp. 1–11.

Reid, T. (1983) *Inquiry and Essays,* ed. R. Beanblossom and K. Lehrer. Hackett, Indianapolis. (Includes *An Inquiry into the Human Mind on the Principles of Common Sense* (1764) and *Essays on the Intellectual Powers of Man* (1785).)

Robinson, H. (2001) *Perception.* Routledge, London.

Rorty, R. (1979) *Philosophy and the Mirror of Nature.* Princeton University Press, Princeton.

Rostropovich, M. (1995) Sleevenotes to EMI Classics: Bach's Cello Suites. EMI 724355536426.

Rowlands, M. (2003) *Externalism: Putting Mind and World Back Together Again.* Acumen, Chesham.

Russell, B. (1912) *The Problems of Philosophy.* William and Norgate, London.

Russell, B. (1921) *The Analysis of Mind.* Allen and Unwin, London.

Russell, B. (1948) *Human Knowledge: Its Scope and Limits.* Allen and Unwin, London.

Ryle, G. (1963) *The Concept of Mind* (1949). Penguin Books, Harmondsworth.

Sartre, J. -P. (1965) *Nausea* (1938). Penguin, Harmondsworth.

Sartwell, C. (1991) 'Knowledge is Merely True Belief', *Philosophical Quarterly,* 2, pp. 157–65.

Sartwell, C. (1992) 'Why Knowledge is Merely True Belief', *Journal of Philosophy,* 84, no. 4, pp. 167–80.

Scarre, G. (1996) *Utilitarianism.* Routledge, London.

Schwartz, R. (ed.) (2004) *Perception.* Blackwell, Oxford.

Scruton, R. (1986) *Sexual Desire: A Philosophical Investigation.* Weidenfeld and Nicolson, London.

Sellars, W. (1997) *Empiricism and the Philosophy of Mind* (1956). Harvard University Press, Cambridge, Mass.

Seneca, L. (1925) *Ad Lucilium epistulae morales* (62–5 AD), trans. R. Gummere. Harvard University Press, Cambridge, Mass.

Shoemaker, S. (1984a) *Identity, Cause and Mind.* Cambridge University Press, Cambridge.

Shoemaker, S. (1984b) 'Persons and their Pasts', in Shoemaker (1984a).

Shope, R. (1983) *The Analysis of Knowing: A Decade of Research.* Princeton University Press, Princeton.

Singer, P. (1993) *Practical Ethics*. Cambridge University Press, Cambridge.

Singer, P. and Singer, R. (eds) (2005) *The Moral of the Story: An Anthology of Ethics through Literature*. Blackwell, Oxford.

Skyrms, D. (1966) *Choice and Chance*. Dickenson, Belmont.

Smart, J. (1973) 'An Outline of a System of Utilitarian Ethics' (1961), in Smart and Williams (1973).

Smart, J. and Williams, B. (1973) *Utilitarianism: For and Against*. Cambridge University Press, Cambridge.

Smith, G. (1970) 'In the Imagicon' (1966), in Aldis and Harrison (1970).

Smith, M. (1984) *The Moral Problem*. Oxford, Blackwell.

Sosa, E. (1991) *Knowledge in Perspective: Selected Essays in Epistemology*. Cambridge University Press, Cambridge.

Sosa, E. (ed.) (1994) *Knowledge and Justification*. Dartmouth, Vermont.

Sosa, E. and Kim, J. (eds) (2000) *Epistemology: An Anthology*. Blackwell, Oxford.

Stalker, D. (ed.) (1994) *Grue: The New Riddle of Induction*. Open Court, Chicago.

Steup, M. and Sosa, E. (eds) (2005) *Contemporary Debates in Epistemology*. Blackwell, Oxford.

Strawson, P. (1992) *Analysis and Metaphysics: An Introduction to Philosophy*. Oxford University Press, Oxford.

Stroud, B. (1977) *Hume*. Routledge and Kegan Paul, London.

Stroud, B. (1984) *The Significance of Philosophical Scepticism*. Clarendon Press, Oxford.

Stroud, B. (2000) 'Understanding Human Knowledge in General' (1989), in Bernecker and Dretske (2000), pp. 307–23.

Sullivan, R. (1994) *An Introduction to Kant's Ethics*. Cambridge University Press, Cambridge.

Swinburne, R. (1968) 'The Argument from Design', *Philosophy*, 43, pp. 202–15.

Swinburne, R. (ed.) (1974) *The Justification of Induction*. Oxford University Press, Oxford.

Swinburne, R. (1991) *The Existence of God*. Clarendon Press, Oxford.

Tolkein, J. (1954–5) *The Lord of the Rings*. Allen and Unwin, London.

Tomberlin, J. (ed.) (1988) *Philosophical Perspectives 2: Epistemology*. Ridgeview, Atascadero.

Tye, M. (1992) 'Visual Qualia and Visual Content', in Crane (1992).

Tye, M. (1995) *Ten Problems of Consciousness*. MIT Press, Cambridge, Mass.

Tye, M. (2000) *Consciousness, Color and Content*. MIT Press, Cambridge, Mass.

Unger, P. (1984) *Philosophical Relativity*. Oxford University Press, Oxford.

Von Wright, G. (ed.) (1972) *Problems in the Theory of Knowledge*. Nijhoff, The Hague.

Wallbott, H. (1988) 'In and Out of Context: Influences of Facial Expression and Context Information on Emotion Attributions', *British Journal of Social Psychology*, 27, pp. 357–69.

Welbourne, M. (2001) *Knowledge*. Acumen, Chesham.

Whitehead, A. (1926) *Science and the Modern World*. Cambridge University Press, Cambridge.

Wilde, O. (1995) *The Importance of Being Earnest* (1895). Penguin, Harmondsworth.

Williams, B. (1972) 'Knowledge and Reasons', in Von Wright (1972).

Williams, B. (1995) 'Ethics', in Grayling (1995).

Williams, M. (2001) *Problems of Knowledge: A Critical Introduction to Epistemology*. Oxford University Press, Oxford.

Williams, T. (1962) *A Streetcar Named Desire* (1947). Repr. in *A Streetcar Named Desire and Other Plays*. Penguin, Harmondsworth.

Williamson, T. (2000) *Knowledge and its Limits*. Oxford University Press, Oxford.

Wittgenstein, L. (1953) *Philosophical Investigations*, ed. G. E. M. Anscombe, R. Rhees and G. von Wright. Blackwell, Oxford.

Wittgenstein, L. (1967) *Zettel*, ed. G. E. M. Anscombe and G. von Wright. Blackwell, Oxford.

Films

13th Floor, dir. J. Rusnak, 1999.

A la Folie . . . Pas du Tout, dir. L. Colombani, 2002.

Abre los Ojos, dir. A. Amenábar, 1997.

Agnes of God, dir. N. Jewison, 1985.

Amélie, dir. J.-P. Jeunet, 2001.

Bladerunner, dir. R. Scott, 1982.

Brainstorm, dir. D. Trumbull, 1983.

Butch Cassidy and the Sundance Kid, dir. G. Hill, 1969.

Cabaret, dir. B. Fosse, 1972.

Capricorn One, dir. P. Hyams, 1978.

La Cité des Enfants Perdus, dir. M. Caro and J.-P. Jeunet, 1995.

The Crying Game, dir. N. Jordan, 1992.

Dark City, dir. A. Proyas, 1998.

Dark Star, dir. J. Carpenter, 1974.

Dirty Harry, dir. D. Siegel, 1971.

L'Enfant Sauvage, dir. F. Truffaut, 1969.

The Enigma of Kaspar Hauser, dir. W. Herzog, 1974.

The Eternal Sunshine of the Spotless Mind, dir. M. Gondry, 2004.

EXistenZ, dir. D. Cronenberg, 1999.

Extreme Measures, dir. M. Apted, 1996.

Fight Club, dir. D. Fincher, 1999.

Ghost, dir. J. Zucker, 1990.

High Noon, dir. F. Zinnemann, 1952.

The Invasion of the Body Snatchers, dir. P. Kaufman, 1978.

Kiss of the Spider Woman, dir. H. Babenco, 1985.

Last Tango in Paris, dir. B. Bertolucci, 1972.

Lawnmower Man, dir. B. Leonard, 1992.

The Life of David Gale, dir. A. Parker, 2003.

The Man with Two Brains, dir. C. Reiner, 1993.

The Matrix, dir. A. Wachowski and L. Wachowski, 1999.

Memento, dir. C. Nolan, 2000.

On the Waterfront, dir. E. Kazan, 1954.

Once upon a Time in the West, dir. S. Leone, 1968.

Play Misty for Me, dir. C. Eastwood, 1971.

Run Lola Run, dir. T. Tykwer, 1998.

Saving Private Ryan, dir. S. Spielberg, 1998.

Serpico, dir. S. Lumet, 1973.

The Seventh Seal, dir. I. Bergman, 1957.

The Silence, dir. I. Bergman, 1963.

The Sixth Sense, dir. H. Shyamalan, 1999.

Sleeper, dir. W. Allen, 1973.

The Stepford Wives, dir. B. Forbes, 1975.

Total Recall, dir. P. Verhoeven, 1990.

Through a Glass Darkly, dir. I. Bergman, 1961.

The Truman Show, dir. P. Weir, 1998.

Twelve Angry Men, dir. S. Lumet, 1957.

The Usual Suspects, dir. B. Singer, 1995.

Vanilla Sky, dir. C. Crowe, 2001.
The Village, dir. H. Shymalan, 2004.
The Way We Were, dir. S. Pollack, 1973.
Westworld, dir. M. Crichton, 1973.
The Wicker Man, dir. R. Hardy, 1973.
Winter Light, dir. I. Bergman, 1963.

Index